LUCKY VICTIM

LUCKY VICTIM

*An Ordinary Life
In Extraordinary Times
1933–1946*

HANS A. SCHMITT

Louisiana State University Press
Baton Rouge and London

Copyright © 1989 by Louisiana State University Press
All rights reserved
Manufactured in the United States of America

First printing
98 97 96 95 94 93 92 91 90 89   5 4 3 2 1

Designer: Sylvia Malik Loftin
Typeface: Cheltenham Light
Typesetter: The Composing Room of Michigan, Inc.
Printer: Thomson-Shore, Inc.
Binder: John H. Dekker & Sons, Inc.

Chapters II and IV were previously published, in somewhat different form, as
"January 30, 1933: A Memoir," *Virginia Quarterly Review,* LIX (Winter, 1983), and
"How I Fled Nazi Germany," *Virginia Quarterly Review,* LXII (Summer, 1986),
respectively, and are reprinted by permission. Other portions of this book were
published previously as a Lawrence F. Brewster Lecture in History by East
Carolina University in Greenville, North Carolina.

Library of Congress Cataloging-in-Publication Data

Schmitt, Hans A.
    Lucky victim: an ordinary life in extraordinary times, 1933–1946
/ Hans A. Schmitt.
      p.   cm.
    ISBN 0-8071-1500-2 (alk. paper)
    1. Schmitt, Hans A.   2. German Americans—Biography.   3. Refugees,
Jewish—United States—Biography.   4. World War, 1939–1945—
Refugees.   5. Historians—United States—Biography.   I. Title.
E184.G3S297   1989
973'.0431024—dc19
[B]   89-30101
                                                                                         CIP

The paper in this book meets the guidelines for permanence and durability of
the Committee on Production Guidelines for Book Longevity of the Council on
Library Resources. ∞

To the memory of my parents

CONTENTS

ILLUSTRATIONS

LUCKY VICTIM

I   MY ANCESTORS, BOTH RICH AND POOR

Each individual is the product of biological routine, and the sum of cumulative psychological bequests. Our physique reflects the looks of our forebears, and our acts repeat their virtues and vices, often in unpredictable combinations. Finally, this inheritance is enriched and complicated by the succession of accidents that constitutes the course of our life and caps the formation of our individuality.

Autobiography offers a balance sheet on which these factors represent both assets and liabilities. But unlike its counterpart in the science of accounting, the book of history often fails to "add up," let alone balance. Too much remains hidden from view, even in an honest record. What we see is not all there is.

No matter how commonplace, such observations belong at the beginning of every autobiographical work. We must make clear that what follows is a mosaic of fragments. It is not a complete record, but only what we, consciously or unconsciously, wish to recall. When we compare such recollections with a less personal historical account, the chasm separating memory from history is often appallingly wide. To reduce the gap in these pages, I have deliberately enlisted the work of historians, not merely to assure accuracy, but, equally important, to establish the context in which an ordinary life coexisted with extraordinary events. Let us be frank: In the individual consciousness, history is an endless fencing match between person and event, and our own contact with it remains confined to that ritual duel. Everything else is footnoted fiction.

Almost fifty years ago, the ex-Republican New Dealer later fallen from grace, Henry A. Wallace, proclaimed the twentieth century the century of the common man. Without concerning ourselves too much with the meaning of that resonant phrase, we can say that its author expressed not so much the democratic tenor of our age as the remarkable development preceding it: a literate society opening history to the masses and revealing their part in it. Many finally became persuaded that the past had been shaped by the anonymous no less than the famous. This discovery has given rise to a subdiscipline, carelessly and redundantly named social history, devoted to the chronicling of ordinary lives on a wholesale rather than individual basis. Social history has, however, failed to connect the world of the obscure with that of the eminent. Future historians must effect this juncture, and until they do, autobiography will contribute individual small steps toward a general upstairs-downstairs synthesis. That is the justification for telling my story. German dissidence, and the history of great migrations and of frightful wars, are some of the categories of which it is a part. The components of the tale scatter across the entire spectrum of broader subjects, becoming in this way a specimen of that breadth.

At the beginning stand the people from whom I am descended. They were quite as ordinary as I, never rising above respectable obscurity. But they displayed solid talents for survival under various difficulties, and some of them upon occasion defied convention. Except for my father, they always landed on their feet, and my father's mother, more than any of the others, displayed a feisty contempt for expediency, and a stubborn disrespect for authority I have always admired.

As the writing of these pages has prompted me to read more attentively than before the contents of a rich archive of family letters, I have also come to realize that I am the product of a marriage between two very different families, each inhabiting a social territory whose denizens knew little, if anything, of the other. My father's ancestors were Catholic or Protestant Christians, sometimes clashing, sometimes subsiding into uneasy coexistence. My mother's forebears were Jews, ranging from orthodox to assimilated, and on the whole less quarrelsome. They made a living in business, and the less successful among them worked for banks. My mother's father died rich, at least by my standards. On my father's side, the forebears I know descended from Franconian peasants and an atypical, long-extinct line of musicians. In the nineteenth century, they joined Germany's rural exodus to the city, where poverty and occasional misery awaited them. Good incomes and a comfortable way of life bred in the Jewish branch liberal habits of tolerance, while the industrial world hardened the Christian migrants into intolerant, misanthropic victims, friendless and unfriendly, caught in a vicious cycle of low expectations, often exceeded by an even more un-friendly reality. The Jews were full of Christian forbearance; the Christians tended to believe in exacting an eye for an eye and a tooth for a tooth. My own knowledge of each side does not extend much beyond the beginning of the nineteenth century.

My paternal grandfather, Johann Matthäus Schmitt, was born on September 21, 1844, in the Franconian village of Hannberg and died of pneumonia in Nuremberg on May 3, 1887. All I know about him is that he was the son of a farmer, Peter Schmitt, and that he became a coachman (*Kutscher*).[1] Documents after his death continue to des-ignate my grandmother as the "coachman's widow [*Kutschers-witwe*] Elise Schmitt." (In pre–World War I Germany, even the humblest citizen claimed a title.) The first American of the family was my grandfather's sister Kunigunde, who is recorded as having emigrated to "Amerika" on May 13, 1859, the year of the founding of Italy, of John Brown's raid on Harpers Ferry, and of the drilling of the first oil well near Titusville, Pennsylvania. Amidst such portents of a violent, industrial age, Kunigunde's footsteps have been lost, and I do not know what became of her or her descendants.

On my paternal grandmother's side the news is more plentiful, and the family turns out to have been more interesting. The *Kutscherswitwe* was born Elise Barbara Schneider in 1843, the il-legitimate daughter of the master carpenter Michael Christ and Frau Dorothea Helbig, nee Schneider, of Lahm im Itzgrund in Bavarian Franconia, a spot so obscure that I have not been able to find it in any directory. Until she married my grandfather, Elise bore her moth-er's maiden name. One must, however, not assume that her il-legitimacy necessarily constituted a handicap, let alone a tragedy. In mid-nineteenth-century rural Franconia 24 percent of all children were born out of wedlock, and "a girl who had preserved her virginal purity until her 20th year was an exception, not necessarily appreci-ated by her fellow villagers."[2] What makes my grandmother's ante-

---

1. Nuremberg Municipal Archives, C21 (Register of Inhabitants)/IN/277/I, 690.
2. Edward Shorter, "'La Vie Intime': Beiträge zu seiner Geschichte am Beispiel des kulturellen Wandels in den bayerischen Unterschichten im 19. Jahrhundert," in Peter C. Ludz (ed.), *Soziologie und Sozialgeschichte: Aspekte und Probleme* (Kölner Zeitschrift für Soziologie und Sozialpsychologie: Monograph Series, XVI) (Opladen, 1972), 542.

cedents nevertheless unusual was that she sprang from a prolonged liaison between two married partners. Local records do not indicate that either was divorced or widowed at the time, only that Dorothea Helbig bore Michael Christ another daughter the year after my grandmother's arrival.

When she married my grandfather at thirty-nine, Elise Schneider was a housemaid in Nuremberg. By the time she was widowed, four years later, she had borne two sons: the older, Julius, was my father; the younger, Georg, died in infancy, about the same time as his father, victim of the same mysterious "pneumonia." After these bereavements my grandmother resumed her former occupation, supplementing her income by taking in her neighbors' washing.

The independent spirit of her forebears was also alive and well in Elise. Bavarian law permitted confessionally mixed marriages, stipulating that sons must assume the father's, and daughters the mother's, religion unless a marriage contract made different provisions. But Elise assented to marry my grandfather only after the couple had come to the Salomonic decision that half its children be raised in her faith, half in his, regardless of sex. Nothing, however, was put in writing—a coachman and a housemaid could not afford the services of a lawyer—and when Johann Matthäus Schmitt passed away in 1887, the Calvinist destiny of his surviving child was challenged by his brother, Georg, a Catholic priest and now my father's guardian.

My grandmother fought her brother-in-law every inch of the way. As I can testify from childhood recollections (I was eleven years old when she died in 1932), the Reformed catechism was, to her, the only valid prescription for eternal life, and its non-negotiable tenets therefore took precedence over other laws of church and state. Father Georg's authority broke on this rock of faith, and the matter went before the Nuremberg city council.

Protracted litigation accumulated an impressive file of documents, tenacious survivors of war and successive uprootings. Fortunately for my grandmother's case, Nuremberg, like most former free cities of the Holy Roman Empire, had been predominantly Protestant since the Reformation. Despite a recent influx of Catholic migrants from the Upper Palatinate, only one-third of its population was Roman Catholic, and the city's elite dominating municipal government was almost entirely Protestant. The city council decreed, therefore, against only one dissenting vote, that my father should follow his mother's religion.[3]

The Reverend Georg Schmitt, however, whose guardianship the decision did not affect, still had a duty to perform. He turned to the administrative appeals court in Munich. The Bavarian capital was Catholic country, and its justices took a different view. Arguing that matters of salvation could not be decided on the basis of "sociological theory," they reversed the Nuremberg magistrate. My grandmother paid no attention to this second verdict. The frustrated guardian had won his case but lost my father's soul in the process. The courts could do nothing to enforce their decision. They had told my grandmother what church her son ought to attend, but the law did not oblige them to deliver the child to the door. Personal persuasion was my great-uncle's only recourse. His sense of duty and my grandmother's tenacity led to a prolonged war for my father's salvation, whose result confirmed the common sense of the Nuremberg city council's partisan verdict. There existed no way to force a Protestant widow to raise her fatherless child a Catholic. She lived with the child; the guardian resided in his rural parish, a two-hour train ride from the city. Her views permeated every waking hour of my father's life; the priest's only avenue of influencing him was the Royal Bavarian Postal Service.

Although family tradition has depicted Father Georg as an ogre who even tried to use small monetary gifts to effect my father's conversion, a careful reading of a dozen surviving letters from uncle to nephew provides a less sinister impression of the divine's efforts. To be sure, he expressed regret that "mother has removed you from my supervision . . . also after the litigation" and stated that he would have looked after my father had God granted his wish that my father, too, enter the priesthood. For several years he pressed my father to enter the Catholic confraternity of St. Henry, making at one point further financial support contingent on the fulfillment of that condition. But the record also shows that this was an empty threat. Apparently my father procrastinated; his correspondence with his guardian does not establish whether he joined or not. My great-uncle, nevertheless, continued to help both widow and son for the rest of his life, and at times with amounts of money that must have

3. I have recently found an accurate summary of the Nuremberg proceedings in a clipping from the Nuremberg *Zeitung*, December 16, 1893.

strained the material resources of a rural parish priest. Father Georg struggled to find the right path between the Scylla of priestly duty and the Charybdis of Christian charity. I cannot, therefore, blame him alone for the ultimate result of this religious tug-of-war. My father grew into a foe of organized religion. When I wanted to attend Lutheran Sunday school as a first grader, he forbade it at first and relented only after my mother, raised in a more tolerant atmosphere, urged him not to perpetuate the strife that had blighted his childhood. As it happened, my interest in Sunday school proved ephemeral and soon gave way to such secular interests as football and stamp collecting.

My ancestors on my mother's side emerge from prehistoric darkness only during the eighteenth century, which found them settled in the Hessian town of Hanau. After the most important event in the history of German Jewry before Hitler, their emancipation by Napoleon Bonaparte, information is more plentiful. In an autobiographical fragment, my grandfather relates that one of his grandmothers did not remember this event as an unmixed blessing. Acquisition of civil rights forced the men in the family to do military service, and she described to her grandson the shocking spectacle of mature men of substance and learning drilling on the municipal common in the same ranks as young lads and riffraff from all classes of society. Her feelings, one should add, were shared by the gentile middle classes in Germany's large towns, who had grown up to view military service as an occupation reserved for the dregs of society. This bourgeois aversion to the trade of arms disappeared only gradually during the nineteenth century, as affluent and educated commoners gained access to officer training and German unification endowed armies with unprecedented glamor.

My maternal grandfather, Adolf Hamburger, was born in 1841, the fourth of six children. His father was a wholesaler in manufactured goods, whose business was just then beginning to suffer from the changes wrought by the construction of railroads. Middlemen in small towns saw the demand for their merchandise dwindle, and it was not until the 1850s that great-grandfather Hamburger weathered the transition by moving into the retail sector. My grandfather's childish imagination seems to have been deeply affected by these familial vicissitudes, and he grew up worrying whether he had the capacity to survive in a changing world full of threatening surprises. Sometime in the late 1850s, after two older brothers had joined a banking firm in Munich, he, too, left home and eventually arrived in Australia—I do not know exactly by what route—where gold had been discovered in New South Wales and Victoria. The find led to a sixfold expansion of the population during the ensuing decade, from which my grandfather seems to have derived substantial profit, and considerable self-esteem as well. When the gold boom began to languish and was followed by land reforms and a spectacular agricultural expansion, young Adolf started an import-export business in Sydney. This enterprise did so well that he decided in 1889 to turn it over to his brother Julius, the third of the four Hamburger boys from Hanau. After returning to Europe, he married a schoolteacher, Jenny Behr, twenty years his junior, bought two large houses on the Bockenheim Parkway in what is now downtown Frankfurt, and spent his remaining years enjoying the fruits of his adventurous life. Except for an occasional visit to the stock exchange to keep an eye on his investments, and the management of his gilt-edged urban real estate, he was done with toiling and spinning.

My grandfather was fifty when his oldest child, my mother Elisabeth Dorothea, was born on October 28, 1891. A second child, my uncle Richard, completed the family on November 11, 1892. Adolf Hamburger died in November, 1919, a year and a half before I was born, and all I know about the placid and idyllic decades of his long retirement derives from my mother's nostalgic recollections.

It seems that my grandfather had originally planned to settle in Italy and begin a new life as amateur historian and archaeologist. What attracted him in particular was the resumption after unification of excavations at Herculaneum and Pompeii near Naples, two Roman settlements buried in an eruption of Vesuvius on August 24, in the year 79. But when his wife became pregnant, his own country, likewise unified during his long absence in Australia, proved a more potent magnet. The two decided their children should be raised in the resurrected fatherland. As with countless German Jews, devotion to the nation remained the hallmark of their lives. Ever since the crisis of the 1840s had forced my great-grandfather to keep his store open on the Sabbath, to eke out a living for his wife and six children, the family's ties with Jewish tradition had been sundered one by one. It was a gradual, gentle separation, during which all concerned maintained a deep respect, communicated to their children, for the ways that were no longer their own. In my mother's childhood home, however, the family celebrated the traditional secular and religious holidays of their environment, ranging from the kaiser's birthday to Easter and Christmas. Out of regard for some orthodox relatives, my grandfather would not transact business on Yom Kippur, but that was the extent of his observance of ancestral practices. When World War I broke out, he turned in the British passport he had acquired during his sojourn in the Pacific outpost of the Empire, demonstrating once again his undivided loyalty to kaiser and reich.

It was only fitting that my mother's father should not have survived by much the defeat of Germany. His son sold the Frankfurt houses after his death and bought from part of the proceeds an estate, coincidentally in that same Lower Franconian region from which my father's mother came. That property, too, was sold long ago. But my grandfather's interest in history lives on. It was his chief legacy to me, the grandson he never knew. I inherited his inclination for historical study and a few remainders of his library: the works of the Greek historian Ernst Curtius and Theodor Mommsen's Roman history, as well as a shelf of leatherbound, gilt-edged German translations of Plutarch, Herodotus, and Tacitus. Although his children learned Latin and Greek, he never had the opportunity to pursue learning systematically, acquiring both English and Italian through his travels. It was also thanks to this inheritance that I first read as a child the historical novels of such minor but popular German authors as Gustav Freytag and Felix Dahn, to say nothing of the German classics, through whose collected editions I ploughed eagerly, if randomly, to escape drier and less congenial school assignments.

Although first and foremost a German, my grandfather had a liberal and cosmopolitan mind. To his children he was a conscientious and methodical guide through Italy's Greek, Roman, and Renaissance treasures. Both my mother and my uncle learned to speak English, French, and Italian. English was often spoken in their home, and my mother utilized this linguistic skill during frequent trips to England, where she not only visited museums but inspected the grim conditions of industrial towns, sometimes under the guidance of Laborite aldermen whose friendship she continued to cultivate in the 1920s and 1930s. Good liberals that they were, my grandparents worried about the "social question," but they remained confident that their society would eventually find a painless, peaceful way to resolve inequities that they genuinely deplored, without ever feeling their sting.

Nor does surviving evidence disclose that my grandparents suffered disabilities on account of their Jewish birth. My grandfather and his brothers had attended public and nondenominational private secondary schools in Hanau, and grown up in a predominantly Christian neighborhood. My grandfather recalled the belief among Christians and Jews that Napoleon's opening of the ghetto was leading the latter to assimilation into a German society where "in two or three generations no difference would be noticeable." On their street "neighbors stuck together and accepted each other's religious ceremonies as part of tradition."

Still, my grandfather was not naïve, and his reminiscences, particularly on this issue, also strike a worried note, indicating how obstacles were beginning to obstruct this process of Jewish germanization. "In my childhood," he wrote at one point, "anti-Semitism was unknown. No educated man would in those days have spoken against Jewish equality." One concludes from this statement that he and his children, to whom these recollections were addressed, knew that this tolerance was eroding and could no longer be taken for granted. I have no idea what events gave rise to this pessimism. As specialists in German history are aware, Jews like Eduard Lasker had been leaders of German national liberalism in the 1870s and 1880s, whereas "no bourgeois party in 1898, 1903, and 1907 elected a single candidate for the Reichstag who openly identified himself as a Jew."[4] In politics, then, Jewishness appears to have become a handicap. But there was more to it than that. When my uncle entered the military in World War I, he was told that he could become an officer only if he was first baptized. A firm agnostic since childhood, he declined to pretend to nonexistent religious feelings and remained a master sergeant (*Hauptfeldwebel*) for the duration of the war. He seems to have felt no resentment, but was entirely satisfied with his assignment as meteorologist to the Richthofen squadron, so far as I know under both its glamorous founder and his infamous successor, Hermann Göring.

The idyllic household of my grandparents seems to have been ruffled but once, and that was when my mother declared that she wanted to study law. Her father took great pride in his gifted daughter, who generally led her class in academic achievement at Frankfurt's *Elisabethen Schule* for girls. Whatever his precious and precocious little girl wanted to do with her talents seems to have

4. John L. Snell and Hans A. Schmitt, *The Democratic Movement in Germany, 1789–1914* (Chapel Hill, 1976), 274.

9

found his approval. But Frau Jenny, a schoolteacher's daughter and a former schoolteacher herself, had narrower and more orthodox views on the subject of women's careers.

By the first decade of the twentieth century, Germany's changing society affected the opportunities and expectations of millions. Universal manhood suffrage and the rise of Catholic and Socialist mass parties were leveling class distinctions, if not in people's minds, at least in reality. New technology increased the labor force in industry and commerce, and provided new means of gaining a livelihood. Some of these new trades and professions were predominantly staffed by women (such as telephone operators and sales girls), and universal education not only raised the educational levels attained by all members of the female sex but also increased the female share of that labor market, especially in elementary education. A variety of trade schools and commercial academies had flourished in major German cities since the 1860s, offering training and, in their faculty ranks, new openings to women with professional aspirations.

Women's admission to German universities lagged behind not only Britain, France, and Scandinavia but Greece and Italy as well. Although the University of Zurich had enrolled female students since 1867—by 1900 they constituted 28.1 percent of the Swiss university population, including an appreciable minority of "foreigners" from across the Rhine—only Heidelberg and Freiburg in Baden and Munich, Würzburg, and Erlangen in Bavaria followed the Swiss example. Prussia did not allow women to matriculate until 1908, and only then with the understanding that their degrees would not open careers in church and state. In that year the academic scene became really accessible to both sexes, for Prussia was larger in territory and population than all other states of the federal empire put together, and Berlin's relatively new university (founded in 1808) was generally considered the best in Germany. Thereafter the number of women students began to rise rapidly. Only 320 women pursued degrees at German universities in 1908 (out of a full-time student population of over 46,000), whereas by 1910 almost twice that number, 632, were enrolled as regular students at the University of Berlin alone.

This invasion coincided with my mother's battle against maternal conservatism. One might think that the rising tide of female aspirants to academic acceptance would have helped reconcile my grandmother to her daughter's plans, but it seems to have had exactly the opposite effect—perhaps because most female students (2,000 out of 2,300 in 1910) enrolled in the humanities. This majority tended to consist of elementary teachers preparing for a career in secondary education. Medical students, about 10 percent of the female enrollment, were a distant second, likewise accepted in a society that saw women as healers in the home and the nursing profession. In 1910 only 15 women were enrolled in faculties of law, and these figures may have accounted for my grandmother's opposition to her daughter's career choice.[5]

As a next step in this confrontation of wills, my grandmother sought allies outside the home. She wrote to the faculty at the municipal teachers' college of Frankfurt, where my mother had meanwhile enrolled, inquiring what they thought of these capricious plans. The answer undoubtedly confounded her expectations. The director's response praised my mother's "superior gifts" and "indefatigable application," which made her "always the best student in her class." If "there ever was a young lady who deserved every assistance" toward a career, it was my mother.

My grandmother had to give in, but not without exacting one condition: Matriculation in Berlin—where else?—had to be postponed until 1912, when my uncle planned to enroll at the nearby polytechnic in Charlottenburg, where he would combine his own studies with the role of chaperone-designate to his older sister. My mother, no less stubborn, managed to shorten the otherwise wasted year by a summer term at Heidelberg, where she took a vast number of courses in law and art history, and attended Hermann Oncken's famous lectures on the French Revolution and the Napoleonic empire.

In Berlin my mother studied with such notables as Gustav von Schmoller, historiographer of the House of Brandenburg, secret councilor of state, member of the Prussian House of Lords, and father of German social history; Ulrich von Willamowitz-Möllendorf, Theodor Mommsen's son-in-law and his successor as mentor of a new generation of classical scholars; Franz von Liszt, namesake and cousin of the composer and central Europe's premier authority on criminal law; and Otto Hintze, whose works on Prussian history and constitutional law set standards unequaled by subsequent genera-

5. James C. Albisetti, "The Reform of Female Education in Prussia, 1899–1908: A Study in Compromise and Containment," *German Studies Review,* VIII (1985), 35–38.

tions of historians. Her true teacher and *Doktorvater*, however, was Gerhard Anschütz, author of the standard commentaries on the Prussian constitution of 1850 and the Weimar Constitution. When Anschütz left Berlin in 1916 to return to Heidelberg, she followed him to complete degree and dissertation under his direction. Anschütz, writing his memoirs on the eve of World War II, recalled the growing number of female law students in his classes between 1914 and 1918: girls "not merely industrious, but really gifted, and endowed with above average, specifically juristic talents." The "three best" among them included my mother.[6]

On October 19, 1916, less than two weeks before her twenty-fifth birthday, my mother became one of Germany's first female doctors of law. Her descendants cherish the formidable Latin diploma issued on this occasion in the name of the "Augustissimi ac Potentissimi" Friedrich II, grand duke of Baden, rector magnificentissimus of his grand duchy's two world-renowned universities: Catholic Freiburg and Calvinist Heidelberg. Another, more humble document, a receipt for payment of her dissertation fee, unwittingly confirms how much of an innovation her graduation represented. The form reflects the longstanding tradition of male monopoly, proclaiming earnestly that "Mr. Elisabeth Hamburger has paid the fee of sixty Mark for the examination of his dissertation."

Out in the everyday world, beyond castle ruins, beyond the moonlit river Neckar, Philosopher's Lane, and Student Prince, a female *Doctor juris* was hardly received with open arms, even if she was the precious only daughter of affluent parents. This is confirmed by a rather sizable sheaf of references covering the next eight years of my mother's search for a stable place in the social order, revealing that she worked four months in the office of the Frankfurt prefect of police, then for half a year in a local law office, whose partners reluctantly dismissed her after a growing wartime coal shortage forced them to close the section of their office in which she was working. ("The coal shortage has led to conditions under which a young lady of good family cannot be expected to work.") There followed a stint with the State Monopoly for Lubricants (*Kriegsschmierölgesellschaft*) in Berlin, from which she resigned when wartime restrictions on travel threatened to interfere with her freedom to rush home should her ailing father take a sudden turn for the

6. Gerhard Anschütz, "Aus meinem Leben: Erinnerungen von Gerhard Anschütz" (Typescript in author's possession), 222.

worse. After the war she held positions, likewise in rapid succession, with the Reich Clearing Office, the Association of Friends and Patrons of the University of Frankfurt, the newly founded German refuge of the Alsatian University of Strasbourg, reclaimed by the French, and in private industry. Only in 1924 did she find a stable niche in a profession considerably removed from her sector of academic preparation: the education of problem children.

But I am getting ahead of myself. I must now resume my father's life story after the Nuremberg and Munich courts had washed their hands of the salvation of his Christian soul.

My grandmother, despite the premature loss of her husband and the ensuing quarrels with the authorities, both clerical and secular, somehow managed to send her son to the Nuremberg *Realschule*, a secondary school that, according to the sixth edition (1907) of Meyer's encyclopedia, "is distinguished from a *Gymnasium* . . . by a curriculum . . . emphasizing, not Greek and Roman languages and literatures, but the disciplines relevant to the intellectual life of the present (mathematics, the sciences and living languages)." The status of these secondary schools and the degree to which their graduates would enjoy the same professional and social opportunities as the alumni of classical preparatory schools was the subject of unending debates at all levels of the educational hierarchy from the middle of the nineteenth until well into the twentieth century. In general, *Realschule* graduates were admitted to universities, but their degrees only qualified them for secondary-school teaching careers.

For my grandmother and her son, these arcane deliberations had little practical meaning. My father's first year in these bourgeois surroundings ended on a discouraging note. According to his report card, his progress was "mostly mediocre" and his "application not always satisfactory." My grandmother saw and signed this unflattering document and undoubtedly gave her wayward son a solid piece of her mind, perhaps also the back of her hand. His grades improved, as did the next assessment of his levels of application, although neither reached the plane of excellence that my elders later invoked when trying to shame me out of my own mediocre classroom performances. I do not blame them for bending the truth to arouse in me ambitions to excel. Besides, everybody's memory suffers with the passage of time, as I am discovering often enough when comparing my own recollections with the written record. But some of their errors were sufficiently serious to warrant correction here.

If my grandmother in her late eighties transfigured her son's high-school record into an epic of peerless achievement—at a time when he had become a *Herr Doktor*, a successful management consultant, and the owner of a fine house in one of Berlin's most elegant suburbs—she failed to explain why it was suddenly decided in 1897 to terminate his stay at the *Realschule*. Was it because she could no longer pay the secondary school tuition (until 1945 Germany had no free secondary schools), or did my father's rather average grades call into question his aptitude for the careers opened by a high-school diploma? Here again Father Georg Schmitt's letters to his nephew are revealing, indicating at least that this decision involved more than mother and son. Just before Christmas of the crucial year, he wrote my father that "it was no mistake that you left the *Realschule*, for this curriculum benefits only rich merchants who some day can start their own business." Subsequent epistles disclose the old man mobilizing his clerical acquaintances in Nuremberg to help my father find a suitable apprenticeship. One of these clerics even turned to the lord mayor, Georg von Schuh, famous for presiding over Nuremberg's remarkable end-of-the-century industrial expansion, with a request for a position with the municipal administration. (The request was turned down because of the large number of "more qualified" applicants.) A sister of Father Georg found an apprenticeship in Kitzingen near Würzburg, an opportunity my grandmother, who would not part from her only child, undoubtedly persuaded her fourteen-year-old son to refuse. Instead, he signed on March 11, 1898, an apprenticeship contract with the "Electric Society Soldan & Co." in Nuremberg, stipulating the payment of one hundred marks apprenticeship tuition (*Lehrgeld*). Father Georg paid the fee in three annual installments, even though there was plainly no longer any hope that this munificence would turn the beneficiary into a Roman Catholic.

This generosity, and the continuing interest the guardian took in his ward's welfare, saved my father from the marginal existence of his unskilled parents. The episode shows that even entrance to the ranks of skilled labor entailed financial outlays my grandmother, and poor folk like her, simply could not afford. Over the long run, the benefactor attached no strings to his support—he certainly never mentioned repayment—except to ask, as his years mounted and his health began to decline, that his nephew "pray a little" for him, and "that [he] might later on realize who helped . . . [him] in his hour of need."

My father spent the next fourteen years constructing and repairing electrical installations, especially telephone systems. Although he seems to have been good at his craft, other ambitions began to consume him. He saw beyond his workshop a wider world, and economic and political problems and inequities to whose solution he thought he might contribute. After enrolling in evening courses, sponsored by the German National Society, he attracted the attention of Wilhelm Ohr, a liberal activist with political ambitions. When Ohr decided in 1911 to stand as Progressive candidate for the Reichstag district Eschwege-Schmalkalden, he asked my father to join his campaign as a paid worker. My father agreed, "probably more out of friendship for me, than out of interest in political combat," Ohr added, not wishing to taint his working-class protégé with a suspicious and, by German standards, unwholesome interest in politics. After the candidate lost the race to his Social Democratic adversary, his discovery that my father displayed a "conspicuous talent for gaining the confidence of small people, whose assistance seemed to be particularly close to his heart," prompted Ohr to recommend him for the secretaryship of the Protestant Workers Association in Frankfurt. Again my father seems to have fulfilled the expectations of his sponsor, and was appointed director of the youth division of Frankfurt's municipal labor office. On paper he held this post until August, 1919. Actually, he spent three and a half of those five years in the army, from May, 1915, to December, 1918—two years in Russia, and 1918 on the western front with the searchlight detachment of the 200th Infantry Division.

As a topic of conversation the war was taboo in our home. Neither my father nor my uncle nor my mother's cousin Heinz Loewen, decorated for escaping from a French prison camp and then volunteering for renewed front-line duty, ever discussed his experiences in my presence. I grew up to regard war as an unspeakable, indescribable horror. This silence kept military service beyond the purview of my imagination. I never wondered whether it might someday become part of my life, certainly not until after I left Germany. My grandmother, who recalled the revolution of 1848 as one of the five wars through which she had lived, believed that wars, like plagues and droughts, happened at regular intervals. Although she had numerous biblical quotations to buttress her argument, her dark view of life failed to depress or worry me. Even as a child, I saw her as the aged, toothless remnant of a past not destined to be reenacted.

How my grandmother had faced these, in her view, inevitable and recurring trials can be seen from the countless letters she sent my father during his active service. They hardly document her piety, but rather her distrust of the powers that be—not kaiser or army, but rent collectors, the municipal food-distribution system, and an unjust society in which a neighbor's son came home on leave every six months while her Julius, at this particular writing, had not set foot in her apartment for more than a year. These letters totally lack patriotic enthusiasm. The war was a great misfortune. It separated her from the only human being who provided her with will and reason to live. The scourge of nations kept him in constant danger and freezing in distant trenches, where lice and other vermin threatened to consume him. The war interfered with the regular delivery of the mail—"Why don't you write," "Why don't I hear from you," constitute a persistent epistolary refrain. The conflict reduced her, once again, to the poverty of her early widowhood, forcing her to subsist on a quarter pound of meat a week and an uncertain supply of potatoes and cabbage. (In June, 1917, she reported that she had lost sixty pounds.) Besides hunger, war brought a cold apartment, and when she received a desperately needed allowance of wood or coal, the physical task of picking it up with a rickety handcart at the dealer's yard left the seventy-five-year-old woman too exhausted to leave her bed the next day. From these low moments she was roused to protest reductions in her survivor's allowance, annual increases in rent, and other afflictions imposed by a hostile world. It is no wonder she had no time to hate the British, the French, or the Russians. One letter reports that someone broke into her storage room in the basement and emptied her vegetable bin. Such tragedies pointed to less distant enemies: one's own neighbors. One in-house collision even went to court, when one of the tenants accused the landlord of stealing her coal.

Added to unending material worries were a mother's inchoate fears of losing her son to forces other than shot, shell, or privation. My father's correspondence with an elderly female colleague, a municipal social worker, called forth obsessive tirades against "this woman" who turned my grandmother into "the fifth wheel on the cart" and "left her completely alone in the world." This object of maternal jealousy must then have been past fifty; I remember her as a bedridden invalid whom my mother and I visited regularly on holidays until her death in the early thirties. My father was thirty-four years old when my grandmother wrote this letter.

These chronicles of misery contain little good news. Only the flowers in May and the harvest in August remained perpetual sources of pleasure for the Franconian farm girl, and once in a while a sermon delivered at the local Reformed church calmed her angry heart. And then there were always the misfortunes of others to draw on for consolation. When a neighbor's son, the recipient of those semiannual furloughs, was "hit right hard in the leg," my grandmother noted with righteous satisfaction that "there still was a just God." Yet even these comforts proved intermittent, drowned in days and nights of "ceaseless weeping" and hours spent morosely looking out of her living-room window (the same window at which I was to sit on her lap, six or seven years later, watching the passing traffic and the children in the schoolyard across the street). Nothing could console her when she did not hear from my father as often as she thought she should.

Surely these untutored, ungrammatical, and extravagantly misspelled, often daily letters constitute the source of an entirely different history of the war, one even recent accounts by such social historians as Jürgen Kocka in Germany and Denis Winter in England have only begun to explore.[7] They draw back the curtain on a politically silent majority, taking no emotional or conscious part in the struggle, accustomed to being of no account and never considering the alternative of rebellion. They enlarge Kocka's conclusion that war divides nations by aggravating hostility between classes and entrenched interests, by pitting neighbor against neighbor, turning families inhabiting one apartment house into envious competitors for survival.

A letter from the other side of the family merely adds to these annals of division. Although my mother's parents also had a son in the service and—for a time—a nephew in French captivity, their daily menu offered more than potatoes and cabbage. This epistle, sent to their daughter toiling in Berlin for the State Monopoly for Lubricants, announced the dispatch of a nourishing symbol of as-

---

7. Jürgen Kocka, *Facing Total War,* trans. Barbara Weinberger (Leamington Spa, 1984); Denis Winter, *Death's Men* (London, 1976).

similation as well as affluence: a piece of ham they hoped would not be too fat for the recipient's taste. They also assured their daughter that this gift did not expose them to undue hardship: "We continue to get our meat from Balz [the family butcher] and if we occasionally want some poultry or venison, we can get that also on Sunday, so that we enjoy fat days from Saturday to . . . Wednesday. Yesterday, today and tomorrow are meatless days which do not hurt us either. Today we had soup, carrots and potatoes, [and for dessert] *blanc mange* and fruit sauce. Tonight . . . we shall have potato pancakes and apple sauce." I also suspect that my maternal grandparents had their heating fuel delivered to the door. Their letters record no complaints about suffering from the cold. They were honest people and patriots; I doubt that they received more than their rations. But poultry and venison were not rationed, did not have to be, because they only figured on the shopping lists of those happy few who could afford them.

This affluent middle class thought and talked about the war constantly and believed in eventual victory. In July, 1918, the newly appointed Heidelberg professor of comparative law, Karl Neubecker, passed through Frankfurt and visited my mother's parents. According to Jenny Hamburger's report to her daughter, he "considered the peace with [Soviet] Russia still too weak." (Concluded at Brest Litovsk on March 3, 1918, it stripped Russia of 386,000 square miles and more than half of her developed raw materials and industrial resources.) "He hopes," she went on, "that we shall soon overcome the French, and [control] the open road from the Baltic to the Black Sea. Then the English will also give up. He thinks this will happen in Autumn. May God grant it." My father's mother also seems to have heard of Brest Litovsk, for it figures in her letters, but not as a code word for peace and total victory. She knew that it was a headquarters town, where privileged staffs, including the husband of yet another neighbor, enjoyed comfortable quarters and all the food they could eat. Interested in neither the hatreds of war nor the intricacies of treaties of peace, Elise Schmitt only wanted her son back. She craved for him no triumph, no Iron Crosses, no Russian, French, or British surrender. The wartime pipe dreams of the bourgeoisie remained beyond her experience or understanding.

My paternal grandmother's detachment was not visibly affected by the German defeat. If she took no notice of the ephemeral Peace of Brest Litovsk, my father's mother also, it seems, did not have time for outrage when Germany was forced to sign the Treaty of Versailles. Once her son had returned, life remained hard, in line with her unchanging expectations, but her world was whole again, and she was as satisfied as she could be.

The residents of the elegant villas and apartments of Frankfurt's west side, on the other hand, saw their world collapse with the western front, and the surrender of their, not the enemy's, armies. These untoward disasters left them distraught and disoriented, and many of them remained at war with their own country and the phantasmagoria of a sinister conspiracy that had inexplicably robbed the nation of the glory they thought it deserved.

This juxtaposition omits the third universe making up the fragmented nation—the millions of men in uniform. My father's responses to his mother's frequent letters have not survived, except one that speaks of the retreat in September, 1918. He describes in stark, touching terms the cruel fate visited upon French and Belgian civilians who were forced to abandon what was left of their homes and join the enemy's eastward march. My father's account reflects a deep disillusionment with the German cause. He was ashamed to be cast in the role of a scourge to these peaceful, innocent people, whom the actions of his army drove into deeper and deeper misery. I frankly do not know how typical his views were. Every student of history has learned at some time, however, that many young officers of any retreating army, as well as the top civilian echelons most afflicted by defeat, may fail to come to terms with its reality. Although he had little contact with that company of bitter-enders among Germans, my father did confess to me much later, when relentless history was about to separate us forever: "When I came home from the war, I believed in nothing. I was ready for anything. I might have become a Nazi, if I had not met your mother."

My father returned to his duties at the Frankfurt labor office and drifted into the Social Democratic party, where he met my mother in the spring of 1919 at a party in the house of a mutual friend: the new Social Democratic corporation counsel of Frankfurt. Thus I owe my existence to two revolutions: the French, releasing my Jewish forebears from their ghetto, and the German, providing the opportunity, if rarely taken, for bourgeois and worker to mingle as equals. Only at this point was it possible for the coachman's dour widow and the tolerant, hedonistic Frankfurt *rentier* to take their places amidst my ancestry.

19

In keeping with their own tolerant dispositions, my mother's parents seem to have raised no objections to their daughter's engagement to a former mechanic. My grandfather even persuaded his future son-in-law to resign his job with the city and continue his education, offering to pay the bills of all concerned for the duration of my father's studies. Now thirty-six years old, my progenitor did not even possess the high-school diploma needed to enter a university. There was no time to correct that deficiency. Instead, his application to Frankfurt's faculty of the social sciences cited his professional experience as an adequate substitute for this document. He now had supporters in the right places, particularly the city government, where his superiors certified that he was about to be promoted to greater responsibilities. On the basis of this record, the faculty voted unanimously to admit him. He enrolled in September, 1919, and my parents married two months later.

All was ready for the wedding when my grandfather died. This loss cast a pall over the beginning of my parents' life together, and was followed by the hasty and ill-advised sale of family property. Cash proceeds from these transactions rapidly melted in the inflation of the early 1920s, when the German mark was finally quoted at four trillion to the dollar. Thus the new household soon shared the pecuniary lot of millions of German middle-class families: expropriation by fiscal disaster. My father's escape from a careworn existence was blocked once more, and my mother—for the first time—had to work, not to satisfy ambitions, but to earn a living.

These events also forced my father to find work before he had completed his dissertation. My own arrival in June, 1921, interrupted my mother's career, and other family subsidies dried up. My father nevertheless finished his manuscript, which was accorded "distinction." It was published within a year of its completion. Next, my father did what society expected of a middle-class paterfamilias. He assumed the chief responsibility for the support of his growing family (shortly before my sixth birthday in 1927, my brother Richard was born) and joined the Hoechst Dyeworks' accounting division as an expert on social legislation, employment, and retirement questions. (In 1925, the firm became a major component of the German Dye Trust, I.G. Farben A.G.)[8] Hoechst was ten miles downriver from

8. Julius Schmitt, *Tarifverträge in der Landwirtschaft* (Schriften des Deutschen Landarbeiterverbandes, XIII) (Berlin, 1922); Joachim Flechtner, *Carl Duisberg: Vom Chemiker zum Wirtschaftsführer* (Düsseldorf, 1961), and "Die Duisberg Denkschrift zur Vereinigung der

the Frankfurt suburb of Eschersheim, in whose green and peaceful precincts my parents had chosen to raise us, and my father left the house every morning at dawn to commute to his distant workplace. By the time he returned in the evening, we children had been fed and were being put to bed. His absence from our everyday existence made him to us a somewhat austere, distant authority figure, rarely entering our daily lives, but invoked to maintain discipline whenever necessary.

My mother, anxious to reconcile profession and motherhood, began during these years a tutorial practice at home, first preparing adult law students for their bar examinations, and then shifting gradually to the tutelage of local teenagers who could not satisfy the demanding requirements of secondary schools. My recollections of this unusual evolution of her career are naturally dim and sketchy. Her first youthful clients came from the homes of friends and acquaintances. Thanks to my mother's efforts, these problem children graduated, and as word of her success spread, her parish expanded and occupied most of her time.

This did not mean that I was neglected or starved for affection. My parents loved me. They demonstrated it by words and actions, and I never doubted their devotion. Besides, my life included other adults, who gave me constant proof of their regard. My father's mother was a frequent visitor in our apartment. She never arrived without a present, often a bag full of red "American" apples, particular favorites of mine. On occasion I could stay overnight with her and enjoy various forbidden pleasures. She would give me pieces of cold cuts, especially a Hessian specialty, "Pressack," a sausage my parents considered too spicy for a child's diet. She also let me play with my father's tin soldiers, against his express instructions (he wanted nothing introduced into our lives that might glorify war). Another frequent visitor was "Uncle" Karl, no uncle, not even a relation by marriage. A bank manager, he had been a childhood friend of my mother's mother, and was the only Christian ever to attend and graduate from Frankfurt's lone Jewish secondary school, the Philantropin. Since both of my grandfathers had died before my birth, he volunteered for that role in my life. A tall, well-dressed gentleman, with an old-fashioned, neatly trimmed white beard, he lived well

deutschen Farbenfabriken aus dem Jahre 1915," *Jahrbuch für Wirtschaftsgeschichte*, III (1966), 236–70.

21

into his eighties, and his unfailing kindness and good cheer like-wise added to my feelings of security and contentment as a child. Finally, there was Babette, the maid, who entered my parents' house-hold at the age of seventeen, after they returned from their honey-moon. She was my mother during the work week. By the time I became conscious of my surroundings, she was "going" with Gus Schwab, who drove a delivery truck for a local department store. But she told him, and my parents, that she would not marry until I was old enough to go to school. We remained friends until I left Germany, and since she had no children of her own, I was still an important part of her life. In 1945 I looked for her, but nobody in her neigh-borhood could tell me where she was. I regret that I never had an opportunity to thank her for what she had contributed to a placid, quiet childhood.

While I lived this carefree life, completely insulated from the storms shaking Germany in the 1920s, my uncle was founding a management-consulting firm in Berlin, the Organisations-Institut, G.m.b.H., and in 1928—the most prosperous year of the Weimar era—he asked my parents to join this enterprise. My father was to become part of the consulting staff, and my mother was to edit a semimonthly journal, *Organisation-Betrieb-Büro* (*Organization-Enterprise-Office*), which my uncle planned to inaugurate as an aux-iliary undertaking. An agreement was quickly reached, and at the end of my first school year, in April, 1928, we moved to the distant capital, where, for the first time, I experienced the pain of separation from familiar surroundings.

The ensuing four years included a time of passing affluence, for my family and, to a lesser degree, our country. At first the move looked like another successful chapter in my parents' unconven-tional lives. Both had jumped the traditional barriers erected by society: my father had broken the fetters of class; my mother had at least bent those of gender. It was hard to say which was the greater accomplishment. Recent analyses continue to emphasize lack of social mobility as a characteristic of twentieth-century German soci-ety and to confirm that the Weimar Republic did little to increase career opportunities for women.[9] For the moment, both pioneers anticipated even wider prospects and increased rewards. They

9. As far as I know, Renate Bridenthal, in "Beyond *Kinder, Küche, Kirche:* Weimar Women at Work," *Central European History,* VI (1973), 148–66, was the first to draw attention to this paradox.

looked forward to joining a new vanguard of business enlightenment, the apostolate of rationalization founded in the United States
and now carried to Europe by an army of proselytizers.

So far as I was concerned, this next chapter in my parents' professional life varied from the preceding years in that my mother now
went to a downtown office, too, at least three days a week. I saw less
of both of them than before and had no precise idea what they were
doing. Berlin being a sprawling metropolis with much green
space—its city limits enclosed 328 square miles—the trip to work
by train and bus consumed an hour each way. In addition, my father
spent much time traveling, visiting and counseling the management
of the firm's clients, as did my mother, though far less frequently.
Their customers included such well-known companies as Teekanne
Tea, Odol Toothpaste, and Persil, maker of Germany's most popular
laundry detergent. Shortly after my parents' arrival, my imaginative
uncle decided to publish a series of monographs, each describing
how his consultants' advice had transformed a stagnating enterprise
into an efficient, profitable undertaking. Called *Model Enterprises of
the German Economy (Musterbetriebe deutscher Wirtschaft)*, it
comprises thirty volumes and is an interesting, if perhaps overly
optimistic, record of the wonder-working powers of rationalization
on the eve of the Great Depression.[10] I possess only two of these
volumes, both written by my father. Volume 10 describes the rise to
higher profit margins of Teekanne, then in Dresden, and the other,
Volume 23, the salvation of the Mercedes Business Machine Corporation of Zella-Mehlis (Thuringia), not to be confused with Daimler-
Benz, the maker of Mercedes automobiles, which was also a client
of the institute.

Meanwhile, I joined the second grade at the 18. Primary School,
whose members were far ahead of me, especially in arithmetic.
Catching up involved much sweat and toil, and left me no time to
wonder about my parents' pursuits. My new teacher, Herr Weber, a
former sergeant in the imperial army, took inordinate pride in his
class's peerless recitation of the multiplication tables. After an inter-
minable day in the hostile territory of the school, I had to endure
additional hours under the supervision of my harrowed mother,
trying to raise my additions, subtractions, and multiplications to
Herr Weber's inexorable standards.

10. The National Union Catalog of the Library of Congress lists 9 volumes of this series,
including 4 written by my father and 1 by my mother.

That these trials unfolded in a physical setting of unaccustomed luxury gave me little solace, especially since our new way of life made additional demands on my scant spare time. From a modest apartment in Frankfurt, we had moved to the suburb of Frohnau, at the northernmost city limits of Greater Berlin, where we rented a two-story villa. The house was surrounded by a large garden, whose lawn, strawberry patches, and vegetable beds became the weekend hobby of my city-bred parents and the bane of my existence. During the short weekend respites from school, I had to contribute my share to this diversion, without prior inquiry into my preferences. Weeding and watering became obscenities for me, and all tillage a pursuit I still gladly leave to others. Our new, expanded quarters were intended as a temporary haven only, while the remnants of my mother's dowry were poured into the building of our own house.

Frohnau (still called a "garden city" and opulent as ever, as I discovered on a visit in 1986) was first developed in 1910 by the owner of Silesia's largest mining and manufacturing complex, Guido Henckel, prince of Donnersmarck, hereditary member of the Prussian House of Lords, and hunting companion of the last kaiser.[11] At that time, dense pine forests covered the dunescape of Berlin's northern city limits, and although there had been a good deal of clearing by the time we moved to this settlement of some five-thousand inhabitants, pine trees still dominated the skyline: gawky, thin trunks topped by fardels of somber green. A few oaks and linden trees struggled for survival in a skimpy park stretching northward from the suburban railway, while many streets were lined with luxuriant chestnuts, whose white and pink blossoms glowed in the spring sunshine like countless chandeliers. Magnificent, publicly maintained rose gardens gave luster to an otherwise drab, little business district near the railway station. The roses are still blooming; the number of businesses has more than doubled in the last fifty years.

Berlin as a whole was "red," and as late as the elections of March, 1933, the Nazis ran behind in the German capital, outnumbered by Socialists as well as Communists. Frohnau differed from that norm, returning nationalist majorities, and Hitler's men—notably the elo-

---

11. Walter Möller (ed.), *50 Jahre Gartenstadt Frohnau* (Berlin-Hermsdorf, 1960); Konrad Fuchs, "Guido Georg Friedrich Graf Henckel von Donnersmarck, 1830–1916," in Ulrich Haustein, Georg W. Strobel, and Gerhard Wagner (eds.), *Ostmitteleuropa: Berichte und Forschungen* (Stuttgart, 1981), 237–51.

quent Nazi *Gauleiter,* Joseph Goebbels—were more welcome than Social Democrats, even in the late twenties. It was also horse country. Most of the local elite belonged to the Jockey Club, whose premises included a large, elegant clubhouse and Germany's only polo ground.

To be sure, we watched this world of polo games, steeplechases, foxhunts—and right-wing rallies—from outside. My parents were busy making money, gardening, and building a house that was to become an object of local opprobrium. In 1930 a young architect, just graduated from the *Bauhaus* of Walter Gropius and Mies van der Rohe, was hired to design a home in a sparsely settled section where the Tegel state forest halted the urban sprawl. In stark contrast to the gingerbread architecture of the Wilhelmine villas around us, the innovative structure was a light gray, quadratic stucco block with huge steel windows and an almost flat roof, tilted only slightly to allow the rainwater to drain. The inside was equally sober. Instead of sporting the customary flowery paper, the walls were painted in soft, solid pastels. The corridors were paved with terrazzo. Except for tables and chairs, everything—even the beds—was built in. We children were particularly impressed that the maid did not have to carry the dinner dishes to the kitchen. Instead, she put them into a compartment of the built-in dining-room china closet and took them out on the other side. Neighbors called our place the "residential machine" (*Wohnmaschine*), and on Sunday in spring and summer, when hundreds of Berliners flocked to the Tegel woods, much of this holiday crowd coagulated on our street, gaping silently and—so we thought—disapprovingly at our home. My father did not let this unsolicited audience interfere with the cultivation of a stately border of dahlias hugging his garden fence. He nonchalantly went about his digging and weeding, outfitted in stained and well-worn *Lederhosen*, hardly the proper garb for a conservative Frohnau property owner.

Intervening decades have, of course, modernized local architecture. Our house still stands, obviously well maintained by its present inhabitants, and two doors down a newer, larger habitation of almost identical design indicates, as do many other Frohnau dwellings, that the *Bauhaus* style has ceased to scandalize the community. Like so many Nazi victims, *Bauhaus* values have survived Hitler. I still saw no one dressed in humble *Lederhosen*, however. On the contrary, parked in front of our former pride and joy was a gleaming white Mercedes Benz, one of many symbols of affluence on this quiet, prosperous street I had not seen since 1932 as a boy of eleven.

My father's leather shorts not only symbolized defiance of conservative suburbanite neighbors but expressed his Bavarian contempt for Prussians in general. I think they also represented something else: his inability to forget his social origins. He always remained quick to take offense at real or imaginary slights from people whom he suspected of holding his lowly antecedents against him. Regional prejudice and suspected condescension on the part of professional associates coalesced into one hostile environment. "I can stand those Prussian pigs no better than the devil can the sight of the cross," he would say, and as the depression began to make inroads on our short-lived prosperity, these outbursts against his proliferating demons multiplied.

In a totally different way, I also viewed our years in Berlin as a sentence of exile. At age seven I seem to have had an unusually fixed view of the world and my place in it. Frankfurt, my home town, was the center of my universe; my friends with whom I had lived and played since I could remember were society *tout court*, the people with whom I expected to grow up. As soon as I entered the second grade of Frohnau's elementary school, there came tangible reinforcement of my misery. Not only was I forced to struggle to catch up, but my Frankfurt dialect was the object of general derision among peers who considered the arrival of a stranger quite as much an intrusion as I no doubt would have, had the roles been reversed.

I must admit, at the same time, that these resentments born of ostracism and scholastic humiliation do somewhat unfairly overshadow the fact that better times ensued before the school year had progressed beyond the halfway mark. It did not take long before I had an opportunity to display talents that prompted my teacher to take favorable notice of me. What I lacked in arithmetic I made up in composition, where my productions were often read aloud as an example of precocious and lively narrative writing. This was also the time when my interest in religion revived. German schools provided religious instruction for Protestant, Catholic, and Jewish children. Only students whose parents had left church or synagogue could be excused from these exercises. In proper, conservative Frohnau, I found that I was the only member of my grade sent home early on days when the last class hour had been set aside for the ministrations of pastor, priest, or rabbi. Feeling that I was sufficiently "different" as it was, I requested to be allowed to join the second-grade Lutheran majority, of whose ranks I became a zealous member. I bore the rote memorization of the catechism stoically, while relishing Bible readings and following with genuine enthusiasm our partisan excursions through the annals of the Protestant Reformation. I wrote earnest compositions on the life of Luther, and delighted my teacher with the enthusiasm I displayed when we took field trips to local sites connected with the Thirty Years' War. (Needless to say, none of our studies mentioned Calvin or such refractory sectarians as Menno Simmons or Thomas Müntzer.) None of this added up to piety, but to a decision set down in a second-grade composition book, miraculously preserved with other family treasures, announcing that "if all goes well, and my family is not overtaken by catastrophe, I want to become a professor of history." The intimations of catastrophe turned out to be prophetic, but I reached my goal despite them. And while I came to view organized religion with an indifference that matched my father's hostility, I have no doubt that religion first awakened in me the interests that gave content and meaning to my life.

In due time, life outside of school became more agreeable, too. The social ostracism that had initially greeted me waned quickly. As my birthday approached in June, I boldly invited to my party what appeared to me to be the leaders of my class, and to my surprise and relief, they all came in their Sunday best, bearing suitable gifts. Henceforth I was one of them.

Although Berlin was not Frankfurt, and never could be, it had its interesting aspects. I cannot say that I found its renowned art museums fun. Looking at rooms full of paintings seemed to me a dull way to spend the day, and I would have preferred the military museum, the *Zeughaus,* off limits, of course, in our family. But I enjoyed the department stores (Wertheim, Tietz, Karstadt) and the fairgrounds near the *Funkturm,* Berlin's half-sized answer to the Eiffel Tower. I remember seeing early demonstrations of talking pictures and television, exhibits of the first streamlined automobile designs, and experimental versions of a prefabricated house, capable of being assembled within twenty-four hours.

I also became an avid newspaper reader, and by the time my family left Berlin, I knew the names and—vaguely—the goals of Germany's major political parties, the identity of their leaders, the

27

chancellors, and major ministerial personalities. I became especially conscious of the violent hostility permeating party factionalism, the battles between Right and Left after political rallies, resulting in dead and wounded, particularly on May Day. On such occasions my father would stay home from the office, because he did not want to be hit by a stray bullet or struck by a stray blow from a policeman's rubber truncheon. I remember the elections of 1928, often viewed as a kind of Indian summer of Republican efflorescence, when I accompanied my parents for the first time to the polling place. The next day I scrutinized the papers for returns. Although "our party," the Social Democratic, emerged from the contest with 30 percent of the vote, a following ten times that of Hitler's party, I also realized how much Frohnau, where the established residents voted nationalist (the postwar label of conservatism), departed from the norm of nationwide results. The brownshirts cast an ominous shadow early, and the reality of their threat came home to me one day in 1931 when they buried one of their comrades, killed in a brawl with Communists, in the local cemetery only a few blocks from our house. A large number of neighbors and fellow suburbanites attended the burial, including my teacher, Herr Weber, who passed our house attired in the accoutrements of deep mourning. In my world Lucifer was no longer at the gate; he was well ensconced in our classroom.

So, all things taken together, Berlin has left me with a mixture of memories, which still add up to the conclusion that none of us belonged there. I do not remember that my parents had many friends. The exceptions were Carl Schott, the secretary of the Metalworkers Union, and his wife Bertha, and the Druckers, a mixed couple whose Jewish husband was a physician and whose gentile wife, like my father, was an avid and tireless gardener.

Anti-Semitism also reared its head in school. I recall one Jewish boy in my class, Herbert Jacoby, not much of a student and even less of an athlete. His failings in the gym evoked unanimous ridicule and prompted me one day to ask my mother whether Jews might possibly suffer from a congenital ineptitude for such manly pursuits as track and games. My question produced one of those unforgettable "serious talks" between mother and son, not concerned so much with poor Herbert as with the news that my own mother was Jewish. I concluded from that revelation that Jews obviously possessed many substantial virtues, and promised to treat my classmate more kindly in the future. The next day I told Herbert and my friends what I had just learned, adding that he was henceforth, if not one of us, at least under my protection.

That my mother's origins made me half Jewish (and thus set me apart in yet another way) never entered my mind, not even during the German presidential election of 1932, during which the main candidates were Hitler (whose party had by then replaced the Social Democrats as Germany's largest party), the eighty-five-year-old incumbent Paul von Hindenburg, and the leader of the Communist party by grace of Stalin (as we did not know then), the Hamburg dockworker Ernst Thälmann. Nazi anti-Semitism and chauvinism ruled out a family vote for Hitler. But although Hindenburg had lost to the mustachioed corporal with the Iron Cross the Conservative support that had elected him in 1925, and become instead the lesser-of-two-evils candidate of the republican parties, my father bristled at the thought of supporting the greatest war hero of the vanished empire. There was much dinner-table discussion during which my parents could reach no accord. I never heard anyone point out that if reelected, Hindenburg would have been ninety-two at the end of his second term. So far as I know, my mother voted for the former field marshal, while my father voted Communist.

There were, of course, other reasons for my father's radicalization. By 1932 the darkness engulfing us had become economic as well as political. In a country with an adult population just short of forty million, the number of unemployed had increased from three million in January, 1930, to more than six million by the beginning of 1932. Plant closings and bankruptcies became daily events, and the management-consulting business was being ravaged by a rapid disappearance of its clientele. Early in 1932 my uncle beat a skillful retreat from independence by accepting an executive position with the large electronics firm Telefunken; the Organisations-Institut closed its doors, and my parents joined the swelling and socially heterogeneous army of the unemployed. This happened only a year after we had moved into our custom-designed *Wohnmaschine.*

My father tried to keep us afloat as a door-to-door salesman, first of life insurance, then of "noiseless" Remington typewriters. He might as well have tried to sell automobiles in a country without filling stations. These were make-work activities of the most pointless kind. There was no denying it—the recently high-flying son of the penniless washerwoman had become a penniless bourgeois. He was crushed. Not only did he speak of "making an end of it all," but he felt now even more strongly than before that "my mother's friends" had suddenly ceased to be his. He loudly remembered his proletarian antecedents and on every occasion explained what unbearable burdens these placed on not only his wife but also his semibourgeois sons.

Finally, my mother took a trip to Frankfurt to see whether old friends and family connections might not come to our rescue. She was gone for a week, and I still remember the Saturday in early spring of 1932 when my father took me to the Anhalt railway station in Berlin to meet the train on which she was scheduled to return. When she emerged from her compartment, a broad smile suffused her face. The trip had been a success, and before we retrieved her suitcase she told us the good news. One of her former employers had indeed a position for my father as head of a new quality-control department in one of his ventures: a bicycle tire plant. The pay would not approximate his former income, but my mother had also seen the teachers at the Eschersheim *Oberrealschule*, whose problem children she had so miraculously rescued from failure before our move to Berlin. They promised at once a new supply of such children to help her resume her old tutorial practice.

We rented our *Bauhaus* palazzo and said good-bye to our well-weeded suburban paradise, exchanging it for a three-and-a-half-room apartment (two bedrooms, a small living room, kitchen, and bath) only a few houses from where we had lived until 1928. It was the converted upper story of a one-family residence whose owner likewise suffered from straitened circumstances. This bare description cannot convey—I doubt that anything can—how deeply this retreat shook my parents, my father in particular. My recent walks through Frohnau's timeless elegance have reminded me once more of the steepness of our sudden social and economic descent. Yet I greeted the move with undisguised joy. My only loss, and I mourned it sincerely, though briefly, was our dog, which stayed behind in Berlin with the house.

Once back in Eschersheim, I soon forgot the faithful beast and everything about our affluent past in uncongenial surroundings. I was back with my old friends, as I saw it, and life resumed its proper course. My father left early in the morning for a worksite halfway between Frankfurt and Hanau, even more distant than the old job at I.G. Farben. My mother was kept busy by an incessant parade of teenage boys and girls in search of academic healing. We no longer had a maid, and my own life out of school was dominated by household chores of the most varied kind, everything except cooking, including the supervision of my five-year-old brother, whom I had to keep quiet and occupied while my mother gave her lessons.

Fortunately, my mother's standards of housekeeping were not rigorous, for my own skills were modest. But I became a fairly adept dishwasher and sandwich maker. Otherwise I did little to ease the transition to shabby gentility. My parents had little time to supervise my schoolwork, and the unequal distribution of my interests soon resulted in serious problems. Instead of doing my homework, I read history. I frequently went to class unprepared, and periodic conferences that called my mother to school on behalf of her charges came to include discoveries of her own son's derelictions. She had to face the painful reality that she was saving other people's children from failures threatening her own. She kept most of these grim revelations from my father, for which I was grateful, but not grateful enough to rouse myself to higher standards of performance.

Occasionally my transgressions became too much for her. I well remember her reaction to my unwritten biology essay. After enduring several procrastinations and pleas for more time to refine my paper, the teacher had asked me to read to the class the offering so often postponed. My notebook was empty, and I had no choice but to recite from a blank page. Suddenly my teacher was standing behind me, looking over my shoulder. I was kept after class and ordered to complete under supervision what I failed to do on my own. Luckily, as I thought, I arrived home before my mother's last pupil departed. But a few days later the mail brought a note, exposing my malefactions. When I returned from school, I found my mother shedding tears of despair, as a parent might whose son has just been convicted of robbing a bank. I was contrite and genuinely sorry to cause her pain, but I cannot say that my conduct improved notably. I was in a not unnatural state of rebellion against a world that considered it necessary that I spend my time in pursuits to which I was indifferent. I dreamed of leading a life without teachers, without adult authority—a paradise of adolescent anarchy. Many years later, when I myself was a professor, I overheard my mother telling my wife about this episode. By then she claimed to have been amused by her son's "creative reaction" to being cornered.

So there we were, at odds with the world and with one another, cheerlessly hanging on to the lower rim of middle-class existence. Ambition had temporarily died in me, and my parents had lost faith in the future. I should perhaps add that I never failed outright. I advanced on schedule from grade to grade, always by small margins, displaying neither my father's mythical nor my mother's documented penchant for excellence. My elders rightly warned that hard times demanded more than German equivalents of gentlemanly C's, and despaired when they saw that despite their entreaties a mere satisfaction of elementary demands in such distasteful subjects as mathematics was all to which I aspired.

What none of us realized—certainly I did not—was that our situation would soon change for the worse. The conflicts, the economic hazards, the career setbacks, in short, the widening chasm between talent and performance in both generations, would continue. The surroundings in which these frustrations flourished would become more hostile than ever before. Almost twelve years of my life had passed at this point. I was about to enter the second dozen, which would prove so utterly horrifying for some of us that it was well that no member of the family was endowed with the gift of prophecy.

II JANUARY 30, 1933

Great events throw long shadows whose complete outlines are only visible at a distance. I doubt that many Frenchmen, taking their after-dinner promenade on May 5, 1789, realized that future generations would remember the day as the beginning of a new era, or as the prelude to what our increasingly short-sighted university catalogs call "modern history." Elizabeth Greicus wrote in her dissertation on Russia's Progressive Bloc and its attempts to affect the conduct of World War I:

Thursday, February 23 [1917], was . . . International Women's Day. Later it became known as the beginning of the February Revolution. At the time, however, no one recognized it as such. Trotsky pointed out [in his autobiography] that not even the most militant socialist organizations had called for strikes and demonstrations on the 23rd. The movement began in the industrial Vyborg section when crowds of workers demanded bread. Others joined the demonstrations and overflowed to the Petrograd district. There were occasional clashes with the police, but the day ended without serious conflicts. Most people did not consider the disorders significant and expected them to pass.[1]

January 30, 1933, too, was just another workday in ordinary German lives. In that part of the world, the next-to-last day of the month is invariably unpleasant. If the sun should shine, in defiance of all meteorological odds, it would illuminate a world lashed by crackling cold. If the clouds that rule the central European heavens from September to May claim this day as their own, as they generally do, then sleet or slushy brown snow covers the pavement. Children amble to school, and their elders walk purposefully to work through

1. Elizabeth A. Greicus, "Efforts of the Progressive Bloc to Influence the Conduct of the War in Russia, 1915–1917" (Ph.D. dissertation, Tulane University, 1969), 298–99.

a world suffused in a spectrum ranging from black to gray. The best holidays of the year are over, and before every German schoolchild there stretches an expanse of dreary, homework-laden days before the academic term ends at Easter. It is the time when youngsters pray for an attack of influenza, or measles, indeed any affliction that promises to lighten life with an unscheduled holiday.

When I woke that morning, I felt the deep depression engendered by the approach of another day of educational misery: my geometry homework was only half done, the assigned passage in Ernest Lavisse's *Histoire de France* (simplified and expurgated beyond recognition) imperfectly understood. I was to face a scene with the German master for defiantly writing, once again, a composition in Latin rather than in German script. French irregular verbs were the only burden that the dismal morning found me ready to carry with a degree of authoritative ease. The day promised to be like any other day in school life, a day hardly worth living.

But wait! I swallowed and my head jerked upward, jolted by a sudden pain. Could it be? Eagerly, I swallowed again. No doubt about it—my throat hurt. I repeated the process several times. I wanted to be sure that this was no dream. Evidence mounted: I had a sore throat. Lying back, I closed my eyes and prayed that the symptoms would not go away.

I remembered at once that the morning of a school day never found me well. I always suffered from a matutinal heaviness of limb, coupled with slight dizziness. These were symptoms of chronic disaffection, the protests of a disconsolate soul. But the sore throat signaled a distempered body, and while the world of authority around me, my parents and my teachers, cared not about my psychic sufferings, it kept a twenty-four-hour watch on my physical health. Every sport I enjoyed was proscribed from time to time as a source of potential injury. As soon as the daily rounds of school and chores had been completed and I seemed ready to claim a life of my own, other rules and curfews intervened. When I began the initiation into the mysteries of the English language in my fourth year of *Gymnasium,* "Early to bed and early to rise makes a man healthy, wealthy and wise" was the first Anglo-Saxon maxim my classmates and I were forced to recite in unison. Duty without end promised a long, useful life; a gram of pleasure portended decay.

Now the time had come to turn the obstructive wisdom of my elders to my own advantage. Indifferent to sufferings of my spirit, they would rise to the challenge of bodily disease. I bolted out of bed to carry the day's first medical bulletin to my mother. By now it must be clear that I was not looking for sympathy. The world in which I grew up gave none. It was divided by a two-party system that pitted the eternal majority of school and home against the child. Both harnessed me into a six-day curriculum of joyless obligations from which Sunday, now punctuated by familial excursions, since we had lost my albatross the garden, and indiscreet paternal inquiries into scholastic progress, offered little relief. There was no escape, except vacation and illness, the latter afforded only after thorough tests by thermometer, careful examination of relevant parts of the anatomy, and, in case of doubt, an earnest consultation with a third, part-time member of this grand coalition of adults: the family physician. These tests made up a daunting obstacle course separating the claim of illness from corroborating adult diagnosis, but the defeats of life had not extinguished my will to tackle it once more.

"Open your mouth," my mother commanded. She peered intently down my throat. "Your throat is red," she announced. "I shall take your temperature." Under the covers I squeezed my thumbs between the second and third fingers of each hand, the German equivalent of keeping my fingers crossed. The first test had been passed.

German home medicine in those days decreed that body temperature be measured, not by the easy introduction of the thermometer under the tongue, but by a far more degrading maneuver. Instead of sitting or lying on his back, the victim, in my case a pubescent boy of eleven, lay on his stomach waiting to learn whether submission to this indignity would turn out to be justified by the results. Having thus impaled me, my mother hurried off to prepare my father's breakfast and supervise my younger brother's daily mobilization. She returned after half an hour and disclosed the thermometer reading: "You have a temperature. Cover up well and stay in bed. I shall call Dr. Wetzler." I pulled up my pajama trousers and slipped under the covers. Life had its moments, after all. January 30 would pass without geometry, without joining Caesar on his forays into Gaul. (Lavisse's summary was at least a kindlier guide than his Latin source, whose reading the modern-language curriculum of my school spared me.) It would be a day of peace, spent alone, interrupted only by surreptitious reading of my latest favorite: a German translation of that congenial classic *Tom Sawyer*, the recent gift of an understanding friend of the family.

The morning passed gently in dozing, daydreaming, and reading. Whenever steps echoed outside my room, I deftly slipped *Tom Sawyer* under the mattress. The doctor appeared in time to confirm my mother's diagnosis and to prescribe that I stay in bed until the temperature was gone. He agreed, however, that she should call the home of my friend Fritz, asking that he bring me the day's assignments, confirming that I was certainly not too ill to keep up with schoolwork.

At one-thirty Fritz duly appeared with a depressing list of new tasks. After my mother had left the room, not before warning him to keep his distance from my bed to avoid contamination, he leaned over with understandable unconcern and whispered excitedly, "Do you know what I heard?"

"What?"

"Hitler has just become chancellor."

We always whispered. It was a convention of our age group, inured to live in constant opposition. Secretiveness was our way. We whispered to each other in class, when talking was naturally prohibited. We whispered in the schoolyard when exchanging a limited, unchanging repertory of anal and sexual jokes, or swapping derogatory remarks about teachers, parents, or other members of the adult world. Our existence was a furtive, resistant, sneaky microcosm of trivial secrets, our own only so long as it remained hidden from our elders.

"Is it true?" I asked.

"It went around school, and I saw storm troopers everywhere on my way home. Reif, the milkman, was in uniform today. You know, he wouldn't wear that get-up on his route unless it was safe."

Fritz was excited. Throughout the past year he had not passed a brownshirt on the street without sidling up to him, raising his hand, and whispering, "Heil Hitler." Sometimes his low-voiced greeting had been noticed and returned, sometimes merely acknowledged with a condescending smile (the Nazis proclaimed their commitment to youth but treated children no better than did other adults), sometimes disregarded. His father, with whom I seldom heard him exchange a friendly word and whom we avoided even more doggedly than we were wont to avoid fathers in general, was a Jewish lawyer whose sister had married a colonel in Germany's purportedly 100,000-man army. Fritz envied his cousins for having a father in uniform. He bragged about his uncle, and in our class he was the resident authority on Germany's glorious future in arms. We accepted his claim to being privy to all kinds of exciting martial secrets that his uncle, "who knew what was going on," supposedly passed on to him.

By the time my exultant friend left, the personal triumph with which the day had begun had soured. My uncle, too, stood in my own mind apart from the hostile adult phalanx. Since we had left Berlin, I no longer saw much of him, and we no longer spent Sundays at his elegant house in Wannsee, Frohnau's counterpart on the west side of Berlin. Although I did not know enough to recognize it then, he was a fair reincarnation of my maternal grandfather: ambitious and active, always curious to learn far beyond the needs of his business, but at the same time a disciplined hedonist, loving good books, good music, good food, and good wine. He never asked me how I was doing in school. I wondered what he thought of the news Fritz had brought me.

For the rest of the afternoon I left *Tom Sawyer* under the mattress and brooded—about what had happened, about Fritz, about myself, about my family. There was nothing precocious about my behavior. As I have explained, politics was a commonplace subject of conversation. Unlike many proverbially nonpolitical Germans, my parents subscribed to several newspapers and talked about what they read. In our home, adults and children possessed a working knowledge of the shifting panorama of current affairs, including the major questions before parliament and the frequent rise and fall of governments.

I therefore understood enough of what had happened to reflect uneasily on what the investiture of a Hitler government might mean. I tired to translate apprehension into personal terms. What effect would the new government have on me and on my friend? Here was Fritz and his harsh, querulous Jewish father with the martial connections. Here was I with a Jewish mother and a gentile father who since the depression had barely kept us afloat on the shallow waters of bourgeois gentility. The members of Fritz's family would be pulling even harder in opposite directions. What would happen to us? Would my mother's ancestry put her, and us, outside the pale? It was a reasonable question, for no one knew at this point what action to expect from Hitler. Was his anti-Semitism serious or merely verbal?

My father was a Social Democrat, not very active recently but of an intractable, intolerant, and choleric nature, an outsider by inclination. How would he react to the latest news?

I found out that evening when he came home from the office. As soon as he heard that I was ill he came to my room, followed by my mother and brother. He began speaking, hesitated, and then abruptly barked at my brother, "Close the door." I shrank back in my pillow. Ordinarily that phrase served as prelude to a tongue lashing or a whipping for something I had or had not done that day. Doors were closed to muffle stormy passages. Surely he was not going to give me hell for missing a day of school?

After my brother had carried out his order, my father burst out, "So that old asshole the field marshal has gone and done it!"

Never in my life had I heard my father use such language. Never in the lives of any of my friends had any father used such language, at least not in the hearing of his children. My world was transformed. I sat up, barely restraining myself from jumping out of bed. What excitement to hear my father describe a person of authority in terms with which we expressed our alienation from the adult world around us.

Only he was not whispering. He had flung the word loudly into the room to characterize the eighty-six-year-old president of the republic, Paul von Hindenburg, respectfully designated by the press of all political shades (except the Communists) as "aged," which was correct, and "venerable," which in some quarters was secretly qualified as a matter of opinion. So far as I was concerned, my father was the first to call him an asshole. Astonishingly, my mother, who, according to my view of the world, did not even know the word my father used, uttered neither protest nor reproof.

"You voted for that senile bastard last year," my father turned on her. "I told you this would happen. I told you. My God!" He sat down on the chair by my writing desk and pounded it with his right fist. The long discussions at the dinner table during the previous year's presidential election came back to me. Faced by two serious choices, Hindenburg and Hitler, my mother, like most citizens supporting the fragile republic, had cast ballots for the old soldier of the vanished empire. My father, veteran though he was, voted for the Communist candidate, as much, I am inclined to think today, in defiance of my mother's imperturbably rational arguments against

38

such a step as from conviction. Now he thought that he had been vindicated, for it seemed that a vote for last year's winner had also turned into a mandate for his closest rival.

While my father raged and my mother remained inscrutably silent, I looked at my brother. He winked. His round cheeks were even redder than usual. He shared my excitement of discovery. At that moment we both loved our father as never before. What a man! Asshole indeed. That's what they all were, principals, teachers, school janitors, and neighbors who confiscated soccer balls we had kicked, quite unintentionally, over garden fences into their flower beds.

Assholes ruled the world, but my father had drawn the line now. He was no longer part of that coalition of oppressors. I looked at him in speechless admiration. He glanced at me and then at the floor, suddenly embarrassed. "Well, how are you feeling?

"Better," I said firmly and to my own surprise. It was a diagnosis one ordinarily left to adults.

"Good. Then let us go down to dinner."

"Don't you think he should have his meal in bed?" my mother interposed, speaking for the first time now that the conversation had shifted to her jurisdiction.

Before I could protest, my father declared firmly, "No, tonight we all eat together." He rose and led the procession out of my room. This time he left the door open.

From that evening on, closing doors and windows before speaking became an undeclared general order in our household. What we had to say to one another at the end of a day was henceforth shielded from alien ears. Maids, repairmen, and passersby represented the ubiquitous enemy, not merely oppressive, but threatening and brutal, bent not on controlling but on destroying. The struggle against the tyranny of authority and custom had been turned into a struggle for survival. Inside the family bastion, however, the barrier between generations had been lowered. After January 30, 1933, we children and our parents moved closer together as the distance between ourselves and the outside world increased rapidly.

We could not know this as we ate our dinner that glum, historic evening, just as we could not know what a divide the day would forever constitute in our lives. My father's reaction had not brought us to such a prophetic understanding. But when he asked my

39

brother to close the door, he had responded to an inner voice, to a sensible warning. He had begun to prepare for our survival before he knew that it was threatened.

III   THE FIRST MONTHS OF THE NAZI ERA

In Berlin, January 30, 1933, was more eventful than in my home, but even there it was not a day of turmoil and violence. At about eleven o'clock in the morning, the twenty-third cabinet of the Weimar Republic was sworn in at the presidential palace. Only three of its eleven members, Adolf Hitler, Wilhelm Frick, and Hermann Göring, were National Socialists. Three other ministers were hold-overs; another had served in an earlier cabinet. The new vice-chancellor, Franz von Papen, predicted, "In two months we will have pushed Hitler into such a corner, he will squeal." In the afternoon, Göring and Frick held a strategy session with two Catholic leaders: Ludwig Perlitius and Hans Bell, the latter a signer of the Treaty of Versailles. Certainly the liberals and Socialists were uneasy. The Nazis that evening celebrated their apparently legitimate and peaceful capture of the chancellery with a torchlight parade. But nobody saw this day as the beginning of Germany's destruction, or could imagine its eventual impact on Europe and the rest of the world.[1]

Since my home town was the place of publication of Germany's most respected newspaper, the Frankfurt *Zeitung,* I have recently been able to recapture some details of what was to follow Hitler's investiture within the year, and to merge this record with my own view of the first mad months of the Hitler regime.[2] The printed pages yielded some troubling surprises. From January until September, the *Zeitung*'s editorial responses to the new order ranged from rejection to a descending trajectory of acceptance. At the beginning stood the classic editorial of January 31 in which the paper declared Hitler

---

1. Elliot B. Wheaton, *The Nazi Revolution, 1933–1935* (New York, 1969), 213–25.
2. All events recounted herein that I did not witness personally have been reconstructed from accounts in the Frankfurt *Zeitung* of 1933.

unfit for high office. A devious and timid rumination about the Nuremberg party congress in the September 7 issue, pleading that no German citizen deserved ostracism on account of his birth, closed the paper's seventy-seven-year history as the mouthpiece of south German bourgeois democracy.

But before the curtain fell, too much was told to allow any literate Frankfurter to claim that he did not know, or could not know, how different the new Germany was from the old. For the first time since 1918, streets were renamed on a scale confusing native and tourist alike. Heine, Mendelssohn, and Ebert gave way to Hitler, Göring, Horst Wessel, and names of other heroes of the "movement." Several new holidays replaced Constitution Day, and instead of one national banner, the black-red-and-gold of the revolution of 1848, two were adopted by the new government: the black-white-and-red flag of the empire, to gain the approval of Germany's fuddled conservatives, and the true symbol of the new state, a red flag with a black swastika on a white circular field in the center. For the first time in German history, school was closed to observe a chancellor's birthday.

By themselves, these symbolic and ceremonial innovations were harmless enough. Other changes seemed, at first, more comic than tragic. Clubs and organizations of every kind rushed to proclaim solidarity with national socialism. From stamp collectors to cactus fanciers, from hikers to vegetarians, everyone likened the change in government to a second coming. Teachers' organizations proved particularly susceptible to the herd instinct. Within three months all of them had been assimilated into the National Socialist Teachers Union. By June, even the Association of German Teachers of the Dance got in step, promising earnestly that it "stood firmly . . . behind the people's chancellor Adolf Hitler."

These acts of homage were accompanied by the expulsion of Jewish members from the ranks of the conforming organizations. One day my father came home more than ordinarily depressed. Germany's big-league soccer clubs had joined the procession and ousted all Jews from their rolls. Sad and indignant, he turned in his membership card to the First Football Club of Nuremberg, whose burgundy jersey and black shorts he had worn on the playing field during most of the eleven years of his active career.

At German universities a wave of student militancy created bizarre conditions of a more sinister cast. The young seized the fugitive moment to get even with their professors. At the Johann-Wolfgang-

Goethe University in Frankfurt, students called for the dismissal of twenty-eight professors (not all of them Jews) who did "not enjoy [their] confidence." In Berlin, student leaders published twelve theses demanding that works of Jews be henceforth published in Hebrew or, if published in German, labeled as translations. The government decided in April that non-Aryans must be kept at 1.5 percent of total enrollment, children of World War I veterans excepted, but revolutionary enthusiasts in Frankfurt subjected this minority to constant molestations, including the lifting of academic identity cards, from which no agency of the educational establishment made any move to protect the victims.

The older generation was not slow to take its cue from those very students it was charged with educating. Frankfurt's new rector (the equivalent of a university president in the United States) announced that his university's chief mission was to disseminate the "ethnic idea," whose exact tenets he was careful to leave undefined. The University of Münster gave an honorary doctor of laws to the provincial party chief of Westphalia. When Göttingen's internationally esteemed physicist, James Frank, protested the mistreatment of Jews, he was hastily disavowed by the rest of the faculty. The culmination of this sordid chapter in the history of German learning, of which the forgoing constitutes only a microscopic sample, came on May 10, when students throughout Germany took the day off to burn the books of authors whom the new Ministry of Propaganda had declared to be offensive to the new government: works by Jews, liberals, cosmopolitans, sophisticates, men and women gifted with a sense of humor, an odd assortment of undesirables, among whom Thomas Mann and Hermann Hesse are probably the best known, at least in the English-speaking world. In Frankfurt this auto-da-fé was supervised by University chaplain Fricke, whose presence lent both secular and divine sanction to the bonfire.

The book burning has become the best remembered single event of the early Nazi era. I think its importance has been vastly overstated. In our technological age, the burning of a book does not necessarily affect its circulation. Instead of eradicating, it calls attention to ideas the public might otherwise never have noticed. What was done to men and women shackled liberty far more effectively, and while many atrocious excesses were hidden, some were deliberately publicized to intimidate people.

Although 1932 had witnessed two parliamentary elections and

the septennial campaign for the presidency, the former called to bolster two short-lived minority cabinets (Papen and Schleicher), the new government decided to dissolve parliament once more and consult the voters anew on March 5, 1933. Only a week before election day, arsonists set fire to the Reichstag building in Berlin, gutting the edifice. On the smoking premises, midst the milling crowd, police arrested a Dutch vagrant, the Communist Marinus Van der Lubbe, who was charged with entering the building, dousing the furnishings of various strategic sites with gasoline, and then, singlehandedly, starting conflagrations in all of them. At his trial a large number of witnesses, including experts of Berlin's fire-fighting services, agreed that this fanatic, who struck everyone as rather slow-witted, was completely incapable of carrying out such an enterprise. The nature and extent of the fire indicated, instead, that the building had to have been carefully prepared by more than one conspirator. Both contemporary and subsequent analysts have insisted, furthermore, that the structure was practically burglar-proof and accessible to the incendiaries only through a subterranean passage that led from the official residence of the Reichstag's presiding officer.

That presiding officer was none other than Hermann Göring, by February, 1933, also minister-president of Prussia, who has gone to his grave insisting that he took no part in the burning of the Reichstag. Why would he insist on his innocence, even at the Nuremberg trials, after admitting to countless other crimes? I believe there is only one explanation. National socialism was founded in Munich, a city that had endured a brief Soviet government in 1919, and from the very beginning anticommunism had been a favorite sales pitch of the party. As time went on, Hitler recognized that this aspect of his program appealed, not only to German property owners of all types, but to conservatives abroad as well. As late as 1937 the British lord president of the council, Edward Frederick Lindley Wood, first earl of Halifax, praised Hitler, who "had not only performed great services in Germany, but also . . . had been able, by preventing the entry of Communism into his own country, to bar its passage further West."[3]

But had Hitler prevented a Communist takeover in Germany? German election returns from 1928 to 1932—specifically, the percent-

---

3. Quoted in Hans A. Schmitt, *European Union from Hitler to De Gaulle* (New York, 1969), 98.

age of votes gained by each of the key parties during that time—are revealing.[4]

Party	1928	1930	July, 1932	November, 1932
National Socialist	2.6	18.3	37.3	33.1
Conservative	14.2	7.0	5.9	8.8
Catholic Center	15.1	14.8	15.9	15.0
Liberal	13.6	8.3	2.2	2.9
Social Democratic	29.8	24.5	21.6	20.4
Communist	10.6	13.1	14.3	16.9

The erosion of conservatism, the near disappearance of the liberals, and the decline of democratic socialism are evident. At the same time, the meteoric rise of national socialism was feebly paralleled by a slow, steady increase in the number of Communist votes. While the Nazi total grew by approximately 1,100 percent, Communist strength mounted about 50 percent, and continued to grow even in the November, 1932, election, when some Nazi supporters appear to have returned to the Conservative party.

The Communists had thus become the third-strongest party in Germany, obviously draining votes from the Social Democrats. Many Germans believed that almost six million Communists would not accept without a fight Hitler's elevation to the chancellorship. Today we know that this assumption, no matter how plausible, was completely mistaken. Germany's Communist leadership followed the Kremlin line, which welcomed the victory of fascism in Germany. They interpreted Hitler's rise as symptomatic of the last stage of capitalism, leading to war, catastrophe, and eventually Germany's overdue proletarian revolution. German Communists remained silent and passive, because they saw Hitler not as an opponent but as the progenitor of Germany's eventual conversion to bolshevism.

In the short run, there was only one way out of this Nazi embarrassment. The Communists might not revolt, but the Nazis had to pretend that they were about to. If Germany, and Europe, were not in danger, a threat had to be staged. Evidence suggests that government agents approached Van der Lubbe and persuaded him that setting fire to the Reichstag would be the signal for a workers' uprising throughout Germany. The slow-witted victim swallowed the bait

4. The designation *liberal* in this table refers to two groups, the German Democratic and the German People's parties.

and may actually have believed that his feeble efforts set the building on fire. Some of the details remain murky and may never be resolved. In any case, the fire broke out on schedule, and Hitler's government proceeded according to plan. President Hindenburg, who knew nothing of the plot, promptly authorized a decree "for the protection of people and state," suspending constitutional freedoms, including freedom of speech, press, and assembly, inviolability of mails, and property ownership. The same edict introduced the death penalty for many crimes ordinarily carrying a life sentence, arson among them.[5] The fact that no evidence of a Communist conspiracy ever came to light was quite irrelevant, for the law was designed to launch open season on political opponents. First in line were the Communists themselves, whose party was outlawed and its leaders seized. The party's second-in-command, Ernst Torgler, was arrested for conspiracy to burn the Reichstag, as were several Bulgarian Communists living in German exile. Their and Van der Lubbe's trial lasted until December 23, resulting in everybody's, except the hapless Dutchman's, acquittal. The unlikely arsonist was executed and the Bulgarians deported, while Torgler disappeared from public view. Despite this anticlimax in the courts, the operation served its purpose. By the end of the year organized dissent had ended. The myth of the Nazi crusade against communism took its place in Western folklore, from which no rational argument is likely to dislodge it.[6]

So far as the election went, the Nazis certainly gained from the elimination of a fairly formidable rival. Having convinced many Germans that a Bolshevik takeover had only barely been prevented, they no longer needed to camouflage their own terrorist methods. Only days before the voting, Hermann Göring rode into Frankfurt, accompanied by squads of SA (*Sturmabteilung*) and SS (*Schutzstaffel*) and eighty members of the regular police. He told a cheering crowd that respect for the law would not be allowed to interfere with persecution of the "enemy": "My business," he cried, "is not to dispense justice, but to destroy and exterminate."

But the election results appearing in newspapers throughout Germany on Monday morning, March 6, indicated that many voters still

5. Ernst Rudolf Huber (ed.), *Quellen zum Staatsrecht der Neuzeit* (2 vols.; Stuttgart, 1951), II, 152–253.
6. This is the contention and the thrust of the copious documentary evidence assembled by Walter Hofer *et al., Der Reichstagsbrand: Eine wissenschaftliche Dokumentation* (2 vols.; Berlin, 1978), the most comprehensive work on the subject.

refused to climb on the bandwagon of the self-styled national revolution. The Nazis received 44 and their Conservative allies 8 percent of the votes, providing the government with a precarious margin of victory. In Frankfurt the Social Democrats and the smaller middle-class parties attracted some supporters lost the previous year. Municipal elections held the following Sunday reinforced the impression that the opposition retained a core of allegiance impervious to the heat of Nazi rhetoric and violence. Social Democrat strength almost reached the figures of 1919, before the incorporation of numerous suburbs; the Catholic Center's following had never been greater. Even the Communists, never as strong here as in the industrial centers of north, central, and eastern Germany, lost only 10 percent. Only a record turnout, combined with the melting away of liberal support since the last city council contest in 1929, gave the Nazis 48 percent of the vote and 42 of 85 council seats, one short of a working majority.[7] Many municipal governing bodies throughout Germany emerged with even larger opposition majorities. Storm troopers and police soon stepped in to correct these results. Frankfurt's lord mayor was arrested "to protect him from the wrath of the people." The next day armed men occupied all exits of city hall, while the same fate overtook the mayor's deputy and the municipal superintendent of schools.

Similar Nazi disappointments attended factory council elections in the Ruhr, where only one-third of local miners and steelworkers endorsed National Socialist candidates. To remedy this error, a new law stipulated that two-thirds of all such councils must henceforth consist of Hitler's followers.

The government continued to waive rules as need arose, and to find new ways of persuasion. On March 20, less than two months after the swearing in at the presidential palace, the German Ministry of the Interior, the only major federal department headed by a Nazi, announced the opening of Dachau concentration camp. The bulletin explained that the facility was to convert Communists into useful members of society. If these enemies of the commonwealth refused to be salvaged, the minister consoled his readers, their detention would at least protect the nation from the threat they posed to its well-being. Once again the popular policy of anticommunism prompted public acceptance of concentration camps as

7. Barbara Köhler, "Die Nationalsozialisten in der Frankfurter Stadtverordnetenversammlung, 1929 bis 1933," *Archiv für Frankfurts Geschichte und Kunst,* LIX (1985), 439–84.

legitimate components of the law-enforcement machinery. Even before all parties (other than the National Socialist) were outlawed in June, the new detention centers became human warehouses for non-Communist political dissenters as well. Jews at that time constituted only a small percentage of the inmate population, and most of them faced arrest, not because of their origins, but because of their political beliefs. A revealing directive, issued by the Saxon criminal police in August, 1933, decreed, for instance, that "officials and . . . spiritual leaders of marxist organizations [no longer just Communists], and persons with serious criminal records," were to be dispatched to the Hohenthal concentration camp, the state's repository of enemies in that particular region, thus making political dissent synonymous with crime.[8]

At this early stage, newspaper coverage was not confined to ministerial announcements. The stories were clearly intended to drive home the positive social and humanitarian tasks performed in concentration camps. The commandant of the Heuberg installation near Stuttgart—a storm-troop leader, who still preferred to be identified as a retired army major—waxed eloquent when describing the burdens and responsibilities of his office. On Sundays, he complained, when ordinary citizens rested, he and his staff faced many troubled individuals inquiring after missing relatives. As a result of the mounting number of arrests, his records were chaotic, and many questions remained unanswered. But he assured the newspapers that the camp leadership, though exhausted from its ongoing labors of human reclamation, did its best to satisfy all petitioners. Major Kaufmann seems to have been unaware that Heinrich Himmler solved the same problem in Dachau by announcing that every inquiry for the whereabouts of an inmate would earn the victim an additional day's confinement. Heuberg's facilities were turned over to the Wehrmacht before the end of the year, but not until that camp, founded to accommodate the overflow of political prisoners from regular penal institutions, had within a few months become temporary home, torture chamber, and, in some instances, graveyard to fifteen thousand Germans. That the most famous of its occupants, Kurt Schumacher, lived to resurrect the Social Democratic party

8. New York *Times*, March 21, 1933; American Association for a Democratic Germany, *They Fought Hitler First: A Report on the Treatment of German Anti-Nazis in Concentration Camps* . . . (New York, 1945), 13, quoting Edgar A. Mowrer in the New York *Times*, November 11, 1933; Raimund Schnabel (ed.), *Macht ohne Moral: Eine Dokumentation über die SS* (Frankfurt am Main, 1957), 106.

after World War II, indicates once again that the camp's population from the very start included more than Communists.[9]

Meanwhile the government mounted a vigorous campaign against foreign "fairy tales of atrocities" (*Greuelmärchen*). With flagrant impudence it rejected foreign claims that 100,000 Germans were being detained for political reasons, not denying detentions altogether, but merely reducing the figure to 16,000 for Prussia and 22,000 for the entire country. Yet even government statistics could not explain why anyone should suffer imprisonment without so much as an indictment or the prospect of a trial for actions never considered punishable before. Several years would go by before an eager law student's dissertation, fittingly dedicated to the "Reichsführer SS and Chief of the German Police, Heinrich Himmler," explained that in the Nazi state, opposition was a "symptom of disease" and that the police as guardian of national well-being was authorized to eradicate every such manifestation "by every suitable means."[10]

Quickly Hitler was establishing a framework of German unity whose authoritarian uniformity would have appalled the nation's nineteenth-century founding fathers. To be sure, persecutions were nothing new. Jews had been treated with great cruelty as late as the seventeenth century; civil rights were denied Christian minorities as recently as the nineteenth. Between 1820 and 1850 a host of independent spirits, like Heinrich Heine and Karl Marx, had preferred exile to German prison cells. But the total exclusion of a majority of representative groups from public life, decreed by a central government whose draconian orders were reinforced by tens of thousands of random arrests, was without precedent, at least in Germany.

Even deeper gloom descended over our home. It was only a year since my father had found work again, after two years of unemployment. Now this. Never of a happy disposition, he succumbed to chronic dejection. As a family we withdrew into our own world, alienated from our immediate surroundings, suspicious, weighing every word spoken within hearing of a stranger, revealing only to one another our outraged reaction to the day's events. Slowly, but obsessively, the concern about escape came to dominate our

9. Julius Schätzle, *Stationen zur Hölle: Konzentrationslager in Baden und Württemberg* (Frankfurt am Main, 1980), 9–16.

10. Otto Geigenmüller, *Die politische Schutzhaft im nationalsozialistischen Deutschland* (Würzburg, 1937), 23.

thoughts—very slowly, because for a man like my father, who spoke no language other than German, any foreign refuge spelled the end of his life as a breadwinner. This was not true of my mother, fluent both in English and French, a fact that made the topic even more delicate. Would we emigrate one day without our father? It was unthinkable. Whenever the conversation edged in the direction of that fearful issue, my mother changed the subject before my father could launch into what became increasingly familiar and depressing tirades lamenting his uselessness to us all.

We had friends who persisted in believing that this new government of incompetent rowdies would not last long. I remember the father of Heiner M., who went about his daily tasks with a fixed, confident smile until Christmas Day, 1934, when he locked the door of his study, drew a pistol from his desk, and blew out his brains, leaving behind a widow and four teenage children. Suicides of civil servants, professors, and other professional men, dismissed because of ancestry or political beliefs, became epidemic. Once again, it is worth recalling that we learned this, not by some secret grapevine, but from our newspapers.

In this grim world only children retained the capacity for laughter. Proliferating public holidays, another shrewd public-relations move by the new government, provided one source of relief and amusement. After the March 5 elections endowed Hitler and his Conservative allies with a slight 52-percent majority in parliament, our homeroom teacher read to us the announcement "that the historic turning point implicit in the overwhelming [sic] victory of the national front" would be observed by a school holiday on March 8. Government bombast had always tickled our irreverence, and my memories do not match stereotypical views of Germans bowing seriously and without question to every word of authority. Still, we were more than willing to meet halfway anyone bearing the gift of another holiday.

The Nazis catered to this hankering for more circuses. If a narrow election victory called for a holiday, then the opening of the new parliament deserved more elaborate celebration. Because of the Reichstag fire, the parliamentary premiere was to be staged in Potsdam, the Berlin suburb that had been, since the seventeenth century, the second residence of the electors of Brandenburg and the kings of Prussia. The newly elected deputies would gather in the

Garrison Church, in whose crypt the most popular Prussian king, Frederick the Great, lay buried.

Parliamentary openings had heretofore gone largely unnoticed. The new minister of propaganda and popular enlightenment, Joseph Goebbels, explained why that practice was going to change. According to his proclamation, the recent election had at last united all Germans. "Many millions, all tribes, estates, and confessions," he intoned, "have clasped hands, rising above differences of class and religion." This wonder-working effect of a 4-percent victory margin, a secular loaves-and-fishes miracle, was to be observed in all towns and villages.

Then came the damper on our holiday joy. We would not have to attend classes on March 21, but we would have to gather in the school auditorium to witness the unfolding of this programmed rebirth. Our principal was to explain the historic significance of the day, followed by a broadcast of the ceremonies, including speeches by President Hindenburg and Chancellor Hitler. Schools lacking a radio were ordered to procure one. "The festivities must be so arranged," the proclamation concluded, "that all students realize that they are witnessing the beginning of a new epoch."

At our worm's-eye level the impact of the ceremony was largely lost. We never had paid much attention to the orations our principal was required to deliver on national holidays. The routine obsequies to history, teeming with allusions to German greatness, never moved us. We dozed, yawned, and fidgeted through all of it. March 21 turned out to be more of the same. The broadcast was a dismal failure. Our school's loudspeaker was adequate for classroom use, but its emanations barely reached half the auditorium audience. The transmission drowned in static, and the speeches remained incomprehensible, even to the front rows. A radio reporter's breathless account of Hindenburg's and Hitler's descent to the church basement, where they gazed briefly and wordlessly at the casket containing Frederick the Great's bones, was likewise punctuated by electronic noise. Fortunately, it was all over by one o'clock, and we ran home as fast as our feet would carry us to salvage what we could of the holiday.

What did the "national revolution" actually mean to us children? Recently, social historians have claimed that our generation had found in Hitler a new father. These scholars reason that our elders returned defeated from World War I and therefore failed us as authority figures, and the führer stepped into a void that had surrounded us since birth. This arresting hypothesis elicits no recognition in my memory. I only remember that my school chums and I feared our fathers more than we feared any dictator. Wherein had they failed? They had fought a hostile world to a standstill and to the end protected Germany from invasion. Their heroism became the stuff of legends and myths. We needed no surrogate father. The American historian Daniel Horn has set the record straight in pointing out that by 1935, when membership became compulsory, only half of Germany's eligible boys had joined the Hitler Youth.[11]

In my class joining such organizations was not fashionable. Of about forty boys, three entered the Hitler Youth or its auxiliary, the *Jungvolk,* in 1933. A somewhat larger number belonged to the Protestant Bible Circle until it was dissolved. School and society preempted so much of our day that we were unwilling to surrender any more time to organized activities. Our ambition was to evade, not conform. Once one reached the age at which career worries necessitated submission, this independence wilted, but in our early teens grades were all that mattered to our parents, and personal liberty was all that counted with us.

I remember, therefore, no individual or collective surge to join a real or imaginary vanguard of history. We had no revolutionary ambitions, no conscious desire to be remembered by future generations. Our acknowledgment of the events of the spring of 1933 consisted of an obscene, two-line joke: "Why is the führer not allowed to fart?" "Because the whole nation stands behind him." It began to make the rounds after the "day of Potsdam," and constituted our "cohort's" most significant contribution to the folklore of the new era.

Most of us continued to play the same games. With adults they remained games of evasion; with each other they expressed friendship or rivalry, depending on our relationships. The political theater around us was mysterious and absurd, as the adult world had always been. But the revolution wanted us, of course, and did its best to penetrate our secret universe. Late in April, the new Prussian minister of education issued a directive exhorting school faculties to

11. Daniel Horn, "Youth Resistance in the Third Reich: A Social Portrait," *Journal of Social History,* VII (1973), 31–45, and "The Struggle for Catholic Youth in Germany: An Assessment," *Catholic Historical Review,* LXV (1979), 561–82.

My father, Julius Schmitt, about the time of my birth

My maternal grandfather, Adolf Hamburger, with his children Elisabeth and Richard, *ca.* 1908

Elise Schmitt and I, her grandson, 1925

The first-grade class at Eschersheim Elementary School in 1927. I am in the front row, third from the right, clutching the remainder of my lunch. Behind me, in a sailor's blouse, is my boon companion, Rainer.

A father with his sons, Berlin, 1929

The house my parents built in Berlin, 1930

Before my departure for the Netherlands,
September, 1934

The photo of Rainer that accompanied his gift
of *Friedrich der Grosse,* September, 1934

Katharina Petersen, headmistress at Eerde

Jan Boost

On the road to Brussels in 1935. Second from the left is my roommate Hans Lüdecke, the bell ringer. I am fourth from the left, Jan Boost fifth.

Afternoon tea on the bridge over the moat at Eerde, Whitsunday, 1937

Golbyshka, 1938

The day of my departure for the United States,
August 25, 1938

Paul Morrison and I on graduation day at
Washington and Lee

Fresh from officer candidate school and just
married, 1944

My mother, Elisabeth Schmitt, shortly after my father's death

My brother, Richard Schmitt, *ca.* 1941

Florence in 1945

My uncle and aunt, great survivors of the war

My uncle and I, reunited in Amsterdam

reconsider failing grades whose recipients had "devoted their entire strength to the liberation movement of Adolf Hitler." Slyly, his excellency left the final decision to the teachers, but he encouraged them "to take into account the greatness and the needs of the times, and to judge generously." So far as I was aware of it, parental reaction to this ukase was hostile, chiefly because our progenitors feared that such policies would devalue our diplomas and obstruct our path to personal success. No one could tell how long this regime would last. Once it was gone, the practice of passing students for membership in Nazi youth organizations might leave behind a generation with worthless or suspect diplomas. That was the common view. To us it made little difference. The injection of politics into grading certainly created no rush among my peers to devote their "entire strength to the liberation movement of Adolf Hitler."

My own next brush with the new reality came one afternoon in May, shortly after the book burnings. My mother was entertaining some friends at tea while I sat in my room, banished from the cream cakes and tarts, halfheartedly decimating my homework. Suddenly the bell of our second-story apartment rang—not in the ordinary manner—but as if someone of great weight, or in a great hurry, had simply planted his thumb on the button and left it there until his summons was answered. I rushed to open the door and found myself face to face with two storm troopers and a civilian who identified himself as a member of the state police. Without invitation the strangers entered the hallway, where the civilian asked me if I knew the whereabouts of Fräulein Hildebrand. She was the maid in the other household sharing our duplex, and I only knew that I had not seen her for quite a while. I also knew that she was a member of some militant left-wing organization—I have quite forgotten which—and therefore lucky to have cleared out before the visitors arrived. At this point my mother emerged from the drawing room, but the civilian, a rotund, jovial sort, glanced over her shoulder at the party and told her in a soft voice that invited no contradiction to resume the entertainment of her friends. He followed me to my room, sat down, patted me on the shoulder, and asked whether my father possessed any forbidden or subversive books. He was not the least bit frightening; the two storm troopers, standing rather forlornly in the hall, even less so.

The entire mission struck me as a waste of time. Did my interrogator expect to find Fräulein Hildebrand in our apartment? Did I look to him like a son who would denounce his father? But I knew that adults needed humoring and assured the uninvited visitor that my father did not read anything he was not supposed to. The plainclothesman smiled at that and left me to my homework. Then he and his martial followers rummaged in the bookcases and after a while departed with an armful of volumes they told me were unfit for the library of a good German household. I cannot remember what they confiscated. One book that turned out to be missing, I gathered subsequently from my parents, was a legal treatise of great technical intricacy, by a former Frankfurt professor named Sinzheimer. What they left behind was much more remarkable. They did not touch the works of Heinrich Heine, Germany's greatest Jewish writer, a luminary of the Romantic movement, who died an exile in Paris. Another book for which I had trembled was Emil Ludwig's biography of the businessman and amateur archaeologist Heinrich Schliemann, the slipshod excavator of Troy. It was a recent Christmas present, and I knew that its author was proscribed because he was a Jew and because of his derogatory biographies of the kaiser and Bismarck. But our uninvited guests had not touched my property, nor—wonder of wonders—had they laid a hand on Marx's *Das Kapital*. I still possess the copy that eluded their zeal, and although it has never figured among my favorite reading, its escape from Gestapo vigilance has made it a treasured relic of my childhood.

This was the only call the secret police paid us. I might add that they did not find Fräulein Hildebrand. Several years later, I thought I saw her on a street in Amsterdam, pushing a baby carriage. She gave no sign of recognition, and I made no effort to approach her.

But to return to school: Since universities were obviously adopting national socialism with such speed that the government could barely keep up with their enthusiasm, the authorities could turn their attention to the secondary sector. On May 9, new guidelines for secondary education emerged. This time the set of directives originated in the German Ministry of the Interior, indicating that the jurisdiction that individual states had traditionally exercised in this field was now being usurped by the national government. A custom of centuries, identified with those national founding fathers whom we were constantly exhorted to emulate, had been abandoned. But, while that may have troubled some of our elders, it was the message, rather than the strategy of its dissemination, that affected us. The minister handed down four commandments:

1. "The German school must form political man."
2. Historical instruction must emphasize events after 1914.
3. Students' "vision of racial differences must be sharpened."
4. Greater emphasis must be placed on physical fitness, to educate German youth to increased prowess in arms.

We first felt the impact of point four. More physical education was a popular prospect. All it actually meant was one more hour of physical education per week. Content of these classes changed only minutely. Instead of putting a small shot (weighing five metric pounds), we were taught to throw dummy hand grenades. The sinister and martial implications of the exercise were, however, largely obscured by the fact that the object remained to throw the dummy as far, rather than as accurately, as possible.

Next in importance for us was point two. As it happened, I advanced from sixth to seventh grade just before these new policy instructions appeared. History was therefore about to make its first appearance on my lesson plan. I had looked forward to this enrichment of my school day, but found my expectations once more disappointed.

History, like every other school subject, was stolidly taught from dreary manuals, whose content and method had not changed since the days of the kaiser.[12] It started with the Egyptians and a year and a half later, when I left Germany, had not progressed beyond the beginnings of imperial Rome. Thanks to my grandfather's compendia of classical lore, I was quite familiar with the standard subjects of antiquity. I did reasonably well in class, therefore, but the ancients—on both sides of the Mediterranean—did not actually interest me, even though I spent much of my childhood in a part of Germany teeming with reminders of Roman glory. In the neighboring suburb of Heddernheim, householders digging in their flower beds still exhumed shards of Roman pottery. An entire subdivision of that locality, called the Römerstadt, included streets named after Hadrian and other Antonine emperors whose legions planted their standards in our native soil.

Farther north, in the wooded hills of the Taunus near Bad Homburg, stood the Saalburg, an elaborate Roman fort from the second

---

12. Kurt-Ingo Flessau, *Schule der Diktatur: Lehrpläne und Schulbücher des Nationalsozialismus* (Munich, 1977), 12–18, 53–54, 66–98, shows how little changed—indeed, needed to be changed—in this sector to turn education into a faithful servant of the new regime.

century A.D., first excavated in the 1870s and then restored at the initiative of William II during the first decade of the twentieth century. The last kaiser wanted to remind his subjects that Germans had not always stood tall and united, and in a more distant age of tribal divisions had been colonized like Africans and Asians.

Why did none of this interest a child so intensely and precociously fascinated by the past? The answer was simple. Part of the excavation included a cemetery of three hundred Roman graves, and no family excursion to the Saalburg was complete without my mother testing my fractured Latin on one of the surviving gravestones. I dreaded these exercises, and silently cursed the Romans and their confounded language, dead so far as everyday life was concerned, but not dead enough to stay out of my weekends. What I am leading to is the confession that starting the study of history with the events of 1914 would have suited me to the ground. The war and the revolution were interesting. However, I do not doubt that our teachers would have succeeded in making even these events as dull as they made the history of the ancients.

The first year of history passed, little affected by the maxims of the national revolution, except that we gathered from our teacher, a horsefaced, perpetually unshaven individual named Meyer, that the peoples of the Near East—except the Egyptians—were entirely too much like Jews to deserve respect and that their decline in the face of Greece and Rome confirmed current beliefs about Nordic superiority. Thus it was only proper that straight-nosed Hellenes defeated hook-nosed Persians at Salamis, and that Romans should eventually throw salt on the ruins of Carthage.

While *Herr Studienrat* Meyer used every opportunity to sharpen our "vision of racial differences," he seemed to entertain no suspicion of my own tainted blood. I was blond and had inherited blue eyes from my Jewish grandfather, to whom I also owe my middle name Adolf. (My Aryan father had brown eyes.) Nothing in my appearance indicated any ties with Asian Semites or North African Phoenicians. However, when our biology teacher began to take seriously the intent of the third point on the ministerial blueprint for education, the battle between the new "ethnic idea" and my own hybrid origins had to be joined.

As soon as Hitler began housekeeping in the Berlin chancellory, talk of race filled the air. Nordic man began to spook every half-educated brain. Girls began to bleach their hair, and—for all I know—so did men. But since most Germans are not blond, in fact not Germanic, other categories of physical respectability had to be devised to maintain the myth of the nation's ethnic cohesion. Terms such as *Saxon, alpine,* and *dinaric* became euphemisms of racial respectability for members of the brunette majority, reassuring them that their antecedents excluded Semitic, negroid, and other unforgivable defects. (In view of the growing friendship with Japan, it was never decided where Orientals fitted into this scale of racial values.)

After the publication of the ministerial ukase, these preoccupations also entered our classroom. Herr Döring, who taught us biology, decided to put his science at the disposal of national reeducation. Our dreary sallies into botanical classification suddenly stopped. Instead, we were subjected to protracted measurements of all parts of our physique not covered by clothing: arms, hands, noses, and craniums. The results were painstakingly recorded on sheets of graph paper. The proceedings delighted us, of course. While this went on, we had no homework; all we had to do was appear in class, have our dimensions recorded, and keep reasonably quiet while our teacher accumulated a formidable set of numbers about each of us.

Once again, my recollections do not indicate that any of us took this experiment seriously. It made us more aware of one another's physical characteristics, and there ensued endless banter over a flat head, a bulbous nose, or a set of bowlegs. It was no more or less cruel than countless other taunts we flung at one another, and it gave no unusual offense to the victims. Certainly nobody displayed anxiety regarding the results of our teacher's inquiry. No one showed any desire to "pass" as this type or that. We assuredly did not recognize that even as Germans were called upon to celebrate total, if spurious, unity, this new "racial science"—soon legitimized by creating university chairs for its practitioners—was the beginning of new divisions, eventually between two fixed classes whom no Hegelian synthesis could reconcile. survivors, and victims marked for extinction.

But first came the great day when the meaning of all Herr Döring's calculations was to be revealed to us. I do not doubt that he consumed much midnight oil drawing new and exciting lessons from his columns of figures. How extensive a presentation he had planned will never be known, because the new Linné ineptly began his talk with the most sensational item on his list of findings. Our teacher started with a flourish by announcing who among us belonged to the elect, whose cranial, skeletal, and dermatological characteristics confirmed membership in the Nordic race. To whet our expectations, he announced that only 7.7 percent of the school population (Had he measured every child from grade five to twelve?) resided at the blond and blue-eyed apex of the human race. After the statistics came the names, in alphabetical order. Naturally, my friend and neighbor Fritz Ewald, a wiry, hawk-faced, ash blond lad, was on the list. That was to be expected. But when Herr Döring approached the end of the alphabet, whose name should he call but mine! It was the first time in my so-far-undistinguished school career that I was in the top 7 percent of anything. What added to the thrill, however, was not the honor, neither desired nor prized, but the sudden overpowering joy with which I realized that a teacher had just placed himself completely at my mercy. The minute he subsided, my hand shot up. "Yes, Schmitt," Herr Döring said with an indulgent smile, "What is it?"

"Sir, can persons of Jewish descent be Nordic?" I asked.

"Of course not, my boy. This is the point of our work," he replied. "Our new racial science allows us to identify and separate such people from the national community."

"Then there must be a mistake," I said, as humbly as I could. "My mother is Jewish."

I have no idea what went through my teacher's mind during the ensuing seconds of silence, when the passage of time seemed suspended. Nor do I know what my peers thought of my revelation, which was no news to most of them. I think that some of them were annoyed that I was putting a premature end to our biological holiday. Herr Döring was momentarily speechless, while his hands fiddled nervously with his sheets of graph paper. Then he shuffled them together in a neat pile, took a deep breath, and told us to get out our herbals. Indeed, I had ruined the entire project, and it was back to counting pistils and stamens. Henceforth I did my biology homework with unusual diligence, convinced that this teacher would miss no opportunity to cause me difficulties should I be caught unprepared. But I need not have worried. For the rest of the year, in fact for the rest of my sojourn in this institution, he did not call my name.

Summer liberated all schoolchildren for six weeks during July and August. My mother went to Switzerland and France, exploring employment opportunities and possible havens of emigration, but without success. For me, it was the summer in which I first took an interest in girls and, in the meadow below our house, hidden in the tall grass, first smoked a cigar, one of my father's Swiss *Stumpen.* Contrary to convention, I did not get sick. I learned to enjoy cigars, and have since graduated to inhaling the fumes of choicer leaves. Even the new Germany left us in peace. Despite the government's authoritarian cast, the life of a German child was not as relentlessly organized as an American child's seems to be. No one appeared worried that we would spend six weeks doing nothing that was either constructive or conspicuously patriotic. We played ball, ate fruit from the trees of a neighbor's orchard, and went swimming in the nearby Nied River. In short, we had a thoroughly good time without a thought of tomorrow.

The resumption of school introduced us to a new classroom ritual. We had always risen and come to attention when a teacher entered the class, but now we were to lift the right hand to eye level and hold it there, arm extended, until the person of authority had returned the salute and given us leave to sit down. This perturbed me greatly. No one in my family gave the Nazi salute, the standard obeisance to our new masters. How was I to respond to the new order? My parents explained to me that I could not violate school rules, that I must, therefore, raise my hand with everyone else, but under no circumstance must I ever say "Heil Hitler!" I had a feeling that if I pressed my own preference, which consisted of simply standing at attention, I would cause trouble to my parents rather than to myself. It had become quite clear to me that the national synchronization of political beliefs involved adults, while childhood remained a privileged reserve of irreverence and irresponsibility. No informer listened to our conversation; no law demanded of us new commitments and explicit changes of attitude. The fact that children did not count suddenly turned into an advantage. But I realized that I must not use this discovery to jeopardize my parent's safety.

The last great event of 1933 was Hitler's visit to Frankfurt. It took place on September 23 and was to open construction of the Frankfurt-Darmstadt leg of the new, grandiose north-south *Autobahn.* The führer was to make his way from the airport to the work-site, turn the first spade of earth, make a speech, and dash back to his plane.

By then the government's stagecraft knew how to turn even so brief a visit into an epic occasion. At seven o'clock in the morning a battalion of some seven hundred unemployed laborers lined up at the Reich Labor Office. On an improvised rostrum, decorated with flowers and flags, the director of the office formally surrendered his control of this contingent, but not before explaining that thanks to Hitler's statesmanship, these men were being discharged from the army of the unemployed to begin work on this Appian Way of the future. After three *heils* to the nation's savior, these chosen helots, preceded by a band of the Frankfurt SA, marched to the square in front of the stock exchange. There followed more speeches eulogizing the unforgettable occasion, and more cheers for the man whom one excited orator described, for the first time, as "the greatest German of all." Then the local party chief handed each of the seven hundred a spade and bade them shoulder it like a weapon. The proletarian battalion closed ranks once again and proceeded in military cadence to the distant site where construction was scheduled to begin the next day.

While the working-class elect tramped to their destination, the notables rushed in their Mercedes Benzes to the airport, where a squadron of planes carrying Hitler, his entire cabinet, and an assortment of party luminaries had just landed. After more panegyrics, and exchanges of bouquets, the motorcade was organized: Hitler by himself in the first car, the flowers in the second, the ministers in the next two vehicles, and so on. At the worksite in the municipal forest, the patriotic sermons continued, including the announcement by the *Gauleiter* and governor of Hesse-Nassau that all necessary rights-of-way in his province had been donated by their selfless owners. Then the chief engineer in charge of the project reported to the führer, in soldierly fashion, that seven hundred German workers had "fallen in" to join the battle against unemployment. He handed Hitler what the papers called an *Ehrenspaten* (a spade of honor, or honorary spade—however one translated it, it did not make much sense), and the "greatest German" seized it "with determination" and thrust it "vigorously" into the ground. He followed this ceremonial labor with a few extemporaneous remarks and shook hands with some of the workmen—a folksy gesture quickly imitated by his retinue of ministers and minions. For a fleeting moment the great fraternized with the humble, in a manner reminiscent of the former kaiser's visits to Ruhr factories during World War I, when he bade the steelworkers to toil as devotedly at their "anvil" as he assured them he labored for the good of the country on his throne.

Easily lost in this chronicle of ceremonies was a brief moment on Hitler's return to the airport when he passed, according to the official report, a "cordon of 35,000 cheering schoolchildren." That was where we came in. The events of September 23, carried by all radio stations, brought us yet another official holiday, half nuisance and half fun. Fun because it meant no classes and some time off, nuisance because most of our day was consumed dawdling through another noisy moment in the hectic pageant of contemporary history. This time, however, we advanced from audience to brief participators. Early in the morning, while the seven hundred former unemployed marched with and without spades, we boarded special streetcars that brought us to our designated spot on the route along which the motorcade was to travel. This logistic miracle, bringing each schoolchild in a matter of hours to a designated place on the periphery of the city, undoubtedly gave many school officials sleepless nights, but our group, at least, arrived at its destination without difficulty and on schedule. Then we stood for hours awaiting the great moment when Germany's leaders would pass before our eyes.

I recollect that our teachers were far more jittery than we. Several of them honored the day by appearing in uniform. Our gym teacher, Herr Reitz, could be seen rushing up and down the street looking both harassed and important in his storm trooper's wardrobe, embellished, as we registered with awe, by the three diamonds of a company commander. We had no idea that such greatness dwelt among us. At the same time, we noted that the leather strap with which his cap was anchored to his chin kept slipping off, until its upward progress was arrested by his nose, which protruded more visibly and effectively than the receding lower portion of his face. Nor was it very clear what agitated him so. After we had been unloaded and lined up along the section of the street that was to resound with our cheers, we had neither inclination nor opportunity for mischief. But poor *Sturmführer* Reitz acted as if each class was competing for a prize in neatness, and he kept jogging back and forth inspecting his sector, pushing us into an ever-straighter line, gradually getting into a profuse sweat. Our math master, Lepke, had draped the uniform of an *Amtswalter* over his copious belly. It included brown jodhpurs and jackboots of the same color as the storm-troop outfit, but his shirt was adorned with different insignia of rank, denoting his membership in the executive committee of the local party organization. *Amtswalter* Lepke displayed more dignity than Herr Reitz. He stood quietly, only occasionally running a wary and threatening eye over our ranks, snuffing out by his very glance any stirrings of levity or unrest.

As the hour of Hitler's arrival approached, an announcement informed us that a deputation of youths would wait on the führer before he passed us, present him with another bouquet of flowers (1933 was a banner year for Germany's flag makers and florists), and ask him to drive slowly so that we could have a good look at Germany's savior. And then the great moment finally came. We heard distant band music, the Badenweiler March, Hitler's reputed favorite, of which repeated performances at every public appearance soon must have made him as sick as Harry Truman was, years later, of the Missouri Waltz. Then the motorcade apparently executed a complicated about-face, because when its first vehicles reached us, their sequence had been reversed. Motorized storm troops began to pass us, and then successive carloads of uniformed, impeccably tailored dignitaries, whose insignia of rank, all polished to a fine gloss, identified them as persons of general rank in SA, SS, and police. Only a few cognoscenti among us recognized among the occupants of the lead vehicles our new mayor, the *Gauleiter,* and other stars of the local hierarchy.

Soon the quality of the cast improved. The familiar faces of Goebbels and Rudolf Hess, the deputy party leader, slowly floated past, each of them transfixed with a beatific smile. We noted that Goebbels had a splendid tan. Another car, filled with a brace of generals and cabinet ministers in civilian clothes, struck us as anticlimactic, probably, in part, because an approaching roar indicated that the führer was nigh. Our eyes turned left in the direction of the cheers, and the man for whom they were intended hove into view. There he was, standing erect in the car, dressed rather like the poor relation of the gilded knights who had passed us in such numbers: brown shirt and black tie, jodhpurs and jackboots, hatless and coatless, raising his hand in his personal version of the national salute—first up to eye level and then bending the arm at the elbow until his hand rested palm upward by his right ear. For the first and only time, I saw Hitler. It struck me that he did not look like the photos in newspapers, magazines, and shopwindows. The ascetic and martial leanness of these likenesses was missing from his fleshy, slightly puffy, immobile, impassive countenance. It was as if he were passing us without noticing our presence, slowly and repeatedly saluting like a wound-up doll, neither frowning nor smiling, looking straight ahead, his gaze riveted on some distant object that only he perceived. He was not taking curtain calls, but giving a performance that would continue until the doors of his plane had closed behind him.

Hitler passed us in a matter of seconds. Before I could articulate in my mind the character of his actual appearance and describe to myself the nature of his visionary aloofness, he had moved on. It was only then that I became aware of my own outstretched arm and my own open mouth shouting, "Heil, Heil," along with the thousands around me. Quickly I lowered my hand. I trembled in a sudden fit of consternation and embarrassment. What on earth had made me act like that? I felt humiliated; I still do when I think of this moment. No one noticed when I stopped cheering. No one would have noticed in this crush if I had simply stood silent. But the fact remained that I had joined this chorus of 35,000 cheeping children though I despised and feared the man they hailed. I had acted without conscious awareness of what I was doing.

When I got home, I confessed to my mother what had happened. She consoled me by insisting that involuntary gestures did not count. I should just remember how easy it is to lose control of one's body and voice. But I did not fail to notice that she did not tell my father of my confession, and I knew better than to share this part of the day's events with him. He must not know of this act of betrayal.

My classmates had enjoyed the spectacle and kept talking about it for days. None of us had ever seen so many famous men in one motorcade; most of us, I daresay, never would again. A great number, as I found out in 1945, would later pay with their lives for this moment of excitement.

Life returned to normal, and our teachers went back to their classroom civvies. My family kept looking for an exit. In 1934, when the school curriculum was drastically altered to do justice to the first of the educational maxims of the national revolution, the formation of "political man," they found an escape hatch for me by sending me out of the country to continue my schooling in Holland. But that is another story, a turn in my fate of which I had no premonition in the autumn of 1933.

IV   HOW I FLED NAZI GERMANY

In the Winter, 1983, issue to which I had contributed, the editor of the *Virginia Quarterly Review* identified me as a person who had fled Nazi Germany. I thank him for dramatizing what has been an ordinary and, by the standards of grand biography, uneventful life, but he is mistaken, and I wonder who provided him with this apocryphal datum. The myth of my escape first surfaced one day in 1938 when William Gleason Bean, chairman of the history department at Washington and Lee University, summoned me to his office. After I arrived, he closed the door, bade me sit down, and asked in a conspiratorial whisper, "Tell me, Mr. Schmitt, how did you get out of Germany?" I answered truthfully, "I went to the Frankfurt main station, bought a ticket, and took a train." His face fell, and he dismissed me with curt thanks. Obviously, I had disappointed him, whether because I had cheated him of a good story, or because my apparent reserve indicated a lack of trust, I cannot say. He never raised the subject again.

There was, of course, no secret to protect. I left Germany on September 19, 1934. It was three months after my thirteenth birthday, and I was on nobody's hit list, nor was I hunted by the Gestapo. Still, it was a dramatic turning point in my life. During the preceding spring the government had decided to add a new subject to the curriculum called "national political instruction."[1] It was to be taught on Saturday and consisted of the history of the Nazi party, the lives of its founders and leaders, and indoctrination in the spirit of the new Germany. Members of the Hitler Youth and its preadolescent auxiliary were excused; they did not need such enlightenment. Chil-

1. Kurt-Ingo Flessau, *Schule der Diktatur: Lehrpläne und Schulbücher des Nationalsozialismus* (Munich, 1977), 20.

dren with at least one Jewish parent, or two Jewish grandparents, were also excluded; they were unworthy of it. Their school week was now shortened by a day, the only instance in the history of the Nazi reign when Jewish ancestry proved an advantage.

According to contemporary statistics, frequent marriages between Jews and Gentiles during the previous century had created a "Jewish problem" that transcended Germany's 600,000 Jews and that included one-and-a-half-million *Judenstämmlinge*, persons endowed with varying ratios of Semitic ancestry. These mongrels complicated the separation of tribes. During its twelve-year tenure, the Nazi government never produced a working definition of Jewishness. Göring is said to have terminated a meeting of legal experts, convened to close this gap in jurisprudence, by pounding the table and shouting, "I'll decide who is a Jew!" The SS required its prospective members to document sixteen ancestors free from Jewish contamination. Not even Hitler could have met that requirement, because his illegitimate father's paternity has never been satisfactorily documented. Rumors also abounded that Reinhard Heydrich, the dreaded chief of the Gestapo, had a Jewish mother.

Racial legislation could, therefore, not bridge this vast gray area. Instead, it subjected many ordinary citizens to a capricious, oppressive game of numbers and percentages. Genealogy turned from popular hobby into fearful revelation. Unpleasant disclosures might suddenly exclude an individual or an entire family from the national community, without offering any social or emotional substitute. Rarely did these products of religiously mixed marriages possess preparation or adaptability to enter the world of Judaism. In our household, too, this new state of affairs prompted a brief, haphazard search for identity. My mother tried her hand at Hebrew until she found that this strange and difficult tongue elicited no vibrations of ancient kinship. I joined the Jewish Boy Scouts and at first had an easier time of it. My certified Nordic appearance was an asset to my troop. I marched in the first rank, the "token goy" who gave the whole outfit a deceptively Germanic appearance. But one day an orthodox member of a sponsoring Jewish community discovered that I was not Bar Mitzvah, and lodged a formal protest against my infidel presence. To forestall more trouble, I doffed my uniform. If and when the showdown came, I would not qualify as bona fide inmate of the new ghetto or be accepted into the multitude of Aryan Gentiles. At the time I did not think much about it. The incident with the Scouts came rather as a relief, since I had quickly wearied of tying knots, building fires, and pitching tents.

The decision of the organization's leadership in 1934 to join the Zionist fold made me even more of an outsider. I still preferred spending weekend spare time with my lifetime friends on the block to preparing for a new life in Palestine. I do not feel any particular resentment today against those elders who protested my presence. They were quite right; I was not a Jew and had no intention of becoming one. Nor did I suffer then from an identity crisis, one of the more fashionable diseases of our time. At this point I was still a German, albeit a troubled one. After I ceased to be a German, I became an American and, what is equally important, a historian. This transition involved passage through material uncertainties and certainly demanded hard work, but never anguished soul searching. I survived and changed without having to sell my soul, and with that I am satisfied.

In school, the first among my peers to join the Hitler Youth tried to recruit me into his troop. He assured me that the local party would not hold my mother against me. It was a gesture of juvenile friendship that nonplussed me momentarily. I solved the dilemma with the German child's standard excuse: "My father won't allow it."

After such a succession of predicaments, including the discovery of my Nordic appearance in biology class, my liberation from Saturday classes was to my parents no laughing matter. They found it intolerable to have their child segregated from his contemporaries, and resolved that I must continue my education elsewhere. In the spring of 1934, English Quakers founded in Holland a boarding-school for children whose parents were suffering political or ethnic persecution. My parents visited the grounds and decided that it was the place for me.

In the short run, their decision freed me from the pressures of academic competition and the fruitless search for alternate allegiances. Being of an optimistic and not overly reflective disposition, I recognized the advantages of my impending transfer, without anticipating the pain separation from my family and friends would cause me. Nothing clouded the delight with which I looked forward to escaping the juvenile prison that was the German *Gymnasium*. I had never flourished in its atmosphere, and the mediocrity of my report cards scarcely presaged the scholarly life I would eventually lead. I disliked most of my teachers and gave them ample reason to reciprocate. With the exception of Dr. Schreuers—my French teacher, whom his subject seemed to have turned into a dynamo of suspiciously Latinate ebullience—they rolled every subject into a tasteless dough of boredom. Before my eyes and ears, these pedagogues picked apart the classics of German literature, like vultures ravishing a decaying corpse. They reduced geography and biology to dreary memorization of statistics and classifications. They were society's lictors, appointed to punish us for being the fruits of original sin.

The pathetic alacrity with which these same teachers yielded to the oncoming wave of new politics increased my contempt for them. During the year and a half spent in the schools of Nazi Germany, I remember only one example of what could today be construed as resistance to the flood tide of national folly. It involved one of those rare Conservatives who kept his head and recognized from the outset the incompatibility of his values and those of national socialism.

Dr. Franz Wegner, who taught us German grammar and composition, was a martinet who never allowed us to forget that he was a reserve officer and a decorated veteran of World War I, as well as a member of the Conservative paramilitary organization the Steelhelmet (*Stahlhelm*). His class was his platoon, and sloppy performers, such as I, did not figure among his favorites. His wife was English, and that explained to us why this crew-cut, ramrod-straight specimen of Teutonic manhood always carried an attaché case, then only used by English businessmen. This eccentricity prompted us to call him "Franz with the suitcase" (*Koffer Franz*), not within his hearing, of course. It was shortly after the institution of the new Saturday curriculum that Dr. Wegner stopped me after class and said to me in his usual drill-ground commander's manner, "Schmitt, if anyone molests you or gives you trouble of any kind, you report it to me!" The son of our Jewish family physician, who was one class ahead of me, told his parents a few days later that Wegner, who was his homeroom teacher, had offered him the same protection.

My other taskmasters turned out to be spineless and unprincipled. I therefore derived great satisfaction watching them wriggle in the net of the national revolution from which I was about to escape. Soon I would be able to thumb my nose at them as well as their führer. Mistaking my parents' wisdom and sacrifice for new and hitherto unsuspected virtues and deserts of my own, I indulged in an orgy of malicious joy.

At home my impending departure occasioned much serious conversation. As they looked at my report cards, my parents must have turned me loose with great misgivings. Who would hold my feet to the fire in Holland? Could boardingschool study halls replace parental authority? They tried hard to meet all negative eventualities by impressing on me that my going away constituted a premature rite of passage: a vote of confidence that my past performance scarcely justified. One day my mother also explained that I was not leaving merely for my own sake. Transfer to a foreign school, sponsored by British philanthropy, was to initiate the eventual escape of the entire family, probably to some corner of the Anglo-Saxon world. I was to be the spearhead of the exodus. Four lives, rather than one, might depend on my success.

I accepted this admonition as a compliment and promised freely to become the savior of our little clan. Otherwise, the prospect of such responsibility did not disturb my sleep. Gathering together my belongings, from sheets to washcloths, from Sunday best to gym togs, absorbed me much more, almost as much as it did my mother, who had to sew name tags into every article of my school wardrobe.

On my parents' instructions, I had told only two of my best friends that I was leaving. There was no law against sending children abroad, but to do so in these glorious times was not an act one wished to broadcast. So the bustle accompanying my move was confined to our apartment. On the day of my departure, I arose early to embrace my father before he went to work. Under the circumstances, he could not think of taking the day off because his oldest boy was leaving the country. Only one visitor came, with a package. It was Rainer, who lived across the street. His parents were, by our standards, immensely rich, but that made no difference to us. An even worse student than I, he had for years shared my fate of being an outsider in a world of disapproving parents and teachers. Since January, 1933, we had added to our repertory of intransigence the refusal to give the Nazi salute outside the classroom. At all public ceremonies, we stood shoulder to shoulder, rigidly at attention, drowning in a sea of extended arms and buffeted by disapproving glares, until one day, during a demonstration for the return of some unredeemed German territory, a frantic teacher whacked each of us smartly across the face and then brought us into his office to explain what dire results our behavior would have for our parents.

"Open the package," Rainer said impatiently. He loved to give

gifts, and he loved to see the recipient open them. The parcel contained a book, *Friedrich der Grosse,* by Franz Kugler, for decades the
best-selling biography of the most popular Prussian king. "Look
inside," Rainer ordered. On the flyleaf I read: "Don't forget me in
Holland. Your boon companion Rainer." "The 'boon companion'
was my mother's idea," he apologized. Since I had for years spent
many gray afternoons reading history, instead of doing my homework, I was very pleased. It was a good present, given by someone
who knew me. But in retrospect, what a gift for such an occasion!
Here I was, leaving to escape the new apartheid with a biography of
Frederick the Great as a souvenir of my past life: a biography the bulk
of which described the wars of the great Hohenzollern, lightly skim-
ming over his musical virtuosity, his sophisticated literacy, his role
as a lawgiver and reformer. What this book represented had been
alien to my family's values long before Hitler, but no one snatched
the superpatriotic confection from my hands. My mother was also
moved, by the gesture as well as my reaction to it; only Rainer left
disconsolate, to report to his keepers at the jail of learning from
which I had been paroled.

My mother and I took the streetcar to the station. If no melancholy
reflections filled my mind as we passed the landmarks among
which I had grown up, it was because, I must say again, this was no
flight. It was only a departure. At the Municipal Theater we changed
to another tram, which deposited us at the entrance of what I had
always been proud to know as Germany's second-largest railroad
station. The hash of sounds with which such terminals reverberate
engulfed us and made conversation all but impossible. First my
mother inquired where my train would leave; then she bought a
platform ticket. Then we went to my train's freight car. The previous
day I had ridden my bicycle to the freight depot and entrusted it to
the clerk for delivery to my train. We made sure that it had been duly
conveyed, so that I could reclaim it at the end of the trip. Then we
found a third-class compartment and, with the help of a kindly
stranger, lifted my suitcase into the baggage rack, and caught our
breath. Now came the worst time, the remaining minutes before the
train squeaked, jerked, and finally moved.

Since I had never traveled alone, this first journey to school was to
be interrupted at Neuss, a small industrial town on the lower Rhine,
across the river from Düsseldorf, where one of my future teachers
lived. Her parents would board me overnight, and in her company I

would complete the trip the following day. The prospect of staying the night and passing an entire day in the company of a teacher was, of course, tantamount to purgatory. But the arrangements had not been submitted for my prior approval, and I really had no time to think much about them. I was entirely absorbed by concern for my bicycle. In Neuss, where the train was scheduled to stop for two minutes, I would have to grab my heavy suitcase, run the length of the train, and retrieve my dearest possession. In my mind I had been rehearsing this operation incessantly since we had left home. I did not want the train to carry my bicycle to some untoward and irreversible destination.

I looked at my mother. "Be sure to thank Mr. and Mrs. K. for their hospitality when you leave," she said. "And be sure to put your knife in your right hand when you cut your meat at dinner. And don't start eating before everyone else. These people are devout Catholics and may say a prayer before their meal." This was going to be more difficult than I had expected. I suddenly realized that I was about to spend a night with strangers, in a town of which I had never heard until recently, in a room and in a bed of which I could form no picture in my mind's eye.

A raucous voice shouted, "Alles einsteigen!" ("All aboard!") I rushed from the car door to my compartment window. My mother was on the platform, and I was in this moving object about to be carried westward into the unknown. I experienced the same feeling seventeen years later in the social science building at the University of Chicago, when the doors of the elevator carrying me to my Ph.D. oral on the third floor closed behind me. I had gone willingly to the point of departure, realizing too late that I was not sure I relished my destination. My mother's mouth crumpled into weeping. She pressed a handkerchief to her eyes. I was moving, and she kept moving with me at first, until the speed of the train pushed her outside the frame of my vision. I kept standing by the window, looking at the railway yards, the switches, the idle rolling stock, the drab houses bordering the tracks, all passing ever more quickly before me. Mechanically, I sat down.

"And where are you going, little man?" The voice of the same stranger who had helped me with my suitcase woke me from my paralysis of thought and feeling. "To visit family," I said, telling the man what my parents had drilled me to answer under such circumstances. I had been trained not to trust people I did not know, because they might have an unwholesome, and to me quite incomprehensible, interest in little boys or because they might pump me for information that I had learned to reserve for relatives and close friends. "You are visiting family in the middle of the school year?" my interlocutor exclaimed. "My grandma is dying," I answered calmly, "and she wants to see me once more. My parents will follow on Saturday." I had lied to adults practically all my life, to parents about school, and to teachers, whom I had treated over the years to an ever more elaborate menu of excuses for not turning in assignments on time. Lying with a good conscience was a new experience. It made the act even easier, and I am sure that I could have expatiated on the sufferings of my nonexistent granny for hours, had need arisen. But the kindhearted gentleman decided not to trespass further on this familial tragedy and opened his newspaper, leaving me to my thoughts.

We had left Frankfurt behind and were racing down the Main toward its confluence with the Rhine at Mainz, the first stop on the journey. I had not seen much of the world, and it did not take long before the sights that passed my window began to engross me. The trip was one of the most beautiful one can take on a German train. The tracks followed a great river through its most spectacular valleys, past a succession of idyllic little towns, framed by steep hills whose crests were adorned with castle ruins. The names of these remnants were known to me even before I saw them for the first time. I have traveled this stretch many times since then and never wearied of its beauty, although later in life I found that the Hudson River between New York and West Point offers sights just as spectacular, even without an occasional ruin punctuating the wonders of nature. After Coblenz the country leveled off, and by the time the train passed Cologne the landscape became monotonous, and the castles were replaced by steel mills and factories. I began to worry about my bicycle again. About one-thirty the conductor announced Neuss as the next stop. I put on my loden coat and dragged my suitcase from the compartment to the exit of the car. My own first D-day was at hand.

Miss K. was to collect me at the Neuss station and take charge of me. Foresightedly she had sent us a recent photo, so I knew what she looked like. I spied her as soon as I got off the train, gave my suitcase a vigorous push in her direction, and made a dash for the mail car. By the time I reached it, the train was moving again, but not, of course, before all mail and freight destined for Neuss had been unloaded. I realized that I could have saved myself much anguish and some exercise, because the German railways were not in the habit of carrying persons or freight one kilometer farther than they had contracted to. There, leaning against a post, stood my bicycle, visibly in the same peerless working condition in which I had surrendered it the day before. Relieved, I seized the handlebars and guided it to the spot where my reception committee of one and my suitcase were waiting.

My chaperone looked younger than any teacher I had ever had. On our trip the next day I would learn that she was to be the new art instructor at my school. From her passport I gathered that she was only twenty-three, thus not really outside the pale. After this revelation I gave her the benefit of my doubt, and found her company to be a great deal more pleasant than I had expected.

For the moment, however, I apprehended that my bicycle had not figured among her travel preparations. "You are planning to take this to school?" she asked, rather foolishly, for I certainly had not intended it as a present for her parents. "Everybody in Holland has a bicycle," I informed her, both reprovingly and defensively. "Well, then, we better dispatch it at once," she decided. In Neuss this was more difficult than it had been in Frankfurt. The clerk at the freight window was still out to lunch, and we had to wait until he returned, or was summoned—I suspect the latter—for he was wiping his mouth demonstratively with a greasy handkerchief as he grumpily opened his counter for business.

The school whose student body I was about to join occupied the eighteenth-century manor of Eerde, in the countryside of northeast Holland, two miles from Ommen, the nearest town. My bicycle, insignificant in official eyes to begin with, had to be charted for a journey far more complex than the clerk seemed prepared to handle. First it had to cross a border, and then it had to be transferred in Arnhem from a fast international train to the jurisdiction of the Dutch railways, and finally to the Dutch version of a milk train that twice a day—as I subsequently discovered—chugged placidly from Zwolle, the provincial capital of Overijssel, through a succession of small towns and villages, including Ommen. The scribe repeatedly shook his head and emitted many grunts of disgust and frustration as he mapped this itinerary on his manifest. After he had written and stamped to his heart's content, he warned us that if the Dutch customs should refuse the importation of this vehicle of dubious value, the matter was, of course, out of his hands. Then he gave me a copy of his handiwork, which took its place in my bulging hip pocket beside my identity card and my ticket. Miss K. sighed with relief and summoned a taxi that brought us to her home.

I have forgotten what the K. residence looked like, nor have I any recollection of Miss K.'s parents. I do not remember whether I committed any social faux pas. Did my hosts pray before dinner; did they pay any attention to my table manners? It has all been wiped from my memory. The guest room in which I slept struck me as elegant, but what stands out most clearly in my mind is a book that my chaperone had given me to read and that I did not put down until darkness overcame the long central-European day. It was a German journalist's tale of his travels in the United States and Canada. One episode has lodged in my mind to this day. It seems that the author found himself one evening all but penniless in a small town of the Canadian west. Faced with the necessity of paying for his hotel room, he went to the local radio station, where he presented himself as a piano virtuoso specializing in contemporary music. The station manager appeared to be impressed and scheduled an afternoon recital for an honorarium that would cover the author's current embarrassment. Actually, the narrator did not know how to play the piano, but he wheedled the money out of his employer in advance and, once alone with instrument and microphone, began to belabor the former in a vigorous, if random, fashion with fingers, fists, and elbows until he and, one presumes, the local listeners were both exhausted and deafened. Then he rushed back to his quarters, paid his bill, and hightailed it out of town.

I think I know why this tale from an undistinguished travel book by an obscure author cleaves to my memory. This was the first account, since my reading of *Tom Sawyer,* of my future homeland that did not teem with trappers and Indians. Like Mark Twain's classic, it reflected a spirit of easygoing enterprise, half rebellious, half larcenous, still adhering to a culture that produced such hybrid heroes, both robbers and revolutionaries, as Jesse James. In Europe one could not cheat and run. Frequent borders, a small geographic space, and one's identity card would lead to quick capture, no matter whither one fled. In the expanse of North America, there was room for genuine escape. I had no way of knowing that it would one day be my home, and that its wide open spaces protected from the sanction of the law not only charlatans but murderers. As a child inured to oppression of many kinds, I empathized with this vision of liberty. It concorded with daydreams in which I defied adult authority and got away with it.

Next morning, after breakfast, my companion and I rode another taxi to our train and began an odyssey of which the completion of my bicycle manifest had given me so daunting a foretaste. The distance we traveled was barely three hundred miles, but with two long stops at each side of the border and two changes, it was evening when we disembarked at the small market town that was as close to our destination as any railway would carry us. The first impressions of this strange, flat country had not been spectacular. Naturally, I had begun counting windmills as soon as we had crossed the border. I had noticed that Dutch houses were roofed with red tiles rather than slate. Dutch trains were drawn by English locomotives with highly polished brass fittings, also bearing the name and location of their manufacturers. By the time we had reached our destination, I had learned that the Dutch word for platform was *perron,* and for train, *trein.* Quickly I had learned to ask "Op welke perron gaat de trein naar?" ("On what platform will the train . . . depart?") Dutch numerals being similar to their German equivalents, I had no trouble understanding the answers. This was reassuring.

In Ommen I discovered, however, that my bicycle was still in transit, and after that indication of this strange country's unreliability, my spirits sank again. The creaky taxi in which we completed the last miles of our journey did little to lift them. After we left the outskirts of the town behind, dark woods engulfed the highway until we turned into a broad, unpaved avenue at the end of which sparkled the lights of the manor. My "flight" had reached its destination.

As we got out of the cab, a handsome lady bore down on us, both hands extended in a gesture of welcome. She introduced herself as Mrs. Petersen, the headmistress, and welcomed new teacher and new student with equal warmth. I had never been placed on an equal footing with a teacher before, and this reception made me so comfortable that I began to realize I had not eaten since breakfast. Besides, Mrs. Petersen looked exactly as I had expected her to look: friendly, stately, and blond, and obviously in charge of things. She brought us both to the kitchen in the basement, where a late dinner awaited. She asked after my parents, and what kind of a trip we had had. While we were eating, we were joined by two boys who were introduced as my roommates. They went by the nicknames of Stippi and Rommel, and I learned only later and incidentally that their real names were Hans Lüdecke and Eberhard Brann. They guided me and my suitcase to our quarters, Room 12, in a separate dormitory building, and after I had extracted my sleeping and washing implements, we all went to bed and, so far as I can remember, to a good night's sleep.

My bicycle, incidentally, showed up soon enough. Two days after my arrival, a telephone call from the local freight agent announced its delivery. After school I walked the two miles to the station and then rode it back, enjoying for the first time a smooth progress on a Dutch bicycle path's level surface of crushed shell.

So much for my first "escape." There was nothing unusual about it, and I would make several such journeys to and from Germany during the next three years. Twice a year the Quakerschool Eerde closed its classrooms: from December 15 to January 15, for Christmas vacation; and for two months during the summer. I generally spent these interludes with my family. There would be nothing to say about these trips home were it not for the changing rules of travel that proliferated during the 1930s. Although my parents remembered the days before 1914 when Russia was the only country requiring travelers to carry a passport, after 1918 few Continental borders could be legally crossed without this document. It was a time when European governments seemed to glory in their power to make the passage of people, capital, and goods across their frontiers as difficult as possible. Before long, earnest bureaucrats discovered the visa: the special endorsement a passport had to contain before it became a valid transit document.

Until 1935, crossing the German border entailed no unusual ceremony. Controls on the German side were thorough and systematic. They may have been a trifle more time-consuming than the border formalities of other Western countries. Then the Nazis added to the inspection of papers and baggage the examination of billfolds. Having raised outlays for armaments to levels that would have led to national bankruptcy had not the printing presses of the state staunched the hemorrhage of deficit financing, the government prevented a second wave of inflation in ten years by insulating the mark from international currency markets. Travelers could take no more than ten marks out of the country unless they secured a special currency-export permit. At the border the amount of cash one carried was entered on one's passport by a suitably grim-faced official. After the beginning of food rationing, especially of meats and fats, in 1936, travelers from such dairy-rich countries as Holland and Denmark usually arrived with packages of butter, ham, and bacon for their German friends, only to find their kindness requited with additional bureaucratic stratagems. The gifts had to be weighed and inspected in an office at the border station to make sure they did not exceed totally arbitrary, government-imposed maxima. One had to leave the train, stand in line, and finally pay a fee before the produce could enter the precincts of the new Germany. Each such requirement extended the border stop by another half hour or so.

It was a dreadful bore, but an inescapable part of the journey. No one cut and ran, no shots were fired, and no exciting chase was enacted, at least within my sight and hearing. On one of these trips home, when I was fifteen, these nuisances became even more burdensome when I had to take charge of a first grader, Mischa, whom I was to deliver to his mother at the Frankfurt railroad station. Since my own brother was not much older than Mischa, this was not an unaccustomed chore. But Mischa was a winning little extrovert, who liked to wander about the train and cadge sandwiches and other diet supplements from kindly avuncular travelers, and when I returned from the obligatory weighing of dairy imports, he was, of course, gone from his seat. Only half an hour after the train had resumed its progress did I catch up with him, cheerfully devastating the candy box left at his disposal, this time by a solitary old lady in a first-class compartment. Luckily he did not get sick before I turned him over to his mother. He seems to have made up for this omission later, for his mother subsequently complained that I had not taken good care of her little boy. He was never entrusted to me again, much to my relief.

I remember two other journeys I took during these school years in exile. My first holiday coincided with the impending Saar plebiscite. This referendum was to take place on January 13, 1935, to decide the disposition of about one thousand square miles of German territory, until 1918 the southwestern tip of the Prussian Rhine province, with a population density of almost one thousand per square kilometer. The Saar district clustered around the core of central Europe's richest coal deposit, producing since the beginning of the century some fifteen million tons of black gold per year. After World War I, these mines had been turned over to France for exploration as part of German reparations. Government of the territory was in the hands of a commission appointed by the League of Nations. Now, after fifteen years, the inhabitants were to vote on their own future, choosing a continuation of the League mandate, French citizenship, or German. The contest created little suspense. The population was German, and no one expected the result of the vote to deny that fact. Saar miners, like miners elsewhere in Germany, had organized into unions before any other group of industrial workers, but under Catholic rather than Socialist leadership. Agitation by German Communists and Socialists, who had taken refuge in the Saar, was not likely to affect their decision. But a world rendered nervous by Germany's totalitarian government smelled trouble ahead, and the Quaker school, therefore, decided to send us home on December 10, so that we could have a month's vacation and still be back by voting day.

In my case these precautions proved unavailing. On January 10 I was in bed with a high fever and a swollen countenance. Mumps, not Nazi troubles, kept me home. On January 13 I sat by the radio listening to the returns. My parents hoped for some magic upsurge in favor of a continued League of Nations mandate, based on the assumption that tales of political oppression would prompt the Saar inhabitants to forgo German citizenship until some miracle had unseated the tyrant. Hope was all one had. It was strong but, of course, no factor in the plebiscite. Some 90 percent of the voters chose Germany, thus giving Hitler his first and most effortless foreign-policy victory. Without delay, the League returned the Saar to German control. The transfer was entirely peaceful, and a few days later I returned to Holland, this time without retinue and, as before, without incident.

My last trip in and out of Nazi Germany remains even more memorable because it coincided with the end of my school days in Holland. It took place in the summer of 1937, after I had taken the examinations for the Oxford School Certificate. Although I was not to learn the results until September, an interim of unpleasant suspense before actual graduation, I was on the way to enjoy my graduation present, six weeks my brother and I would spend with our maternal uncle in the Austrian Alps.

As I try to set down my recollections of this trip, I find it uncommonly difficult to reconcile memory to history. Because of a German-inspired attempt to overthrow the Austrian government in

1934, an unsuccessful coup taking the life of Federal Chancellor Engelbert Dollfuss, relations between Berlin and Vienna were worse than they had been at any other time in the twentieth century. This was the first cold war within the orbit of my experience. Austrian courts condemned to death the assassins and outlawed the Nazi party. In retaliation Germany required citizens wanting to visit the Austrian Alps or the Salzburg festival to deposit one thousand marks (about four hundred dollars) with German customs, redeemable on their return.

When I recall the elaborate preparations my uncle made for our passage to Austria, I also remember that I assumed then that the infamous *1000-Mark-Sperre* was their cause. The study of history has, however, informed me that this particular obstacle was removed in August, 1936, almost a year before our visit. On the other hand, Hitlerian economics had meanwhile created in Germany a serious shortage of foreign currency. As far as Austria went, German travelers to that country were constrained to apply for a currency export permit and then buy their Austrian *Schilling* in Germany before departing. Students of German literature can discover in Erich Kästner's novel *Der kleine Grenzverkehr* (*Commuting Across the Border*) how these rules could complicate an individual's summer vacations. Kästner's tale concludes with the laconic observation that the hero's request was granted in September, long after he had returned from his annual holiday.

We were more fortunate. My uncle spared us all border formalities, but what he had to do and how he did it I can only surmise. Being a Jew, he had in 1933 lost an executive position with the Telefunken electronics firm, but found employment with a Dutch competitor whose board placed him in charge of one of its faltering Austrian enterprises: the Plansee Steelworks in Reutte, only a few miles from the German border. His responsibilities involved frequent trips to Germany and Holland, and I have a dim recollection that he and his chauffeur had a pass that allowed border crossing without having to palaver about visas or currency export permits. In any case, my brother and I boarded the train in Holland, incidentally enjoying the privilege of a 50-percent fare reduction that Germany at the time accorded foreign tourists in order to acquire hard currency to bolster its chaotic finances. We traveled to Augsburg, where the chauffeur picked us up at the station. Whatever arrangements had been made, they proved effective, and our progress, at what seemed magic-carpet speed, was scarcely slowed at the border. The driver exchanged a comment about the weather with one of the German officials, and he merely waved at the Austrian on the other side. They knew the car; they recognized the license plate, and whether they even noticed my brother and me, I have no way of knowing.

I enjoyed not only the vaguely illegal border crossing but the train trip that preceded it. Attired in a new suit consisting of jacket and plus fours, hand-me-downs from English benefactors who periodically shipped cast-off clothing to the school, I decided to use my cut-rate ticket to play the foreign tourist. At the first major stop I bought a copy of the London *Times,* which I studied earnestly while my brother dozed or looked out the window. By now I spoke English well, and before long two English women in our compartment engaged me in conversation. With the reserve characteristic of their nation, they did not ask me personal questions, as Americans might have, but approved of my reading matter, discussed the weather, and were delighted to find me so knowledgeable about travel in the country that they were visiting for the first time. I smiled tolerantly at their expressions of surprise that the state of affairs in Germany did not seem to be as bad as they had expected. The train was clean and punctual, and the service courteous and efficient, not a bullying storm trooper in sight. Predictably, they were enchanted by the scenery—the river, the hills, the vineyards, the castles, the picturesque towns and villages—and I am sure that they decided then and there to disbelieve the tales of horror and oppression their press had been disseminating since Hitler's advent to power.

It was an instructive experience: another reason I have never forgotten the trip and its encounters. A year later, when I conversed in England with a male traveler just returned from his tour of enchanting Germany, I could, without risk, point out that dictatorships do not arrange public executions for the entertainment of tourists. But in the summer of 1937, I merely received and stored away in my mind an abiding impression of the worthlessness of vacation travel as an instrument of political education. The German government was not only gaining financial rewards from its encouragement of tourism. What began with the Olympic Games of 1936 continued almost up to the outbreak of World War II: an open door to harmless voyagers who had great difficulty imagining that this lovely land with its natty, uniformed officials, sparkling hotels, and low prices could, at the same time, be a place of terror. I have never understood why other dictatorships have failed to imitate this ingenious public-relations device. As was to be expected, my sweet-tempered companions left me, not at some grimy, big-city stop, but at Rothenburg, that popular relic of medieval architecture, still a fixture on package-tour itineraries.

Seen in retrospect, my last passage through Germany was also the first time that I began to see my homeland as the foreign country it would eventually become. What was then still a childish and frivolous pose would soon become reality. But even before circumstances dictated such a metamorphosis, as early as the summer of 1937, playing the foreigner among Germans proved surprisingly easy.

For the moment, however, my mind was full of lighthearted anticipation. Ahead of me lay six weeks of what I naturally considered to be well-earned rest: hikes into the mountains, excursions into the surrounding country as far as Innsbruck, and contemplative idleness among my uncle's books, while my brother played with our cousins, who were closer to him in age. This was the summer I discovered Flaubert's *Madame Bovary*, and Mann's *Magic Mountain*, a perfect companion for the eve of the Holocaust. A few days after our arrival, my uncle said he had a surprise for me. My mother was going to join us. She would travel to Zurich, where we would pick her up in his car and take her to Austria, across not the German but the Swiss border. Naturally I was pleased, but then I wanted to know why she could not have come with us from the start. "I can bring you children in at Reutte," he laughed, "but adults present greater problems." Still, would they not stamp her passport at Feldkirch, where cars journeying from Zurich to Innsbruck first entered Austrian space? "I think I have arranged that neither the Swiss nor the Austrians will stamp your mother's passport," he replied with a satisfied smile. "When she goes back to Germany, no one will be able to tell that she has been in Austria."

The next Saturday we departed at dawn, and after a long, beautiful trip—the likes of which I had never taken—through the Lech Valley Alps, Appenzell, and Toggenburg, we arrived at our *hotel garni* in Zurich. The next morning, before meeting my mother's train, my uncle filled his gas tank at, not just any station, but the Hotel Baur-au-Lac, which was festooned that day with the Romanian flag, indicating the presence of playboy King Carol II (and, my uncle informed me, his red-haired mistress Magda Lupescu). I was told to sit up straight and look serious as we drove his Steyr convertible off the premises. "Perhaps people will think you are the crown prince of Romania." My uncle was not only generous and hospitable but full of such unexpected funny notions. At times one could almost forget that he was an adult, a pillar of the business world, and himself a fatherly tyrant to his children.

Since this was Switzerland, my mother's train arrived punctually, and we barely arrived at the station in time. Then we drove off for a border crossing a bit more nervous than we had been at my brother's and mine the week before. Both Swiss and Austrian authorities examined my mother's passport, as well as a piece of paper my uncle held out to them with his identification documents. Although they stamped his papers with abandon, they merely returned hers with a noncommittal nod. Again, I am quite certain about the sequence of events, especially at the Austro-Swiss border. But I cannot explain why so much trouble was taken to keep the officials on both sides from stamping my mother's passport.

In no case, however, do these memories bear the stigma of fear or flight. But one must not forget the many ill-starred victims while dwelling on the good fortunes of an exceptionally lucky one. I was spared even close calls as well as the terrible fate of those who stayed behind.

Eight years were to elapse before I would see Germany again. It would be a different country, and the total paralysis of public life, commerce, and ordinary existence among ruins closed a chapter in history and provided the confused and tragic setting in which I was to take leave of my youth. When I returned to Germany, I would be, not a tourist, but part of a conquering army of an enemy country whose citizen I had become. I would be a soldier traveling in a jeep, not on the Rhine Express of the *Reichsbahn*. Nobody would examine me at the border, and in my relations with Germans, I, not they, would play the role of inquisitor.

V   THE SCHOOL IN THE MANOR

After Miss K. had delivered me into the capable hands of Mrs. Petersen, Eerde "castle" became my next home. I put the word in quotes because the Dutch *Kasteel* Eerde never had been a *castrum,* or fortified place. It likewise lacked the majesty of a princely *Schloss,* and its dimensions barely qualified as a château presiding over a lesser French vineyard. I suppose the term *manor* most accurately describes the size and stature of the edifice completed in 1715 and now turned into a boardingschool. Surrounded by a moat wherein water lilies bloomed in spring and summer, and a noisy traffic of ducks circled all year, the building contained the apartments of the headmistress and two married teachers, school kitchen and dining room in the basement, and on the main floor the classrooms and a few cabinets, tiny rooms usually reserved for upper-class pupils preparing for their final examinations.

A circular drive ringed the courtyard, a greensward with a sundial at its center, framed, in turn, by the main dormitory and the former stables, now converted into a variety of workshops and the music room. The outer moat circumscribed several acres of grounds, surrounding the manor and its outbuildings, that were being turned into a large truck garden, providing the school's produce. Two small eighteenth-century pavilions on these grounds included the domicile of my travel companion, the art teacher, and a practice room for piano and voice students.

Beyond these confines lay the remaining estate of the school's landlord, the Baron Philipp van Pallandt and Eerde, a mile and a half in every direction. Apart from several tenant farmers, this Arcadian paradise contained a clearing of dunes, rampant with wild flowers, which we children called the Sahara. At the north end of the domain,

His Lordship had built for his family a sprawling, one-story, red-brick villa, in what Hollanders then called the "California style." In 1935, the growing school also absorbed this dwelling, and I do not know where the Pallandts lived after that.

At the time of its founding the school had no athletic facilities. Students later converted a large meadow behind the manor beyond the outer moat into two playing fields for soccer, field hockey, and team handball. A more ambitious enterprise, an outdoor swimming pool, still in apparent working order when my wife and I visited Eerde in 1977, took a succession of student crews more than two years to complete.

The staff of the school included the mistress of the kitchen, a massive, unsmiling north German with the face of a pugilist, Frau Kuck (pronounced, appropriately, "cook"), who commanded a team consisting of another German, her deputy Fräulein Emmy, and several Dutch girls, recruited in the surrounding villages. The garden was kept by a quiet, unobtrusive Dutchman, Paul Kruimel, whose skill as a soccer player never ceased to arouse our admiration. One of the housemothers was an ebullient, warmhearted woman from Hamburg, Josi Einstein. At first she was the sole adult in the dormitory, until the enrollment increased and a second housemother joined the staff. The pottery at the south end of the former stables was the domain of Thea Hermanns, a master of her craft and the wife of our history teacher; the carpentry shop was supervised by Mijnheer Brouwer, a blond, handsome, but moody man. He was thin-skinned and quick to take offense at real or imaginary gestures of condescension from colleagues or students. But Brouwer was also a master of his métier, and whether he knew it or not, we liked and respected him.

I have already mentioned the head of the school, Katharina Petersen, a two-fisted humanitarian who hailed from Schleswig-Holstein. She had left Germany, in disgust, to serve the persecuted, but in the late thirties pressures from a brother, whose civil-service career her demonstrative exile endangered, forced her to resign and return home. She was succeeded by Kurt Neuse, the man most responsible for shaping the school into an educational institution equal to any, and the most remarkable teacher I have ever met. (Pedagogic talent ran in his family: his brother Werner inaugurated the language programs that have made Middlebury College famous.) Mr. Neuse was a spare and earnest man, with a craggy face dominated by a Punch nose. Few of us really liked him; compared to many of his more popular colleagues, he seemed cold and distant. In the classroom he was a demanding and often merciless critic, but he taught me enough Latin in one year to enable me to take courses at the junior and senior level in college several years later. Even more important, he taught English, and he taught it so well that those of us who eventually came to the United States knew the language better than did many educated natives of our adopted country. My debt to him remains immeasurable. Mr. Neuse's wife, Rose, was an English Quaker who had come to Germany after World War I to perform relief work. She kept the school's books and entertained us with her unpredictable German pronunciation, particularly her habit of violating umlauts. She adored her husband, who, to her, represented the true Germany. As it turned out, the couple would never return to Germany, and she became as much a disconsolate exile as her husband, indeed much more vocally so.

Another faculty member, Mr. Hermanns, taught my favorite subject, history. I liked him much better than Mr. Neuse, for he was a cheerful, handsome man. Unlike the grim antiquarians of my German school days, he treated history as prelude to the present. In his lively classroom, events of the past became real and meaningful. Mathematics and science were the domain of Otto Reckendorf, who had been forced to leave the faculty of a renowned German boardingschool, the Odenwaldschule, because he was a Jew.[1] (When I arrived at Eerde, he was the only Jew on the faculty.) What every alumnus and alumna of the school remembers best about "Rex," however, is not his subject or his ancestry but his dedication to physical culture. During the first year of the school's operation, our day began with Rex leading the entire student body in barefoot morning calisthenics, capped by a run through the pristine woods. He had his Spartan way until one day in December, when he drove his herd through its shoeless exercises even though the first snow of the season covered the ground. Someone must have complained; we children never learned who, and after the holidays we began wearing gym shoes. I found running over twigs and stones painful and pointless, but I suspect that there was good sense in the Recken-

1. Life before and after Hitler on the campus of that German precursor of the more cosmopolitan Quakerschool Eerde has been recorded in the powerful memoirs of Ernst Erich Noth, *Erinnerungen eines Deutschen* (Hamburg, 1971), 150–68.

dorf method. None of us caught cold during these drills, and running barefoot in any weather left one's feet warm and tingling.

A year later the faculty increased by two English women whose arrival reflected an increasing concentration on the Oxford School Certificate, for which most of us eventually prepared. This scholastic obstacle course typically included examinations in English (composition and literature), history, a modern or classical foreign language, arithmetic, algebra and Euclidean geometry, and a science. A "pass" in these subjects entitled the recipient of the certificate to admission to an Oxford college. A higher grade ("credit," "good," or "very good") turned the diploma into an invitation to any British institution of higher learning.

One of the newcomers, Miss Green, a jolly, homely spinster, also taught English, but always in the shadow of Mr. Neuse, who feared, rightly as I recall, that she was too tolerant of our imperfections. She was, nevertheless, important to our education, for she did not know a word of German and thus forced us to use her language and become at home in it. The other Britisher, Betty Shepherd, who taught math in English to the upper grades, was also unilingual, and intensely pious besides. Every Sunday morning, at the crack of dawn, she would bicycle to the Reformed church in Ommen and for the remainder of the day stay out of sight, reading and praying, no doubt, for such wayward and frivolous pupils as I. She must have been about Miss K.'s age, and I suspect that Eerde was her first post. She was conscientious, but often at a loss to understand why so easy a subject as hers should give some of us so much trouble. A plump, pink, little Dutchwoman, Molly Swart, taught French—then, as now, my favorite foreign language. Two other additions to the staff, also arriving well after my coming in the fall of 1934, were a more immediate influence on my own development: Jan Boost and Billy Hilsley.

Before the school had existed many months, it also began to attract Dutch students, mostly problem children, who could not adjust to the inflexible discipline of our host country's secondary schools. (I never attended Dutch schools, but they sounded similar to those I had left behind in Germany.) Although most of us viewed these natives unsympathetically at first, as intruders into our community of ethnic and political outcasts, their affluent parents helped stabilize Eerde's precarious budget. Dutch parents, however, generally wanted their children to graduate with Dutch, rather than English, diplomas. This required the establishment of a new department, of which Jan Boost became the first staff member. I am not sure that he relished his task of salvaging the unstable sons and daughters of the Dutch upper bourgeoisie. As the size of the Dutch faculty increased, Boost offered to teach advanced French to those of us who had begun this subject in Germany. That is, however, not how I first came to know him.

Our association began outside the classroom, in Boost's bachelor quarters, where he held perpetual open house and where some of us students discussed God and the world-at-large until it was past our bedtime. Boost considered himself a Communist, but when I think of him, the memory conjures up the names of aristocratic anarchists like Tolstoy and Kropotkin, not Lenin. In character with his doctrinal pretensions, as well as the heritage of these two noblemen, he never attended our Sunday meetings, the only teacher who demonstratively rejected Quakerism. I soon discovered that he despised secular discipline as much as organized religion.

Boost had previously taught at a fashionable academy in Lausanne, where the late shah of Iran and his brother had been among his pupils. I have no idea why he left that employment, but whatever the reason, I suspect that the fifty guilders plus room and board, which Eerde paid all employees from headmistress to resident kitchen staff, were not the chief attractions of his new job. He was, no doubt, drawn to the school by the egalitarianism of our community and its commitment to succoring the victims of nazism.

Access to his private library was this teacher's chief contribution to my upbringing. He allowed its contents to circulate freely among students and never kept a record of who borrowed what. I never heard him ask a pupil to return a book. He gave willingly of himself and shared what he possessed, and none abused his generosity. This private reservoir of literature and information introduced me to Upton Sinclair's *Jungle* and *Oil*, Ilya Ehrenburg's fictional accounts of recent history, and Emil Ludwig's *July, 1914*, which, more than thirty years before the work of historians such as Fritz Fischer and Fritz Fellner, condemned Germany's and Austria's aggression on the eve of World War I. From Boost I also borrowed Bertha von Suttner's famous pacifist novel *Lay Down Your Arms*, such banned books as the Berlin physician Alfred Döblin's *Berlin Alexanderplatz*, and the writings of the mysterious Ben Traven, particularly his *Ship of the Dead*. What a lode of new impressions for a receptive adolescent mind, just escaped from Germany! Jan Boost also had me read Erich Remarque's *All Quiet on the Western Front* and Ludwig Renn's more subtle chronicle of demoralization in the trenches, simply entitled *War*.

In the classroom, on the other hand, Boost was what might best be called a stimulating failure. As a convinced antidisciplinarian, he found it difficult to tell students what to do. In his French classes his motto was, "Read what you like and tell me about it," and he, in turn, would tell us what absorbed him. His anarchic methods expanded our literary horizons but proved of little help in passing examinations. His preferred readings were avant-garde, and his choices excited us and prompted us to read much more than we would have, had we been plagued with classics like Molière, Corneille, and especially Pascal's *Pensées,* under whose weight I watched Luxembourg Lycée pupils of fifteen and sixteen groan when I paid their school a visit in the 1950s. Instead, our teacher introduced us to Dadaist poetry and, on the other end of the scale of his broad preferences, to the sound paintings of the three Vs: Verlaine, Verhaeren, and the Dutch poet Albert Verwey, who, of course, did not belong in a French class. Boost also acquainted us with the most commanding presence in twentieth-century Dutch literature at that time, the Socialist and pacifist poet Henriette Roland-Holst, another interloper in the curriculum of Eerde's French studies, and finally to the masters of the contemporary French theater: Cocteau, Giraudoux, and Anouilh.

But Boost was no mere seducer. His anarchic and libertarian missionary zeal introduced into our education literature not yet accepted into the official curriculum. Paradoxically, his one-sided views fostered in us an open, receptive spirit, not encouraged by the orthodox national educational establishments of Europe.

He was also a warmhearted friend. In the spring of 1935, when I fell ill with influenza and spent hours in a feverish delirium, I would wake up in the middle of the night and find him sitting at my bedside, applying compresses and feeding me aspirins. Whatever freedom he granted us, he did not make life easy for himself. After a sleepless night at my bedside, he went on to teach in the daytime. He never missed a class. Still, in the long run—and his devotees sensed this, too—he presented a problem.

Even a community of material equals such as Eerde could not exclude conflict from its ranks. We children were too young to perceive it, but living in relative isolation and close proximity, our elders simply saw too much of one another and not enough of the outside world. As I learned later, for instance, Mrs. Petersen cordially disliked Mr. Neuse, then and for the rest of her life, and he returned this feeling. Prussian schoolmaster that he was, often in the best sense of the word, he probably found it difficult to accept a woman as his hierarchic superior. In the dormitory, the two housemothers vied for the souls of their charges. They were jealous of each other. To this must be added more predictable complications disturbing the school's utopian atmosphere. In 1938, the chaperone of my first journey to Holland, Miss K., had to leave because she was expecting the child of one of her married colleagues. My family archives contain a letter reporting that Fräulein Emmy came to the dormitory early one morning to wake one of the older girls who had duty in the kitchen—just in time to see a teacher, carrying his shoes, tiptoe out of a female staff member's room. More overtly, the ageless Frau Kuck in her subterranean domain found much to disapprove—newfangled methods of education and shoddy discipline—and she was so lacking in tact that she would not hesitate to criticize teachers in front of students, in itself the worst indiscipline imaginable.

It was also in 1935, if I remember correctly, that a fifteen-year-old girl student was caught in the shower with a slightly older boy: an infraction of communal customs for which both were immediately expelled. Boost had no immediate connection with any of these events and potential scandals, but in a stormy faculty meeting he opposed the expulsion of the two students. Not that he advocated promiscuity. His own monkish existence was proof of that. He simply believed that communities should reform, not cast out the wayward. At the same time, he refused to face the fact that an educational institution with a faculty and student body mostly foreign could not survive in puritan, rural Holland any imputation of sexual looseness. Pregnant and unwed teachers or students would destroy the school. Anyone who broke the rules of celibacy, or monogamy where married adults were concerned, endangered the community and lost all claims to its tolerance. (In Miss K.'s case, however, the errant husband retained his post, thanks to the prevailing double standard.) Following the controversy over the incident in the shower, Boost's contract was not renewed. He was replaced by a more staid Dutch *couple* who provided little charisma and, to his disconsolate and abandoned *chapelle,* no commensurate intellectual excitement.

I was too callow to mourn this loss for long, and Jan Boost's place as my *spiritus rector* was taken by Billy Hilsley, at that time still known by his German family name Hildesheimer. Billy was born ten years before me, in 1911. His mother had decided to have her child in England. This decision must have appeared eccentric and dangerous at the time, for the quality of English medical care, hospitals in particular, lagged far behind Germany's. But the risk she took made her a twofold life giver to her son. When the Germans invaded Holland in 1940, Billy, though a Jew, was saved from extermination by his British passport. He spent the war in an internment camp for enemy aliens from which he emerged undernourished, but otherwise unharmed, in 1945.

Billy arrived shortly after me, fresh out of school, another novice teacher. He immediately organized a choir and a small orchestra from which he drew extraordinary performances, considering the size and modest talents of the student body. Thanks to him, I can list singing opera among my accomplishments. Although I have ordinarily found it difficult to carry a tune, Billy made me sing. I was assigned the small part of a moneylender in Carl Maria von Weber's *Abu Hassan,* and even carried a solo part in the one-act opera *Cress ertrinkt* by the Schönberg disciple Wolfgang Fortner. Before the performance, my more talented peers consoled me that in this atonal work, the audience would not recognize my sour notes.

Every Monday morning all students fourteen and older gathered in the music room for Billy's musicological performances. Here we learned a hitherto-unknown foreign language: music. These hours were light years removed from Boost's literary free-for-all. To be sure, our music teacher was no drillmaster. But he had a message to convey; he had a lesson plan from which he never deviated. What he actually taught us, of course, was the history of German music, plus Chopin. We came away totally innocent of Italians, Russians (except Stravinsky), Czechs, northern Europeans, and the French, both romantics and impressionists. But what was left was substantial and exciting enough. We learned the vocabulary of Bach, Händel, Gluck, Haydn, Mozart, Beethoven, and the German romantics, including Wagner. I shall also never forget the last session, when our teacher donned the mantle of the prophet. Conservative that he was, both as a classicist and as a German cultural chauvinist, he found little to praise in modern music. But he instructed us to keep an eye on three contemporaries who marvelously vindicated the standards by which he judged: Stravinsky, Béla Bartók (anything but a familiar name to the public of the 1930s), and Kurt Weill, whose "serious" works are now at last finding a place alongside his more popular contributions to the musical stage. Billy did not teach us everything, but he taught us a great deal well.

I also recall that this Jewish fellow exile had not remained impervious to the prejudices that had long dominated certain sectors of German cultural life. In the course of more than one lecture, he insisted that Jews could excel as performers, as virtuosos, but not as creators. He execrated Mendelssohn, my first "favorite composer," and regarded Gustav Mahler as an adept orchestrator who concealed a barren imagination behind dazzling fireworks of sound. I never discovered, and surprisingly never asked, how Weill escaped these strictures, but then I was old enough to know that every rule, except in mathematics, had its exception.

As in the case of Jan Boost, Billy's influence on me was not confined to classroom or choir rehearsal. In the dining room I sat at his table, where arguments about Mendelssohn continued, and where many other intellectual controversies ignited as we consumed Frau Kuck's solid, predictable, Teutonic cuisine. Early in life Billy had strayed into the outer ranks of the discipleship of the German poet Stefan George, in my opinion a writer with more physical profile than creative talent, but terribly serious, mystical, ascetic, and ultimately mysterious—popular among young people of an idealistic cast. Surrounded by a company of male adherents, who, in turn, showed little taste for female company, George exemplified aspirations of earnest, pure manliness, and clean living. I saw him as a kind of super–Boy Scout, who produced volume after volume of highly polished, formal verse, breathing the spirit of Schiller rather than Goethe. Under Billy's aegis these poems were read by candlelight, amidst the antique furniture and seventeenth-century tapestry of the manor's assembly hall, in grave, sepulchral monotones, each recitation followed by intervals of total, motionless silence. I never became a bona fide member of the "Georgianer" cell at Eerde. I liked girls better than boys, and my own reading of "the master" was merely a reverential concession to a teacher whom I admired.

Many years later I encountered a contemporary judgment of George, written the day before his death on December 4, 1933, which aptly echoes my own feelings: "Is a poet without humor conceivable? A poet who does not cherish woman, and whom no woman . . . cherishes? . . . A poet who requires theater props—wreaths, altars, candlelight, robes . . . and the like—to embellish his poems? A poet who does not love and who fails to recreate the natural setting surrounding him, but [instead invents] an imaginary one? A poet who versifies his failure to experience?"[2]

These dim-lit rituals were sometimes devoted to the work of a genius whom plebeian members of the circle, such as I, found more accessible: Friedrich Nietzsche. I discovered among his poems veritable jewels of German lyricism. This lonely, mad philosopher without system became part of my small company of guardian angels, an essential part of the inheritance with which my lost homeland sent me on my way. It all comes down to the point that Billy taught me to read poetry, as well as music, and thus enabled me to penetrate new continents of the spirit. Not that he approved every stop on my peregrinations. My next discovery was Rainer Maria Rilke, whom he abhorred. More discussions, more agitated readings of passages to prove this or that point, more search for more beauty, more wisdom, and more revelation. On another journey I found Hermann Hesse—again Billy disapproved—whom my generation-in-exile worshiped no less than did American students of the 1960s.

Unlike his idol George, Billy did, however, have a sense of humor and an irrepressible penchant for musical horseplay. After I came to the United States, I soon learned to enjoy the musical parodies of the late Alec Templeton and Victor Borge. Their rather predictable antics could not match those of Billy, who, on a Saturday night, could sit down at the grand piano in the hall and regale us with improvisations of every kind: spur-of-the-moment chansons satirizing the school and its inhabitants, the Dutch, the English, the Germans, and politics in general. A favorite routine consisted of taking a song, popular or folk, and playing it in a dazzling variety of musical styles, from a Bach fugue to an austere Bartók setting. His periodic, and sometimes painstakingly prepared, evenings of musical merriment were highlights of the year and made him everybody's chosen entertainer.

2. Rudolf Binding to Hans Carossa, December 3, 1933, in Rudolf G. Binding, *Die Briefe* (Hamburg, 1957), 226.

Billy Hilsley was a teacher of infinite resources and limitless devotion to his calling. However, after years of internment, he temporarily abandoned teaching to join the Kurt Jooss Ballet as a pianist, and in the spring of 1946, still in uniform, I caught up with him at the Théâtre des Champs-Elysées in Paris, where he was playing one of the two grand pianos that furnished the musical accompaniment to the group's program. Later that year, after my return to civilian life, on Jooss's American tour, my wife and I picked him up at Orchestra Hall in Chicago for a convivial evening. It was the last time our paths crossed. After the group's return to Britain, the Sadler's Wells Ballet sought his service, but he decided to return to Eerde, staying with the school after it moved to Beverwerd Castle near Utrecht. His greatest joy was teaching; it remained his life's work until he retired in 1978.

Jan Boost was less fortunate. We lost sight of him after he left Eerde. At the end of the war, I learned that he had been killed in action against the Japanese in the Dutch East Indies. I do not know how he came to such an end. Although one of his brothers was a regular army officer, Jan Boost as a soldier boggles the imagination. One could have envisioned him plunging with heedless enthusiasm into the thick of the resistance and suffering martyrdom at the hands of the Nazis. But dying for an empire he despised and rejected was a terrible fate for the man who gave me and some of my friends our first acquaintance with a noble pacifism and the utopia of social justice.

Upon my arrival at Eerde on September 20, 1934, the number of students stood at thirty-four. Four years later it had grown to about one hundred, but during the war its ranks were thinned drastically, by emigration and by extermination. I would guess that, during my three years there, more than 80 percent of us were German, and that a majority within that group were wholly or partly of Jewish origin, while the rest were the offspring of unheralded political resisters: parents who often risked a good deal by sending their children to a foreign school. Theirs was an opposition more concrete than the mostly silent disapproval of generals, high civil servants, and bishops, about which so much has been written.

The majority of Dutch children, with their "learning disabilities," represented special cases for which Eerde had not been designed. In continental Europe private boardingschools existed primarily to provide care for the psychologically and mentally handicapped who were fortunate to be born of parents affluent enough to pay for the special attention they required. Some of our Dutch students were mad as hatters, whereas others became as much a part of our community as the other children. I think of Tjot Coster, whose parents, if I remember correctly, lived in the colonies: a quiet, sweet-tempered girl with a beautiful voice and a sovereign command of the recorder. She was among the elect of Billy Hilsley's student congregation. I also remember Rijn, a tall, taciturn boy, my age, from Vriesland. We were roommates until, at age fourteen, I was placed in charge of a larger room of young boys between ages ten and twelve. A few days after this transfer, Rijn threw a large piece of pottery down the stairwell of the dormitory. Luckily he hit no one, and the artifact became the only victim of his outburst. Queried about the reason for his dangerous behavior, he complained that I had "deserted" him. I liked him but had no idea that this silent, undemonstrative lad had become so attached to my company. Therefore I agreed only too readily to move back into the quarters we had shared.

We also had a few English students. One of these, Michael Rowntree, member of a famous Quaker clan, spent a year in Eerde to mingle with students of other cultures, for the good of his soul and the promotion of international understanding. He was a charming, slightly blasé young man who became very popular and whose departure was mourned by all. Three girls, Faith, Margaret, and Penelope, may have been in Eerde for similar reasons, although in Penelope's case I can testify, since she was in my class, that she suffered from a "learning disability" of a common and incurable sort: a lack of brains. When we took the examinations for the Oxford School Certificate in the summer of 1937, Penelope failed so resoundingly that it was considered inadvisable to have her stay on and try again.

Given the composition of faculty and student body, German was the lingua franca of the school. This occasioned some friction. For Dutch students it must have been an astonishing experience to attend school in their own country as an alien minority. What made matters worse was that many of us Germans, both old and young, viewed Dutch as an amusing dialect, a prejudice we lacked the tact to conceal. We spoke Dutch, not only with an accent, but with more than an occasional snicker. Only two territories were closed to this shameful cultural arrogance: the kitchen, where Frau Kuck's native low German met her Dutch staff more than halfway, and Jan Boost's classroom and chamber. After his years in Switzerland, he spoke either German or French with us, Dutch only with his Dutch pupils.

Among the German majority, group allegiances were not political but geographic. Most of us came from Germany's larger cities, notably Berlin, Hamburg, and Frankfurt (where the Jewish community included almost 10 percent of the population). We continued, surprisingly, to cherish our birthplaces, certainly more than our country of origin. We Frankfurters, for instance, missed no opportunity to extol the virtues of our ancient city, the coronation site of emperors and the birthplace of Goethe, at the expense of a grubby hub of commerce such as Hamburg or a smoky rabbit warren like Berlin.

But what made the student body, in retrospect, as extraordinary as the faculty was the gifts and achievements of many of its members. As my contemporaries among the school population pass in review, I cannot claim to have lived among geniuses, but I remember an unusual number of successful talents. Of the fourteen who took their Oxford examination at the time I did, I know of six who went to graduate school and obtained doctoral degrees. Another became a fellow at Harvard. Other Eerde alumni whom I met or heard from again in adult life include Beate Ruhm von Oppen, now at St. John's in Baltimore; Fritz Hoeniger, professor of English and Shakespeare scholar at the University of Toronto; Keith Andrews, who became keeper of prints at the Scottish National Gallery in Edinburgh; Werner Warmbrunn, the American chronicler of the German occupation of Holland during World War II; and Karl J. Weintraub, nationally recognized as a master teacher and later, for many years, dean of humanities at the University of Chicago. Klaus Epstein and my brother Richard, who were classmates in Eerde's elementary school, beginning with the second grade, later received their doctorates at Harvard and Yale respectively, and then became colleagues at Brown University. Klaus had become the internationally acclaimed historian of German conservatism when an automobile accident snuffed out his life before he was forty. Steven Kaufmann became a physicist on the staff of the Argonne National Laboratory; Ruth Gruenthal a practicing psychiatrist in New York.

Not all of Eerde's gifted children lived to maturity. Another Klaus, a blond, dreamy boy, the premier pianist in our ranks, who mastered the solo parts of Mozart piano concertos by the time he was twelve, was one of many whose life was to end at Auschwitz. Klaus Metz, a good-natured, shambling, near-sighted albino, and a whiz at mathematics, took special tutorials in calculus with Mr. Reckendorf while the rest of us still struggled with the Pythagorean theorem. His widowed mother had left him in Eerde and emigrated to Argentina, where she worked as a domestic servant. She fought unceasingly to obtain an entry visa for her visibly handicapped child, but in vain. In my possession is a postcard, dated April 6, 1943, announcing the safe arrival of a group of Eerde pupils, including Klaus, at Vught: one of two Dutch way stations on the road to the gas chamber. Another member of this group, Hermann Isaak, wrote regularly before he left Holland. I do not remember him; I have only his letters to my mother and brother, thanking them for their gift of books—consoling this young man of eighteen during the last weeks of his life. They included the annals of Tacitus, the works of Sallust and Ovid, and the *Chanson de Roland.*

Two of my schoolmates, both offspring of German Quaker families, died for "führer and fatherland." One, a member of the first class to obtain the Oxford School Certificate, died in action in Poland, the other aboard a submarine that never returned to port. One was until his graduation in 1936 my closest friend. Political and professional pressures on his family forced his return to Germany. The other was my brother's classmate in primary school. Although I am not one to place the dead of the Wehrmacht in the same category as the victims of Nazi policies of extinction, I mourn these two schoolmates. What a burden their loss must have been to parents who could have prevented their deaths!

Life at Eerde was full of work and pleasure. We arose at six-thirty, awakened by a bell attached to the outside of the former stable, and rung unfailingly during my years by my first roommate, Hans Lüdecke. It was not without significance that so important a duty should have been entrusted to a student and that it was not difficult to find among us a teenager who discharged this herald service day after day, year after year, without ever being late or remiss.

After a quick, frugal European breakfast, we spent half an hour making our beds and sweeping our rooms, before the first class convened at eight o'clock. Classes lasted until noon. Apart from the three high-school curricula—German secondary instruction for lower grades, as well as the Dutch and English study plan—there was a primary school for children under ten. In all four divisions, however, students were assigned not by age but by levels of achievement. During my first year, for instance, I took math with my own age group, but French at the advanced and English at the elementary level. In 1935, the five oldest German students became the first group to prepare for the Oxford School Certificate. My own group became the second class to negotiate that obstacle course. From the moment we entered this curriculum, all our classes were held in English.

As I look back on my three busy and tense school years at Eerde, I cannot say that it was all fun. Much of it, in fact, consisted of mechanical drudgery. The study of English literature was taken up by "set books," in our case *Macbeth* and the less racy parts of the *Canterbury Tales*. By the time we took the examination, we all knew *Macbeth* by heart, and somehow had not grown to despise it, and my heart still sings whenever I take up Chaucer's epic. That this incessant preoccupation with so small a body of work did not become the mindless grind that the study of literature had been in German schools was undoubtedly due to Kurt Neuse. I do not know how he managed to make us sit up attentively instead of bending with boredom when, for the umpteenth time, he took us back to "that Aprille with his shoures sote," but he made each reading a new experience. His every teaching hour was a master's class. I am sure whoever taught him how to invest his lessons with such variety was not a professor of education.

Mr. Neuse also taught us English composition. This was the most formidable part of the examination; failing composition meant failing everything. We would be required to write on a subject chosen by a group of English examiners, and would be judged alongside native Englishmen. We had to learn to write correctly and idiomatically in a language not spoken in our daily surroundings. Most of us had no difficulty with English grammar, including syntax, it being much more simple than that of other European languages with which we were already familiar. Acquiring a vocabulary was likewise not hard, since the words had familiar Germanic and Latin roots. What stumped us was the idiomatic character of the English tongue. We had to learn it phrase by phrase instead of word by word, and it took a while for us to learn to express ourselves directly instead of by translation. Woe betide the perpetrator of Teutonicisms! "At the evening," Mr. Neuse might recite from one such hapless expectoration, "I sit before my desk and write up in my diary what I have experienced by my friends." "*In* the evening," he would rage, pacing up and down before us, "In the evening I sit *at* my desk, and write—

neither up nor down—in my diary what I have experienced *with*,"
fist on the table again, "my friends." And he would add angrily,
"You'll make fools of yourselves if you cannot get this sort of thing
right!" But we remembered. We were serious, reasonably intelligent
students, and at an age when ridicule seemed the worst of all degra-
dations. Nor did we resent being pilloried. Mr. Neuse played no
favorites; his wrath touched everyone, and in his composition class
no one laughed at another's mistakes. When the showdown with the
examiners from across the Channel finally came, nobody failed
English composition.

Lunch was the main meal of the day. Before each repast, we
observed a minute of silence as we grasped the hands of our neighbors to the left and right, a fleeting, recurrent ritual of total community. We sat at tables accommodating ten to fifteen students, each
under the aegis of a faculty member. Supervision was nominal.
Some table heads would carry out an occasional inspection of
hands and fingernails, and send the unclean back to their rooms for
a second scrubbing; others simply ate with us and joined in discussion and argument.

We were, on the whole, not hard to manage. We respected our
elders, even when we disagreed with them, and the teachers, in turn,
taught and led without authoritarian postures. Perhaps it was the
other way round. Since our teachers were kind and competent, we
followed them willingly. In class we sat quietly at our desks when an
instructor entered the room. We kept discipline without heel clicking and saluting. Even the anarchic proceedings in Jan Boost's
French classes preserved an outward orderliness.

After lunch we usually had a brief meeting on the bridge connecting castle and courtyard, which was taken up with announcements.
The stairs leading to the main entrance served as rostrum. Sometime
in 1935 I persuaded our headmistress to allow me to include a short
summary of the latest news. Ever since the age of seven I had been
an avid newspaper reader, and had kept up the practice after my
departure from Germany into a world free from censorship. Our
school subscribed to a number of first-class newspapers, and not a
day passed when I did not at least glance at the London *Times, Le
Temps,* the Rotterdam *Courant,* and the Zurich *Zeitung.* I think I was,
at thirteen, also the youngest regular attendant at Eerde's "newspaper evenings," which brought together at irregular intervals outside visitors—often parents—faculty, and a few of the older stu-

dents to discuss international affairs. I believed that everyone should take an interest in events that would determine the fate of our band of exiles.

Mrs. Petersen, always responsive to students anxious to assume worthwhile responsibilities, agreed to my proposal, and I became Eerde's anchorman. Five times a week I reported on the rise and fall of French cabinets, the abdication of Edward VIII, the Italian invasion of Ethiopia, the Spanish civil war, and the latest shockers from Berlin. No wonder that I remember the history of the 1930s well. I chronicled much of it for the school as it happened. I must admit, of course, that my range was limited. Only the Japanese invasion of Manchuria and its consequences persuaded me to mention Asia. Africa entered my purview only during the Italo-Ethiopian war, and the United States hardly at all. The New Deal meant nothing to me, nor do I recall announcing Franklin D. Roosevelt's reelection in 1936. Indeed, I remember only one American news item I capriciously decided to include in my daily bulletins: the assassination of Huey Long, an event I interpreted as an enviably healthy response to the ambitions of a would-be dictator; an act of courage that, alas, no German seemed willing to imitate.

These bulletins constituted my own beginnings as a teacher. They are more than a fond memory; they symbolized how far I had traveled since leaving home. One day's train ride had taken me from my German school auditorium, where I was forced to listen to the sermons of one führer, who, like Jehovah, tolerated no gods other than himself, into an open world where each of us could pray at the altar of his choice. Every daily news summary became a step on my personal progress to liberty.

Until two o'clock we students observed a somewhat abbreviated hour of silence. We went to our rooms, to rest, to sleep, to read, even to do homework. It did not matter how the time was spent, so long as it was done noiselessly. Then the bell rang again to summon us to one and a half hours of manual labor. (In German this period was called—somewhat dogmatically, I still think—*praktische Arbeit.* I cannot accept that working with one's hands is inherently more practical than the exercise of the mind.) According to a duty roster, these plebeian tasks rotated at regular intervals between various crafts, such as pottery and carpentry, and work in the garden, less glamorous, but indispensable to the school's survival. A stint in Mrs. Hermanns' pottery was by far the most popular assignment. Here we indulged what many mistook for creative talents, sculpting heads and busts from clay, shaping a variety of primitive receptacles, and learning to operate the potter's wheel, as well as finishing and baking these products in the school's small electric kiln. In time every parental home was awash with these artifacts. My mother carried some of my heavy, graceless creations halfway around the world. Unlike the delicate works fashioned by our professional betters, these ashtrays and fruit bowls never broke. Some of them now gather dust in my attic.

Next door to the pottery, the more talented members of Mijnheer Brouwer's shop crew produced other useful objects, notably bookshelves, endlessly in demand in this bookish community. The young carpenters also repaired cupboards, chairs, and tables as need arose. During the first two years of the school's existence, the older students, under the command of the popular and ubiquitous Mr. Hermanns, served time on another project already alluded to, the swimming pool. This installation became the most impressive achievement of our shop curriculum, and its opening in the spring of 1937 was perhaps the most satisfying moment in the life of the community.

Work in the garden, sweaty digging and scratching, had less appeal. But these exertions helped feed us and therefore merited the drudgery. Here the favorite assignment was Paul Kruimel's pride and joy: the greenhouse. Most valued among its rare products was American corn, and the appearance of its slender harvest on our tables, just enough for a meal or two, constituted the culinary high point of the year.

On Wednesday and Saturday afternoons, the workshops lay idle as we gathered on the playing fields. The centerpiece of our improvised athletic facilities was the soccer pitch, which likewise served as grazing ground for the cows of one of the baron's tenants when not in use. Preceding every match these docile beasts were driven to a nearby enclosure while the current swimming-pool crew carefully removed their droppings before the referee's whistle sounded. This converted pasture also served our Eerde all-stars in matches against neighboring schools and villages. For these encounters we appeared neatly dressed in blue jerseys and shorts.

I cannot estimate to what extent sport built our characters. We certainly learned to cope with the frustration of defeat. Most of the time we bore losses stoically. No coach harangued us at half-time, and no setback resulted in extra practice sessions on the field or at the blackboard. Although some of us harbored preposterous dreams of becoming professionals, we kept these visions, and an occasional furtive tear after a particularly galling defeat, to ourselves. Deep in my heart I prized a goal, scored in interschool competition, more highly than a good grade, but I knew that these were not the priorities established by reality. Games were an escape; we all understood that.

At 3:30 we gathered for tea and cakes, once more on the castle bridge, and from 4:00 to 6:30 did our homework. Elementary students had study hall, while the rest of us worked in our rooms. During my last year I occupied a cabinet in the castle with a walk-in closet, which I shared with the occupant of the adjoining room, an equally privileged contemporary, Hans Joseph Epstein, with whom I formed a steady partnership. We prepared our English texts together, discussed and criticized each other's essays, and groaned in unison over math and physics. Unfortunately, we were equally weak and uninterested in science and, on occasion, when we were at our wits' end, were forced to seek enlightenment from other classmates to whom this sphere was home ground.

After a cold supper of sandwiches and tea, we were free for the evening. Some of us filled the remaining hours of light, if any, with improvised games. Some of us became avid table tennis players, but after our noisy proceedings in the castle corridors disturbed too many people, an outside passageway was whitewashed and outfitted with powerful ceiling lights. Some friends of the school donated two tables, paddles, and balls, equipment that was seldom idle. As the dreaded examinations approached, these freedoms were curtailed by more studying.

We were also allowed to prowl the woods outside the grounds, granting individualists a brief, but necessary, escape from community life. One wanted to be alone every once in a while, even in utopia, or talk undisturbed to a girl. We signed out before leaving and reported to the teacher on duty upon our return.

First and second graders had to be in bed between 8:00 and 8:30; for the oldest among us, lights out was at 10:00. The supervision of the final daily rites was in the hands of the housemothers and the faculty officer of the week, assisted by a student member of the "committee," whose mention brings me to the last important aspect of life in Eerde: student government. I do not know the details of its organization in January, 1935, because my return after the Christmas holidays was delayed by the mumps. When I got back, the students were about to elect the first *Schülerausschuss,* an organization designed to share in the management of all aspects of student life except instruction.

This first election, if I remember correctly, was Eerde's only secret ballot. In subsequent years committee members as well as the chairman were elected at the meetings of the school assembly, composed of everyone on the grounds: faculty, staff, and students. The process was extremely simple, devoid of all secrecy. When a candidate's name was called, every person supporting him rose, and heads were counted. The student with the largest number of votes became not only committee chairman but also presiding officer of the assembly. The six next highest vote-getters in descending order were considered elected to the committee. Despite the all-inclusive nature of the assembly, students ran it, and no adults stood for an office or voted in the open ballot. Our elders did, however, take the floor, and their opinions naturally had great weight.

I realize that student government is a commonplace in American school life. For German and Dutch youngsters at our school, it was an exciting novelty. In the two secondary schools I had attended in Germany, classes annually elected from their ranks a trustee (*Vertrauensmann*) who was to bring all questions and complaints from the ranks to our homeroom teacher. In practice, election to that position was nothing but a popularity contest. The only function I ever saw the trustee perform was keeping us quiet when a teacher was unexpectedly called away in the middle of a lesson. After Easter of 1933, our homeroom teacher in Frankfurt, the portly *Studienrat* and party *Amtswalter* Lepke, opened the new school year with the announcement that the vaunted leadership principle of the new Germany would also apply to the choice of a class trustee. As our führer in education, Lepke would appoint the next incumbent of that office. Thus we lost even the right to designate the most popular member of the class.

At Eerde student government became anything but a farce, despite its limited jurisdiction. It gave us the opportunity to formulate some of the rules by which we wanted to live. Thus we legislated a ban on smoking, binding on students of all ages; that we did not drink went without saying, and drugs were unheard of in our world. In 1935 the school assembly, despite some objections from a divided faculty, put students in charge of the duty roster, governing afternoon work assignments under a triweekly rotation. The same authority established an athletic commission, important chiefly because its chairman kept under lock and key our sparse recreational equipment: soccer balls, hockey sticks, volleyball nets, and so on. When any item in that scant store showed signs of wear, he went to Mrs. Petersen to plead for a replacement. In an important step designed to inculcate, not only pretensions, but habits of exercising authority in a responsible fashion, the assembly recommended, and the faculty appointed, members of the student committee as assistants to the weekly faculty duty officer. This measure charged some of us with the task of putting grade schoolers to bed at the appointed hour.

As a member of the committee from its inauguration to my graduation, I participated in these law-making activities and assumed my share of the resulting responsibility, also as keeper of footballs and table tennis paddles. It was a part of everyday life. We took our duties extremely seriously and actually reveled in playing what seemed to us adult roles. None of this responsibility, however, went to our heads. No chasm opened between the committee and the rest of the student body. It was all part of an education in liberty: We constantly examined our values and assumed responsibility for their preservation. This system worked without the application of force or intimidation.

Finally, we were a Quaker school, but few of us were Quakers. On the whole, I think most of our teachers and pupils represented the secular, if not anticlerical, traditions of Europe's educated middle classes. A devout Calvinist like Miss Sheperd, the mathematics teacher, and a practicing Catholic like Miss K., who attended Sunday Mass regularly, were conspicuous exceptions. We respected them, but their example prompted no conversions. Although a majority of the school population was of Jewish or part-Jewish ancestry, I remember no individual or group observance of Jewish holidays. No one in my class asked to be excused even for Yom Kippur. All of us looked forward to and celebrated Christmas, and since we happened to live in Holland, we also adopted that country's practice of observing the day of St. Nicholas, December 6, a day of gift giving. Some weeks before the holiday, we would draw the name of a fellow student, for whom we bought a present or crafted a gift in one of the workshops. On the evening of December 6 we would gather, names would be called, and the gifts would be presented, often accompanied by the reading of a verse chaffing the recipient. Easter was the other major religious holiday, generally honored with a musical performance under Billy Hilsley's direction.

On Sunday, however, we held our own version of a Quaker meeting. Everybody donned his best and gathered in the manorial hall. Our attire for the occasion included stockings without holes, for we were required to enter the sumptuous chamber shoeless to spare its precious carpets. In contrast to orthodox Quaker practice, our reflections were not interrupted by members randomly rising to proclaim the message of their inner light. Our meeting was less spontaneous and, as a rule, interrupted by one sermon, delivered by an adult; sometimes Billy Hilsley performed at the grand piano. On most Sundays Kurt Neuse occupied the pulpit. After about ten minutes of silence, he would rise from his chair, clear his throat, button the middle button of his jacket, and speak, usually in German. No one watched the porcelain clock on the inlaid Louis XV table between the west windows while he addressed us, quietly, and with his customary authority. All consciousness of time vanished.

Since he spoke without manuscript, the record of these perorations has vanished. What made them so arresting was his habit of explaining that the world and its values did not conform to our assumptions. I remember how he warned us one Sunday that the unprecedented human mobility of our age separated, rather than united, mankind. The more we came to know one another across cultural and continental divides, the more we would find grounds to hate one another. We disagreed, of course, but he turned out to be right, and many who listened to him then would be forced to bear witness to his warning later.

Mr. Neuse's Easter sermon, delivered in 1937, of which I found a typed summary in my mother's papers, illustrates what I mean.

Man is indolent and clings to the accustomed. Man is made of common clay, and habit is his wet-nurse. Obstinately he resists the new. Ordinary communication with our fellow-men never reveals that we live in unheard-of times of material and ideological reversals and of convulsive and continuous revolutions. Everyone is too caught up in the rhythm of his workaday environment, the demands of routine, to sense the rhythm of the world beyond. That rhythm seems not to touch him, even though we assume that it touched our ancestors as we read in our history books about the upheavals of their time.

And yet, as we reflect, we must see and confess that everything, yes indeed, everything, which once appeared fixed for all ages, is reeling and in part already overthrown and destroyed. In a time which we elders still remember, which has already become history to you students, incredible revolutions shook every sphere of politics, society and the arts, and cast to the winds what had been accepted. The same remains true of ideology and religion. The ideas of the traditional world of our conceptual imagination have proved false and become indefensible. What is worse, they have become boring, they no longer enthrall and inspire. What the medieval church offered man, the enthusiasm it engendered, is now cold and dead, and well-meaning attempts to preserve or rekindle any part of its light and warmth are tepid, paltry and doomed.

Need I add that we did not take his jeremiad to heart either? As the ascending sun streamed through the windows on this day of resurrection, some of us were undoubtedly tempted to comfort our teacher and ourselves with the assurance that there awaited us a future of discovery and freedom. We did not mourn his vanished world, and only the disappointments of ensuing decades have forced us to admit that he was both chronicler and prophet. So much of what he said fits our own age now; his observations sound shockingly commonplace at the end of the twentieth century. Over the short term, they forced us at least to consider the worst possibilities. On these Sundays we were called to look at our time and its eventual place in history. Just as our teacher's English lessons drove us mercilessly to avoid degrading errors, so his sermons warned us, week after week, against taking Eerde's community as a norm of human relationships. He gave voice to his own deepest fear, that life in this terrestrial paradise would incapacitate us for dealing with more cruel realities.

I think Mr. Neuse underrated himself and us. Yet his example provided the strength throughout our lives to accept less than we had hoped for. On these Sundays the greatest among our teachers rose above his secular calling, and, as I realize today, he also became our shepherd.

VI   GROWING UP IN EERDE

Demanding and absorbing as it was, communal school life still left room for an individual existence. My second chapter of Eerde recollections calls forth more personal memories: changes in family life, the challenge of an exacting curriculum, travel to other countries, and the climactic final examinations. In the preceding chapter, I referred to myself and my friends as children. When I left boardingschool, I was no longer a child.

The most important single event during my first year in Holland forces me to cast another backward glance at life in Nazi Germany. After Easter of 1934, my younger brother entered the first grade. As the account of my own emigration reveals, children's immunity from adult follies became more and more precarious once the Hitler dictatorship was fully established. My brother had the brown eyes of our parents and my mother's dark hair. He was, therefore, more readily hectored for "looking Jewish." In later years my mother claimed that he often came home in tears, mourning that I, "his protector," was gone. I have come to distrust my mother's family recollections, but I do not doubt that my brother's German school year was unpleasant.

A letter in our family archives from his teacher, addressed to my father, documents what he had to endure. One day, for instance, the lesson plan required the study of the vowels *u* (oo) and *au* (ow). The teacher, quite reasonably, sought to demonstrate the relation between the sound and the vowel's use in writing, asking for words that included the vowels in questions. The first illustrative list included the word *Jude* (Jew), while the examples for the second sound sequence featured, among others, the word *Gauner* (rogue, cheat).

As he wrote them on the blackboard, the teacher commented how well *Jew* and *rogue* went together.

My brother reported the incident at home, and my father exploded. This time he did not close the door. Anger overcame prudence. Instead, he fired off an acid letter in which he accused the teacher of having deliberately elicited these two "complementary" words and of having gone out of his way to humiliate my brother. The reply, far from giving my father satisfaction, called him back to reality. The teacher calmly denied having chosen the offending words, claiming that he had simply written on the board what members of the class had suggested. "Among others," he insisted, "the word *Jew* and immediately afterwards the word *rogue* were mentioned. As a matter of course I put these words on the blackboard and commented, quite spontaneously and without premeditation, that these two words were a good match. Nothing very tragic really happened," he concluded, without the hint of an apology. The remainder of the letter charged my father with misrepresentation but stated—no doubt the writer thought generously—that this adversary exchange would not be held against my brother.

What could my father do? Complain to the principal? Petition the superintendent to take disciplinary action? Sue in a Nazi court? Any of these actions could well have put him behind bars, and perhaps even earned my brother's tormentor a commendation for his ideological orthodoxy. There was no recourse. Had the matter been litigated, no lawyer would have dared take my father's case. Slowly, my family was descending from second-class citizens to outcasts. This discovery drove my father to make another, infinitely more painful decision. My brother, too, would have to leave Germany.

Unfortunately, my parents lacked the means to send two children to boardingschool in a foreign country. There was only one way to manage it. My mother would have to emigrate as well and somehow find a job abroad whose income would raise the money. Ever resourceful, and quick to translate plans into action, she wrote Mrs. Petersen to inquire whether the expanding school might possibly have a place on its staff for her. She offered to work without pay if my brother were accepted at Eerde. The two ladies had taken to each other during the visit that preceded my own enrollment, and there was no doubt that my mother had much to offer. After receiving a doctor of law from Heidelberg, she had become interested in juve-

nile problems and managed to combine profession and motherhood. Thanks to our maid, Babette, a girl of unfailing reliability
and utter devotion to me and my brother, she had been free to build
up a large tutorial practice. As a result, her inquiry bore fruit. The
growing school needed a second housemother, and in the summer
of 1935 she assumed that post. My father remained behind, alone,
continuing to pay for my fees and board, as well as sending my
mother, as spending money, the equivalent of the token salary she
had forgone to gain my brother's admission.

By the time our family broke up, for good as it happened, I had
spent three-quarters of a year away from home. At first I nearly
drowned in homesickness; my spirits matched the weather of the
flat, foggy, drizzly Low Countries. The knowledge that there was no
way to escape their gloom and no respite from separation began to
affect my mental balance. For the only time in my life I lapsed into
perpetual hypochondria; I suffered shortness of breath and stomach
pains, and became convinced that I was slowly dying, far away from
home. I went through the routine of daily life mechanically. What did
school, friends, anything matter to someone marked for an early
grave? The announcement that the Saar plebiscite would advance
the Christmas holidays by ten days picked me up for the first time in
months. It gave me the first happiness since Mrs. Petersen's cheerful
reception on the castle bridge.

And then, while in Frankfurt, something astonishing happened. I
suddenly realized how little the splendors of nature and civilization
in my home town compensated for the hopeless lives we, and people like us, were forced to lead. My place of exile assumed a brighter
hue, and I left home almost as eagerly as I had school, five weeks
earlier. This time I arrived in Eerde at dinnertime, earlier than after
my first journey, when I had detoured through Neuss. My fellow
students, gathered in the dining room, greeted my arrival with
cheers and applause. This reception convinced me that I was where
I really belonged.

My mother's arrival, six months later, intensified the attachment
by combining with it a partial family reconstitution. It freed my
brother from his purgatory and ended our separation. For my parents, however, life held out no such consolations. My father carried
the heaviest load, but my mother also shouldered grave emotional
burdens. She separated from her husband for our sake. Satisfying

one obligation forced her to abandon another, and during the years between my graduation and my father's death, she often considered returning to his side, regardless of the risks.

Community life exacted other sacrifices. We did not live together. My mother had her room on the top floor of the dormitory; my brother and I lived with other students. We took our meals at different tables and went our separate ways during the day. Even after hours or during holidays, my brother and I could not take for granted my mother's undivided attention. Other children sought her out: forlorn, homesick boys and girls who might at all hours knock on her door, in need of a good cry and a motherly word of comfort. Many were the pupils to whom she became a substitute parent.

Finally, I must quite frankly confess that in due time our limited reunion produced unexpected disadvantages. My mother quickly made friends among her colleagues; she worked hard and was, as always, more intent on helping than seeking help. Her success inflicted on me a burden shared by many sons and daughters of teachers and clergy throughout the world. My conduct and accomplishments were forever weighed on a scale calibrated to her stature in the community. If I stumbled, there was always someone to remind me that I had proved unworthy of my mother. Once, after a particularly exhausting and disheartening session in geometry, I told Miss Shepherd that I could hardly wait for the day when I had prepared my last lesson and finished my last math test, and could "just vegetate in the sun." Whereupon that pious, humorless, and earnest young woman fixed me with a sad, soulful stare and said, "If that is all to which you aspire, I do feel sorry for your mother." Guiltily I picked up my books and stole from the classroom.

It was, of course, good for us that the humane, tolerant, and open atmosphere of the school was coupled with great demands, and that our teachers refused to indulge student weakness. Failure was not among our options, and anyone who demanded less than our best was, in the long run, not our friend. Before Christmas in 1935, accordingly, the school urged my parents to agree to my promotion to A Class: the group preparing for the Oxford School Certificate. I was fourteen when this decision was made, one to three years younger than all but one of my new classmates. What was the hurry, one may ask? Clearly, my early graduation would cut our fee and board bill in half and thus remove the reason for my parents' separation. Economic setbacks, which my father suffered in 1937, doomed these hopeful assumptions but validated in unforeseen ways the wisdom of forcing my progress.

It was one thing, however, to put me into the top class; it was another to keep me there. The rapid promotion swamped me with homework until bedtime. Later in the year, I was even allowed on occasion to skip practical work so that I would not fall behind. Before long Sunday and holiday respites had to be sacrificed to maintain this breathless progress toward early graduation. Two weeks before the exams were scheduled to begin, I remained far from confident of success. My mother calmed my growing panic by pointing out that failure would simply mean trying again next year, with a group closer to me in age.

The great divergence of my achievement in different subjects provided grounds for continued uncertainty. In English I often wrote the best essay in class, and my mastery of the "set books" left nothing to be desired. My letters to my father record these small triumphs with particular pride, especially when I had done well by Mr. Neuse's iron standards. When the old Prussian taskmaster wrote under one of my late-dress-rehearsal compositions "remarkable for its fluency," it was as good as scoring a hat trick on the soccer field.

History was pleasure rather than work. German, which all of us chose as the examination's first foreign language, demanded a proficiency in English that I was rapidly acquiring. After that, the clouds began to gather. For a year I prepared Latin as a second foreign language. But my background consisted of only a few months' instruction at my mother's knee when I was nine years old, supplemented by Mr. Neuse's rigorous refresher. As most of my classmates had studied Latin for two years or longer, this scant foundation left me at a distinct disadvantage. All I could do was hang on for dear life, catching up one week, falling flat on my face the next. Finally, in April, it was decided to reduce the risk and allow me to substitute French, of which I had taken almost four years at the *Gymnasium* level. For six weeks I worked at top velocity through a pile of past Oxford examinations to limber up. When the time came, I was confident that the demands made in that subject would not exceed my reach.

Math and science yielded no such assurance. I managed well enough in arithmetic, but my algebra was barely respectable, and geometry never more than marginal. Unless I did better in the exam-ination than I had ever done before, Euclid, Pythagoras, and other assorted Greeks would force me to spend another year at Eerde.

Not every moment of my school life was preempted by such a calendar of anxiety. For the first time I traveled, often with a serious purpose, always with open eyes. Many of these excursions were short trips in Holland. A weekend I spent with my uncle in Amster-dam in January, 1935, gave me particular pleasure. Having been raised in cities, I enjoyed once more the sound of traffic, the sight of elegant shops and shoppers on the Kalverstraat, and a stay in a comfortable hotel near the Leidse Plein. On Saturday afternoon we roamed the ghetto, later razed during the German occupation, and spent two hours in Rembrandt's house viewing his drawings and engravings. In the evening we visited a Dutch business associate whose wife was Danish. I enjoyed being treated like an adult guest in their cheerful and hospitable home. After dinner, the conversation inevitably turned to the nature and importance of Nazi parties in Holland and Denmark. Both our hosts assured my uncle that in their respective countries the movement was quite insignificant, to which my uncle replied with a skeptical shrug, "As recently as 1928 that was also true in Germany."

On Sunday my uncle treated me to another new experience: din-ner in a restaurant of intimidating elegance. The tablecloth and napkins were of heavy, spotless white linen, and as I sat down I gazed upon a bewildering array of eating implements—spoons, forks, and knives of various sizes and shapes, and a profusion of plates and glasses. The menu was voluminous and in French; the waiter, clad in peerless tails, spoke both French and German without accent. My uncle put me at ease by explaining the function of each receptacle and instrument on the table. Then we turned to the bill of fare and after some deliberation ordered "homard froid à la may-onaise" and, for the main course, "châteaubriand garni pour deux personnes." We drank white wine with the first dish, and red with the second—in my case, in consideration of my tender years, diluted with water. The waiter's surgical expertise with crustaceans pro-tected me from the humiliation that often accompanies the uniniti-ated diner's first encounter with lobster. All I had to do was consume the pieces of meat he deftly extracted from the shells. By the time our multilingual majordomo placed before me a plate of filet, surrounded by five different vegetables, I was utterly at peace with the world.

My travels to more distant places were less elegant, but equally memorable. In July, 1935, I joined a party of eight boys, chaperoned by Jan Boost, on a bicycle trip to Belgium, with a five-day visit to the World's Fair in Brussels as its major objective. Laden with knapsack, a couple of changes of clothes, shelter halves, tent poles and pegs (all fastened to our bikes), and fifteen guilders (less than ten dollars), we hit the road, I still on my trusty Frankfurt bike, traversing Holland from northeast to southwest. We pedaled the last leg from the old fortress town of Breda to Flushing at night, across the causeway from the mainland to the island of Walcheren. Along the way we visited the old town of Middelburg (in my memory the most beautiful in Holland but, alas, destroyed during World War II) and then took the ferry back to the mainland, where we crossed the border into Belgium. A history of intermittent common government had established a certain special relationship between Belgium and Holland, even before Benelux, and the *douaniers* on the deserted gravel road on which we were crossing assumed that we were Dutch and simply waved us on. But Boy Scouts, even an ex–Boy Scout such as I, had been taught never to lie, and on this occasion we proved for once loyal to these precepts and stopped to display our German identity cards. The Belgian officials became more distant and examined our pathetic equipment with great care. This sudden change of atmosphere prompted Boost to remind us that Germans were not welcome in the country that had suffered so cruelly from the invasion of 1914, and for once in his teaching life he gave us an order: Speak Dutch or French at all times until we were back in Holland.

Cycling in Belgium was harder work than it had been in Holland. The roads were poorer and full of arduous ups and downs; Holland's comfortable bicycle paths of cracked shell stopped at the border. We eased into these difficulties by dawdling along the relatively smooth and level coastal highway from Knocke-le-Zoute to Ostend. After we reached Blankenberge, and had visited the local war museum that displayed more bitter memories of Belgium's first German occupation, we pitched camp on the beach and decided to spend the night. We ate the standard meal of our trip, bread, cheese, and cold cuts, washed down with water, and curled up in our tents on the sand. Sometime early in the morning, as the sun was just beginning to discolor the horizon, someone shook me. I started up and saw two gendarmes viewing our encampment with somber expressions on their faces, little black books in hand, and pencils poised. They told

Boost that sleeping on the beach was *interdit* and showed him a manual listing the penal consequences of our trespass. Fortunately, they made no move to arrest us but let us pack up and go in search of legal campgrounds on the outskirts of Ostend. There we decided that this adventure entitled us to another respite, and passed the day swimming and loafing.

That evening, Bruno, the brother of my roommate Hans Lüdecke, and I decided to compensate further for these tribulations by sampling Ostend's nightlife. We rode into town, chained our cycles to a lamppost on the city square, and then looked for excitement. We found little of that. After an evening spent drinking lemonade in a harborside *boîte*, whose three-man band, consisting of a saxophonist, a fiddler, and a drummer, seemed to know only three tunes, we became bored and decided to return to our tents. But when we two men of the world got back to the square, our bicycles were gone. That was a poser! Hundreds of kilometers from home, in a strange and not entirely friendly country, with only a few francs in our pockets, and a good hour's hike from our few belongings—it was enough to numb us with momentary panic. For a while we just sat on the curb, helpless and perplexed.

Bruno, two years older than I, was the first to recover his reasoning faculties. "Let's look for the police station," he said. A passerby directed us to that seat of authority, and the moment we entered the building we realized with immeasurable relief that we had come to the right place. There in the corridor stood our bikes. The officer at the desk gave us yet another stern but fatherly lecture, the gist of which was that chaining bicycles to lampposts was likewise an infraction of the law. He was sorry that his men, while taking possession of our errant vehicles, had broken our chains and, to compensate, offered us his blessings and the injunction to pedal as quickly as possible out of his jurisdiction. We took his advice, after expressing our gratitude as elaborately as my French permitted.

The next day we turned our backs on the temptations of resort life and visited Bruges and Ghent before reaching the capital, on whose outskirts a kind farmer allowed us to sleep in his barn. I cannot say that I made good use of our visit to the two former landmark towns of medieval commerce. Because I knew what was expected of me, I gazed dutifully at the ancient quarters of Bruges and visited Ghent's cathedral of St. Bavon, with its famous *Adoration of the Lamb* by Hubert and Jan van Eyck. Modern, vulgar Brussels impressed me much more. I barely noticed the resplendent Grand Place, but marveled at Europe's first parking garage and plunged into the jerry-built magnificence of the Fair. I wandered from pavilion to pavilion, lingering particularly wherever samples of free food or drink were dispensed. This involved frequent stops at the coffee urn in the Brazilian exhibit and at Denmark's fountain of Tuborg beer. I did spend an interesting afternoon in the largest pavilion at the Fair, that of the Congo—my only lapse into serious sightseeing that I can remember. Bruno and I also managed to sneak into the Great White Way section, where a ticket taker, more concerned with profit than with regulations, admitted us to an adult attraction featuring a stripper performing in a cage with six sleepy lions. As the shapely lady stepped gingerly over the lethargic beasts, she dropped article after article of clothing, but when she was about to come to the end of her flimsy wardrobe, the lights went out, and the performance was over.

We also happened to be in town on the Belgian national holiday, catching a glimpse of a parade of Belgian lancers with steel helmets, a bizarre combination, and observing Leopold III and his beautiful Swedish queen Astrid as they passed us in a black limousine. What surprised me, accustomed as I was to the choreography accompanying the public appearances of Hitler, was the seeming indifference with which the public greeted the passage of the royal couple.

Finally, we paid our respects to the statue of Maneken Pis, the legendary hero who is said to have stopped the advance of Spanish invaders by urinating in their faces. Then we took to the saddle again for a visit to Antwerp. I savored this lively city with never a thought of Peter Paul Rubens, and my letters home only expressed boundless admiration for "the most elegant taxis I have ever seen." After Antwerp, we had had enough of Belgian roads and hurried back to the more cyclophile highways of Holland. After three full days of constant pedaling, we returned to the school, sunburned and weary. At this point a good night's sleep in a clean bed seemed equal to any of the attractions we had encountered on our journey.

The following summer I spent in England, just after my controversial transfer to A Class. Thanks to our Quaker connection, the school had procured me invitations to spend six weeks with two English families. This sojourn immersed me in the language of the forthcoming examinations and made me bilingual, or very nearly so. I had just turned fifteen, and the prospect of this trip excited me tremendously. Ordinarily a fairly placid, sober boy, to whom insomnia was unknown, I literally did not close my eyes during the night preceding my departure. In view of my inexperience, the journey to my destination had been carefully planned. My uncle, who happened once again to be in Amsterdam on a business trip, picked me up at the central station and saw to it that I caught the right train to Rotterdam. There the dock was in sight of the train, and it was rightly assumed that I would manage to cross from one to the other without losing my way. Then I would be safe for the night, unless the boat sank, or until we reached Gravesend, where it was likewise only a stone's throw from dock to train. At Victoria Station, German friends, who had only recently emigrated to the British Isles, met my train and brought me to my first host: a family named Smith, who lived in the north London suburb of Finchley. These genial people brought the entire expedition to a successful close by sending at once a telegram to apprise my uneasy family of my safe arrival.

The Smiths made me indeed welcome. As the head of the house explained to me the first evening, they were members of the Fellowship of Reconciliation, a pacifist sect like the Quakers, but with beliefs differing in a variety of arcane ways from those of the followers of William Penn. I understood that Mr. Smith assumed this to be of consuming interest to me, and therefore listened politely, but comprehended little.

My mother had warned me that this trip would make greater demands on my social resources than had bicycling in Belgium. I received instructions on the etiquette of dress and table manners. Up to this point my wardrobe had consisted of knee socks, sport shirts, and navy-colored corduroy shorts. These shorts were the blue jeans of my generation and worn by every German youth organization from the Jewish Boy Scouts to the Hitler Youth. According to our code of manliness, they ended twenty centimeters above the knee, a rule that gave rise to frequent family arguments in wintertime, when parents insisted on covered knees, whereas we preferred frozen limbs to the contempt of our peers. For special occasions a pair of plus fours would substitute for the shorts, and on Sundays a tie would complete my adolescent ensemble. Now, for the first time, my mother took me shopping to buy a pair of long flannel trousers, and preempted from a recently arrived clothing package at the school a hand-me-down suit, the former property of a recently deceased Dutch worthy well up in years. A local tailor reduced this garment to my proportions. Two white shirts and a red tie were likewise added to my wardrobe. These purchases were to prepare me for the ritual of "dressing for dinner." I was to wear the flannels during the day and the suit for the evening meal.

That much done and learned, I found out that there was more to dinner than dressing up. In England, I had been told, an individual does not ask to have food passed to him. His neighbors will supply him unasked whenever they see that his plate is empty. Unfortunately, he is expected to join this watch. Instead of digging into his food, he must keep a constant eye on the contents of everybody else's plate. The moment a neighbor at table asks if he would care for more vegetables, when they are heaped before him while the neighbor has run out, he knows that he has been found wanting. I could see this happen to me, and conversation around the table dying as I groped, red faced, for the vegetable dish. It was a humiliation to be avoided at all costs.

On my first evening at the Smith home, I did not feel the least bit hungry. Throughout the meal my gaze wandered incessantly over the table, keeping constant inventory of everybody's portions: Mr. Smith's (Carlton), Mrs. Smith's (Rhoda), Mrs. White's (the housekeeper), and the oldest son's (John). After the meal Mrs. Smith asked me solicitously whether anything unaccustomed in their diet or cuisine had not agreed with me, for I had obviously eaten very little. I reassured her, and for the next few days worked even harder at being my brother's and my own stomach's keeper. It took some time before I became accustomed to these alien practices, but by the end of my visit they had become second nature to me.

The Smiths had two sons. The younger one, Allan, was sixteen and intended as my companion during the visit. He came home from his public school my first week in Finchley and turned out to be rather young for his age; during the ensuing weeks, we coexisted amiably but had little to say to each other. I explored London on my own or in the company of the older son, John, who was twenty-three, but with whom I got on much better despite the eight years that separated our ages.

To the amusement of his parents, John informed me the first evening of my visit that he was a Communist. His tolerance of the company of a fifteen-year-old was, in part at least, prompted by his obvious desire to convert me. Faithful to Jan Boost's particular version of the century's new secular religion, and the precepts of my maternal ancestry, I usually recoiled from religious and secular dogmatism, but I had sense enough to use John far more than he used me. I encouraged his missionary impulses, which became my introduction to the more flamboyant aspects of political life in London. In John's company I attended an enormous number of meetings. Despite his rigid beliefs, he proved to be an eclectic guide. Perhaps he wanted to demonstrate the worthiness of his favorite cause by giving me an opportunity to listen to the views of communism's numerous opponents. In any case, we spent many evenings attending lively exchanges between Labourites and Conservatives, who debated how Britain should respond to the civil war in Spain. Englishmen of all shades of opinion were greatly troubled by their government's refusal to back a legitimately elected republican democracy against its clerical, military, conservative, and Fascist assailants. British business interests, influential in Conservative councils, and heavily invested in Spanish mining, looked for a Spanish government that could curb unions and break the rising number of strikes disrupting the early years of the republic. Dictatorship was more to their taste than democracy, but they concealed this pursuit of their interests behind frequent evocations of the specter of communism. In Spain's case, theirs turned out to be a self-fulfilling prophecy. As the deserted democracy became increasingly dependent on Soviet support, the Communist party naturally began to dominate its government, and, more particularly, the high command of Spain's citizen army and its international auxiliaries.

Between these plunges into the waters of national division, we paddled among less conformist congregations. Thanks to John I heard and met Willie Gallacher, then the only Communist member of the House of Commons: burly, cheerful, and cocky, very much like the aldermanic prototypes of Chicago politics whom I would watch in action a decade and a half later. I also got a closer look at another British soul burden, the Irish question, when we attended a conclave addressed by a member of the executive committee of the Irish Communist party, a gnarled elf with false teeth, named, almost predictably, Pat Devine.

Consorting with the extreme left was, of course, a particular pleasure. To a German, which I still considered myself at that time, it meant an excursion into forbidden territory, listening to forbidden truths, and tasting forbidden fruit. It was a private act of defiance on my part, which included the additional benefit of involving absolutely no risk for anyone, not even my father, to whom I was careful not to report on this particular aspect of my trip.

One night John and I took the subway out to Hampstead Heath, where Sir Oswald Mosley's British Union of Fascists had scheduled a rally. I had demurred at first, as if such a visit constituted a gesture of sympathy for the organizers of the meeting; but my guide was interested in seeing my reaction to these British "Nazis," and so I was persuaded to go. It turned into a reassuring evening. The frequent hostile interruptions indicated that the black-shirted speaker had few friends in the audience. He expended more energy pacifying the booing, milling crowd than in the exposition of his views. I came away, not with any impression of the Fascist program, but only with the feeling that plain Englishmen did not consider it worth a hearing. I was delighted and relieved. British fascism was not exactly on the march. So far as I could tell, it had just been buried on Hampstead Heath. This set me to wondering why an industrial society like Britain's, as afflicted by depression and unemployment as Germany's, proved so unaccommodating to political extremes. Life in the bosom of the civilized Smith family, whose members I considered for lack of any other evidence to be typical of their nation, convinced me that Englishmen had reached a level on the evolutionary scale that Germans might not reach for ages to come. John's missionary purpose had failed utterly. I simply could not take his confessions of communism seriously. What Communist would take me, an innocent bystander, on a tour that attested to nothing but the vigor of his country's political pluralism? Indeed, he demonstrated that even an English Marxist could be fundamentally tolerant. I concluded that what had happened in Germany could not happen here, among people whom Nietzsche had called the Romans of the modern age.

If I felt warmly toward the heirs of Rome, I was no less stirred by the life and sights of their world capital, still my favorite big city. The thrill actually began as my boat train approached Victoria Station, and I was able to identify from my compartment some of the landmarks I had until then only seen in the pages of my English primer. To see them close up was my first holiday objective, and the day after my arrival I boarded Bus No. 5, passing only one block from the Smiths' cottage, a direct conveyance to Trafalgar Square. Nervously I sat on the edge of my seat, in the upper section, approaching the city and waiting for the appearance of some familiar edifice. After a seemingly endless trip, I discerned Nelson's column, dashed down the stairs, and asked the conductor whether we were approaching Trafalgar Square. This was before the age of mass tourism, and the stupefied man looked as if he heard so foolish a question for the first time. Perhaps he suspected that I was pulling his leg. He nodded curtly, and I jumped off as we stopped by a red light, just in front of St. Martin's-in-the-Fields.

I must have changed since the previous year, for after crossing the street and observing the National Gallery, I had an intense desire to view its holdings. Ascertaining that admission was free, I ventured into the museum. I took my pleasure of its familiar sights: Bellini's *Doge Loredano,* Titian's *Bacchus and Ariadne,* Moroni's *Tailor,* the *Adoration of the Kings* by Jan Gossaert Mabuse, a reproduction of which hung in our living room in Frankfurt, Hans Holbein's *Ambassadors,* and a surprising number of reminders of my temporary home, Holland. Van Dyck's portrait of Cornelius van der Geest resembled several lesser specimens of his school hanging in our classrooms at Eerde. Pieter de Hooch's *Interior and Courtyard* depicted scenes of everyday life I knew well, as did Meindert Hobbema's *Avenue,* with its portrait of the Dutch countryside. I stole a furtive glance at Velasquez' *Venus and Cupid* and then regained the street to continue my exploration of the city. After examining the map in the guidebook my hosts had providently supplied, I walked down Charing Cross Road to Oxford Street and ambled along that thoroughfare, examining its countless shop windows as carefully as I had earlier inspected the treasures of the National Gallery.

Near Marble Arch I stopped at a restaurant of the ubiquitous Lyons chain. It was lunchtime, the place was crowded, and I discovered that my English school readings, ranging from Oscar Wilde's *Happy Prince* to *Richard II,* had not included the vocabulary of an English menu. Everybody seemed too busy to answer questions, and so I ordered a dish of green beans, the only item I could identify. When the waitress solicitously asked me whether this was all I was going to eat, I answered with a curt and embarrassed, "Yes," consumed what she set before me, and then left the chaotic scene, relieved to be in the street again but just as hungry as I had been when I entered.

Once at Marble Arch I ventured into Hyde Park. On weekdays the famous "corner" was empty, no speakers or hecklers were to be seen anywhere, and the park offered nothing except vast expanses of sparse grass. My feet were beginning to ache, and after returning to

Oxford Street, I decided to rest in one of the gigantic movie houses—I was to see nothing like them until I arrived in New York—which happened to be showing Charlie Chaplin's *Modern Times*.

At that time the *uomo universale* of filmdom, scriptwriter, composer, producer, director, and star of this classic, was one American known to practically every European. I had first seen his comic shorts on the home-movie set in Rainer's house and at Sunday matinees in the Palace Cinema in our suburb, a plain hall with wooden chairs. My parents had admired *The Gold Rush* and *City Lights* and promised me that I, too, might see these films "when I was old enough." I fully expected that the box office attendant would ask my age and was prepared to add to the truth whatever years were required to gain admittance. But the girl took my money without so much as looking at me and gave me a ticket. *Modern Times* was chiefly touted as the film in which Chaplin spoke for the first time, singing a little song of nonsense syllables. I became more engrossed by the antics resulting from the encounter of the little proletarian with the horrors of futuristic automation, including a video screen that enabled the bosses to monitor his visits to the washroom. I emerged thoroughly rested and amused, retraced my steps to Trafalgar Square, and boarded Bus No. 5 going in the homeward direction. On subsequent visits I would strike out more boldly. Eventually I even mustered the courage to ask strangers for directions, and by the time I left England I could face the maze of London's streets without a guidebook.

My English holiday also allowed me to share family life in a foreign country, an aspect of existence that school life in Holland gave me no opportunity to experience. The Smith clan was large and in the habit of congregating each Sunday at the home of one of its members. Given their nation's reputation for reserve in social intercourse, I was unprepared for the effusive affection with which members of the family greeted one another at these weekly parties. Everybody kissed everybody, fervently and repeatedly, as if all had just been reunited for the first time in years. I was included in this kissing orgy, but only by the older members of the family. Among its younger offshoots was a sixteen-year-old beauty whom I do not recall ever having a chance to kiss. Her father, recently deceased, was Swiss, and I was told that she spoke German. What she did speak was *Schwyzerduetsch,* a dialect quite beyond the understanding of ordinary Germans. I had to discard the notion of getting to know her because she was both unapproachable and incomprehensible, and mingle with the rest of the company as best I could.

One Sunday, over our cups of tea, cakes, and sandwiches, we listened to a radio broadcast of the unveiling of the Canadian war memorial at Vimy Ridge in France, where the prince of Wales gave a creditable speech in French. I was surprised to find that English audiences hung on the words of royalty with the rapt intensity I later associated with revival meetings. My friend and guide John listened with the rest, silently and respectfully, as if the heir to the throne was reciting from Marx's *Das Kapital* or Lenin's *What Is to Be Done?*

The summer plans for me also included a long look at other parts of England. After three weeks with the Smiths, I was to join the family of an Oxford alderman, Henry Gillett, for a trip to Wales. Of his five children, three girls and two boys, the youngest, Roger, was exactly my age, and the middle daughter, Esther, had just spent a year in Eerde. I had met the parents earlier in the year, when they had visited Esther at school, but I nevertheless remember this Welsh holiday as a time among strangers.

One day Roger took me on a tour of his beautiful home town, which inevitably ended in a punt on the Cherwell. As we struggled with poles and vessel in the July sun, I was suddenly overwhelmed by a wave of homesickness, all the more crushing because it was so totally unexpected. Oxford is one of the most handsome cities I know, but it filled my heart with melancholy. To this day, whenever I see photos or films of it, or whenever I read of students punting on the Cherwell, I am forcefully reminded of this feeling of sudden depression. I can only suggest one explanation for this untoward reaction to hospitable kindness in some of England's most beautiful environs: the Smiths were ordinary people, the Gilletts local big-wigs, whose affluence and grandeur intimidated me, their hospitality notwithstanding.

The problem was compounded by the fact that I had as little in common with Roger as with Allan Smith. I did not seem to click with English schoolboys my age. In retrospect, this is not surprising. In the 1930s, my English contemporaries were still at the beginning of growing up in a secure, self-confident world, whereas I was learning to pick my way through strange regions. In London I had found an older, more congenial companion. My second host family provided no such substitute. I had no choice but to spend my time with Roger: a cheerful, normal chap with whom I shared no interests.

On my first weekend in Oxford, I also met the husband of the oldest daughter, the only married child. As the two outsiders at the family table, we gravitated toward each other despite our difference in age, almost ten years. Like John, Leslie was a professed Communist but, once more, a very English variety of the species. Whereas John was serious and schoolmasterly, Leslie was more outgoing and possessed an inexhaustible repertory of wisecracks about everybody and everything: from Hitler to the royal family, from both houses of parliament to the pacifism of his Quaker in-laws. His wife's family did not look to me as if they approved of him, and during one or two of our conversations, he whined about being odd man out wherever he went. This fitted poorly into my image of British pluralism, but he silenced my objections when he said, "You might just as well accept that no one likes a man who is both a Communist and a Jew."

Unfortunately, Leslie and his wife were not joining the excursion to Wales. I would have preferred to remain with them in Oxford, but of course that was not possible. Such a choice would certainly have deprived me of some memorable sights. We stayed in a cottage near the beach of Pwllheli, a precarious narrow stretch of flat land crowded by mountain ranges that extended almost to the edge of the ocean. I had never seen a seascape like it, and it alternately exalted and dejected me. During the day, when the sun bested the clouds, these elevations rising to the distant peak of Mt. Snowden glowed richly in the summer heat. At night, as fog conquered our surroundings, these same heights loomed like malevolent giants over the little house, threatening to crush the dwelling and sweep it and its inhabitants into the waves like so much refuse.

Since the cottage was too small to accommodate everyone, Roger and I slept outside in a tent. It was probably during that summer that I began to lose my taste for the romance of outdoor life. Welsh nights, as I remember them, were dank and chilly, the weather at the beginning of the day invariably discouraging and pallid like autumn. One evening, as we were about to crawl into our confining shelter, we discovered that some trespassing cattle had broken down one of the poles and torn one of the shelter halves. Henceforth we took care that the gates to our yard remained closed and secured with a chain.

On Friday of the second week, we struck our tent and returned to Oxford. I still feel ungrateful when I recall with what pleasure I anticipated my return to London, where I was to spend four days with the German friends who had picked me up at the station at the beginning of my sojourn. Now a confident habitué of the London scene, I was full of plans to satisfy my wide-ranging curiosity. A trip to a radio exhibition, which included my second look at a television transmission, a visit to the Venetian porcelain collection at the British Museum, and a soccer game were to figure among the entertainments.

Two encounters during my last Oxford weekend remain in my mind. Upon our return from Wales, I met another house guest of the Gilletts, an exiled German professor. He was a handsome, extroverted gentleman who spoke, loudly and effusively, execrable English. Roger took an immediate dislike to this sophisticated, Olympian visitor, who spoke so poorly and who also monopolized the family telephone. I still see him in the library, making calls while Roger and I hung around. Being a stranger in the house, he could not tell us to leave; instead, he sought to foil our ill-mannered curiosity by speaking French, not realizing that I understood every word he said. So far as I could tell, he was not exchanging startling secrets with the other party on the wire, but later I would translate to Roger the gist of what I had heard, even embellishing the conversation somewhat. At that point, just before our ways parted, the youngest Gillett and I finally found a common ground of mischief.

On Sunday, Roger's older brother James took me to visit yet another German exile, whose name I am not sure I ever knew. He was a massively built man whose huge head, topped by an unruly gray mane, reminded me of pictures of Beethoven. While James went on some errands, we made the usual refugee conversation: How long have you been here? Where are you from? Why did you leave? How do you manage to get along among strangers? When James returned and I rose to leave, the old gentleman put his hand on my shoulder and said, still in German: "Would you please come again? I am so terribly lonely." I expressed my regrets and explained that I was leaving Oxford the next day, and England the following week. As I spoke, I was overcome by a feeling of sorrow and guilt, which accompanies any act of desertion. Although what I said was, of course, true, I was torn between relief and regret as I left. Relief because my departure spared me the depressing task of listening to the lugubrious reflections of an unhappy man. Regret because I could not make even the most ineffectual gesture of consolation. Finally, I was embarrassed because I realized, even then, how much it must have cost this elderly, forlorn stranger to beg for the company of a fifteen-year-old boy. It was the first time, though not the last, that I realized what strong ties united exiles, regardless of years and achievements. Among us involuntary travelers, class, age, in fact any distinction that separates members of an established society, ceased to have meaning.

Four days later I was back at Victoria Station, boarding the boat train to which my parents' friends had conscientiously, though this time needlessly, escorted me. Their good wishes, supplemented by a giant supply of sandwiches, sent me on my way. As I left London behind, I had no way of knowing how soon I would see it again.

The following year the summer's expedition to Austria, described previously, was preceded by my final examinations. They began on June 5, 1937, the day before my sixteenth birthday. Timidly, those of us being examined entered our classroom, whose chairs and tables had been rearranged, each removed from the other by a distance sufficient to foreclose cheating. The door was then locked behind us, and complete silence settled over the room, broken only by the proctor, a total stranger designated by the sponsoring university, who noisily opened with a large knife the envelope containing the questions. Each of us received a copy, printed on paper of a venomous green, the like of which I have never seen since.

Luckily, the first immersion was gentle. The subject was German, and all of us emerged at lunchtime satisfied and optimistic. Next came composition, and again I turned in my paper, confident that I had written an essay deserving far more than a minimal "Pass." Indeed, everything went well, and my spirits rose with every ordeal. The trial turned out to be easier than its preparation. Even the geometry test contained none of the problems that had given me such headaches in class. Only afterwards, when I triumphantly recapitulated one of my solutions to my mother, did both of us simultaneously realize that my exposition had skipped a crucial step. This troubling disclosure caused us to forgo further post-mortems. Physics confronted me with more impenetrable mysteries, but it was my sixth subject and would not affect the outcome so long as everything thing else had gone well. There was nothing left to do but await the announcement of the results at the end of the summer.

My determination not to let examination worries spoil my holiday in the Alps pushed speculations about the eventual outcome of my June ordeal into the back of my mind. But there remained other matters to be considered. What if I passed? Where would I go; what would I do? These were much more difficult questions. Failure would simply mean that I had to try again. Success, on the other hand, opened several roads demanding a decision which to take.

My desire to study history seemed beyond reach. There was no money. In the spring of 1937, my father's Jewish employer had seen the situation in Germany for what it was, and sold out. The new owner considered my father a dangerous liability: an executive with a Jewish wife, unwilling to join the party, refusing even to greet his coworkers and clients with a routine "Heil Hitler!" when entering and leaving the office. As a manufacturer of tires, the firm depended on increasingly strict allocations of rubber and other scarce raw materials, more than ever in jeopardy if the enterprise acquired the reputation of employing dissenters. He decided to solve the problem by ridding himself of this uncomfortable associate. My father was fired, and my uncle assumed responsibility for my brother's and my school expenses until my father found another job. This took longer than any of us anticipated. As German rearmament went into high gear, unemployment gave way to a shortage of labor, but wherever my father went (and the opportunities were, of course, concentrated in industries benefiting from the military boom), his wife and his politics turned initial interest into regret. He turned out to be "politically intolerable" (*politisch untragbar*). He learned what hell on earth was like as the practical reasons for his separation from us had been invalidated by his unemployment.

The least I could do under the circumstances was to prepare for a less esoteric career. A variety of schemes came and went. Since my father was a talented photographer, now planning to use this gift to try and build a new existence, and since I had also shown some aptitude with the camera, my parents considered my learning this skill under his tutelage. But this would have required my return to Germany, to which my father would not agree. Next, the ease with which I learned languages suggested I might expand my repertoire to include Slavic or Oriental tongues, and try my luck as an interpreter. Eventually, my mother and I decided that I should think of exploiting my facility in English. I had discovered that the University of London had a school of journalism. Deciding that recording the present was the next best thing to studying the past, I felt this field offered an alternative with more immediate prospects of a decent livelihood.

124

Before we reached this decision, however, I floated still another idea. Two of my classmates had already found sponsors for their emigration to the United States and were applying for admission at American colleges. Both had decided to major in German and use this strategy, together with the prospect of advanced standing often granted to graduates of European secondary schools, to earn a degree in considerably less than four years. But this proposal of mine found no second. Neither my parents nor my uncle would even consider sending me three thousand miles across the ocean, at age sixteen, to make my way in the fearsome and distant West.

During my stay in Austria, therefore, I wrote to the University of London to find out more about its journalism program. I learned from the reply and the accompanying catalog that, unlike many other English university programs at the time, this one did not require Latin for admission, and that the Oxford School Certificate and competence in one modern language would gain me entry. The university authorities also pointed out that if I wanted to spend another year in my present school, to prepare for and take the examinations for the Intermediate School Certificate, I could then enter college in 1938 as a second-year student. That struck us all as a most economic and sensible solution. No Eerde student had ever taken this examination, but Mrs. Petersen and Mr. Neuse were willing to let me pioneer. I could not have been more pleased. Another year in Eerde: it sounded too good to be true.

This is how matters stood when my brother and I returned from Austria. On the last leg of our journey, the half-hour train trip from Zwolle to Ommen, we met a Dutch teacher from Eerde who rose from his seat when he saw us, warmly shook my hand, and congratulated me on having passed the Oxford School Certificate with nothing but "goods" and "credits." I was elated. When our taxi rolled into the schoolyard, my mother rushed from the dormitory, waving her hands and shouting "You made it" as she embraced me. "Even in geometry," she exclaimed as she followed me to my room. "What a relief," I responded. "Now I won't have to memorize another theorem for the rest of my life." Mine was not the only good news. Twelve of us had passed; only our Dutch classmate and poor Penelope had foundered.

That evening we celebrated, and Mr. Neuse contributed a cigar to my enjoyment of the festivities. No longer a student in the ordinary sense of the word, I broke rules without pangs of conscience. This smoke was the closest I came to a formal rite of passage. The next day I began a new, and this time more solitary, grind.

The following weeks do not stand out clearly in my memory. What books did I read and with whom? What kind of discipline held me to the routine of pursuing another diploma, this time all by myself? I cannot recall, but no matter: In the middle of September, chance intervened and ended my stay in Eerde, abruptly and on the same day on which I had arrived three years earlier.

VII   TOLERATED, BUT NOT WANTED: MY YEAR IN ENGLAND

On the evening of Thursday, September 18, 1937, my mother bustled into my room with unexpected news that would drastically alter my life. A delegation of English schoolboys, visiting Eerde, was planning to return home the next day. One of their members had fallen ill and been sent back the previous week. Now I could fill the vacancy on their group ticket and travel to England with them. My mother had known of this opportunity only long enough to call my uncle in Austria, who readily agreed to underwrite the one hundred pounds hastily calculated to keep me fed and housed during a year's study in Britain. The Intermediate School Certificate was shelved, and I had from nine o'clock that evening until eight o'clock the next morning to pack and clear my cabinet in the castle.

I was thunderstruck by this change of plans, and cannot explain to this day why a free ticket on a channel steamer should have convinced my elders to abandon plans preceded by so much discussion and careful thought. But I did what I was told. Experience had made me a quick if somewhat untidy packer. My books and other immobilia were stowed in a small attic next to my mother's room; my bedding returned to the school storage from which I had drawn it three years earlier. The suddenness of my departure spared me extensive, emotional farewells, from people and places. One day I sat at my study table overlooking the moat and the manorial garden; the next I was on the high seas.

It would be almost a month before I had time to look back, for the next weeks presented not only a host of new experiences but also a chain of misadventures. Things began to go wrong as soon as my channel steamer reached the open sea. For the first and last time in my life, I endured a violent attack of seasickness. I spent most of the passage bent over the railing and recovered only when land was sighted, barely in time to compose myself and retrieve my baggage before the ship docked.

Passing through customs and immigration confronted me with new obstacles. Indeed, I did not pass. My precipitous trip had left no time to plan exactly what I was going to do once I reached Britain. I carried with me the letters I had earlier exchanged with the school of journalism at London's King's College. But I had not applied, of course, and could produce no evidence that I would be admitted. All I had on my person was a passport, issued by the German consul general in Amsterdam on my fifteenth birthday, and five English pounds (about twenty-five dollars), by my childish standards a princely sum. I had no permanent address and no visible means of long-range support. That my family, above all my uncle, would finance my stay was established in my own mind, but documenting it to the satisfaction of the immigration officials at the port of Harwich was another matter. A sober-faced interrogator looked at my capital and observed that it was not sufficient for a year's study at the University of London. I asked him to call Friends' House in London, where I knew two Eerde trustees who would vouch for my fiscal trustworthiness. But it was after five o'clock in the afternoon; nobody was answering the phone. In fact, as I suddenly realized with alarm, it being a weekend, no one would answer until Monday. The Home Office had no intention of providing me room and board for the interim, at the taxpayers' expense. Instead of admitting me to the United Kingdom, the authorities decided, posthaste, to send me back to where I had come from. A huge policeman escorted me to the ship, to a cabin below deck. He kindly wished me a good night as he locked the door behind him.

Alone in my cell, I reflected on the fate that seemed to await me. I saw myself on the Continental side of the Channel once more, facing a Dutch functionary who would, in turn, examine my papers and my lean purse, ask the same questions his English colleague had just asked, and then have a Dutch guardian of the law convey me back to my floating home away from homelessness. Like a latter-day flying Dutchman, I visualized myself journeying back and forth, forever adrift on the channel waves between Europe and the British Isles.

In the meantime, however, there was nothing specific I could do to prepare for the reenactment of the ghostly seafarer's saga. I undressed, went to bed, and as I reported to my parents a few days later, "slept splendidly despite everything." When I awakened it was light. I washed, dressed, and tried the door. It was no longer locked, and I went out. A kindly sailor gave me coffee and some bread and butter. After that no one took any notice of me, and I went on deck. It was a pleasant day, and the docks were quiet as I gazed longingly at England's unattainable terra firma. I do not know how long I had been standing thus when my ruminations were interrupted by a short, pudgy civilian, who suddenly materialized below within easy shouting distance. This apparition addressed me in impeccable German, inviting me to get my belongings and come down the gangplank.

I leaped into action, got my suitcase from the cabin, and descended to where my savior was waiting. There had been a call, he told me—now in English, after my conversance with his mother tongue had been established—and all difficulties had been resolved. "Just in the nick of time," he added. "In the what?" I asked, perplexed, for I had never heard this expression before. "Im letzten Augenblick," he translated.

I had no idea whose call had engineered my rescue, but I thought it best not to complicate my situation with needless questions. My liberator led me into an office where another official resumed the inquiry into my immediate intentions. Once again my capacity to answer questions to which I really had no answer, first tested in the German *Gymnasium,* proved useful. How long did I intend to stay in England? I had no idea but suggested, confidently, one year. Where did I intend to go then? This was an even greater imponderable, but no matter; I explained that I planned to settle in the United States. This second improvisation went over particularly well. The inquisitor nodded and wrote for several minutes on an official-looking piece of stationery. Then he stamped on my passport that I had been granted permission to spend one month in the United Kingdom, provided that I accepted no employment "paid or unpaid." It occurred to me at once that this arrangement left most of the next year unaccounted for, but the immigration office at Harwich was not the place to vent my misgivings. I thanked my second benefactor, picked up my suitcase once more, and walked to the nearby railway station.

No boat had recently arrived, so it was five hours before the next train appeared; but at nightfall I beheld the London skyline for a second time—now in a more subdued frame of mind than the previous year. From Victoria Station I called the people who had launched me on my 1936 vacation. I was to stay with them until I found permanent lodgings. My hosts had been exceedingly disquieted by my apparent disappearance and were relieved that I had called just as they were about to wire my parents. This telephone conversation also revealed the identity of the mystery caller whose intervention had sprung me from my cabin in Harwich. She turned out to be Mrs. Else Cappel, the mother of one of my classmates, who was on his way to study engineering at University College in London. She, her son, and I had traveled on the same steamer. So far as they were concerned, we had simply lost one another on the boat train. But then Mrs. Cappel, a habitual worrier, decided the next morning to make sure I had arrived safely. Upon learning I had not appeared, she called the immigration people in Harwich, who apprised her of my detention. This news tempted her to offer her informant any financial guarantee needed to expedite my entry. That cavalier assurance, coming from a resolute, foreign voice on the telephone, inexplicably melted official resistance and led to the sudden termination of my shipboard confinement. When I visited Mrs. Cappel a few days later, to thank her, she laughingly confided that she would have been hard put to make good her bluff. Her own financial resources were barely sufficient to secure temporary entry for herself or permanent admission for her son. We both rejoiced that British immigration authorities had revealed themselves to be more credulous and softhearted than had at first seemed to be the case.

On Monday I paid a visit to Friends' House to see about an extension of my residence permit. A secretary there assured me that this would be granted routinely once I was settled and enrolled in school. Then I went to King's College, where a new disaster awaited me.

I had no trouble finding the institution, down Woburn Place and Southampton Row to St. Mary-le-Strand, where the college buildings barred further progress. Locating the school of journalism likewise proved easy. After a short search, the secretary there found my file and ushered me into the office of the head, a Mr. Harrison. I presented my Oxford School Certificate and asked to be admitted to the program. My vis-à-vis seemed satisfied with my credentials, adding merely a few routine questions: place of birth, date of birth, and so forth. That is where the hitch developed. When I told him my age, Mr. Harrison asked, somewhat severely, whether I had not read the catalog he had sent me last summer. I assured him that I had. "Don't you know, then, that our minimum age for admission is eighteen?" he inquired next. I had seen that provision, I confessed, but assumed that the satisfaction of the academic requirements for admission would take precedence. In this I was quite mistaken, he informed me. I should come back when I was eighteen. Could I not apply for an exception? No, the college rules knew no exceptions. Many years later, in 1974, before I delivered a paper in Small Hall of the University of London's Senate House, a King's College historian introduced me as a scholar who shared Lord Acton's experience of having been denied admission to his college. A chuckle went through the audience, who, of course, could not apprehend how inconvenient a distinction this setback was in 1937. I left Mr. Harrison's office, not knowing what to do next.

I could not possibly spend two years in England just waiting for my eighteenth birthday. I also saw that even if I returned to Holland and took the examination for the Intermediate School Certificate the following summer, I would still be under age so far as King's College was concerned. As I slowly retraced my steps along Southampton Row, I chanced to pass Pitman's College, a business school founded by the father of English stenography. Having nothing in hand except time, I went inside to inquire what this institution offered, besides instruction in shorthand.

After a short wait, I was able to see the principal. I explained to this austere gentleman that I had come to England to study journalism but that my age prevented the immediate satisfaction of that ambition. His first response was to direct me to his college's branch facility for foreign students on Tavistock Square. After I had shown him my Oxford diploma, however, he agreed that I ought to attend the main college, whose curriculum he then proceeded to explain. He recommended that I pursue a rather formidable program: shorthand, typing, bookkeeping, business French and Spanish, and another course, vaguely described as "commerce." If I could provide evidence from King's College that I was indeed a prospective student there, he also promised a reduction in fees.

I was immensely relieved. My next step was a return visit to Friends' House, where one of the Eerde trustees, Bertha Bracey, took time to see me and put her stamp of approval on my alternate plans. At King's College, Mr. Harrison showed his humane side when he agreed to write Pitman's College qualifying me for the discount. So, in the course of an eventful day, I had been both crushed and up-lifted. I had experienced both aspects of a Janus-faced England: its forbidding as well as its benevolent side.

Friends' House next gave me a list of respectable and inexpensive boardinghouses, and the following day I went in search of a room. After hours of comparison shopping, extending from Chelsea to Camden Town, I decided on Bloomsbury, whose less fashionable squares teemed in those days with establishments offering cheap room and board to students and budding geniuses. I pitched my tent at Gowardene House, Torrington Square, whose lady owner offered me room, breakfast, and supper for thirty-five shillings a week.

The following week I moved into a cubbyhole furnished with a metal bed, a folding table and chair, a chest of drawers, and —for decoration—a faded engraving of Lady Hamilton at the spinning wheel. It was not until November that I realized the room was un-heated, a common defect of London inner-city housing in the 1930s.

After paying my rent for the first two weeks, I deposited the shrunken remainder of my capital in an account with Barclay's Bank on Euston Road. Then I dispatched a rather urgent bulletin home, requesting funds to pay Pitman's tuition and to meet my future living expenses. My call for money was heard; Pitman's received at once the fourteen guineas due, and twenty-five pounds were said to be on the way to Barclay's. The Home Office extended my residence per-mit without delay. Finally, I paid a visit to the Bow Street police station to satisfy the regulations established by the Aliens Order of 1920. There the police issued me Certificate of Registration No. 645155, which revealed that I had arrived in the United Kingdom on September 19, 1937, a day I was not likely to forget, that I held German passport No. 2444, issued in Amsterdam on June 12, 1936, that I resided at 60 Torrington Square, and that I was enrolled as a student. The little gray booklet also recorded that I had initially been granted one month's stay, but that this provision had been extended to July 18, 1938. Now I was right with everybody and as respectable as any ordinary foreigner was likely to become.

But my troubles were not quite over. On Monday of my third week at Gowardene House, I returned from school to discover on the hall table an envelope addressed to me. It had not come through the mail. It was a note from my landlady to which was attached my check for the second half of the month's room and board—returned by the bank because of insufficient funds. "What next?" I thought. What had happened to the twenty-five pounds whose mailing my mother had announced two weeks earlier? My Danish landlady, Mrs. Holbeck, promised to wait for the balance after I showed her my mother's letter promising to send money. The bank, however, opted for cold-hearted reason. A personal letter from a family member had no standing as a letter of credit, and their records showed no deposit to my account since I had opened it. At sixteen one learns quickly, and though I had not dealt with such institutions or their managers before, I understood at once that the dapper, tweedy, pipe-smoking head of the Euston Road branch of Barclay's Bank could not have acted otherwise. I left his office subdued, with a personal capital of twopence, enough for a subway ride to Bayswater. I sent home another SOS, which, fortunately, solved the emergency within a week. In the meantime, I stopped eating lunch. The lost check never reappeared. My second visit to London was certainly turning into a reenactment of Murphy's Law: Whatever could go wrong did. Who could therefore blame me for becoming impervious to the glamor of the world capital, seeing only the reality of my immediate surroundings, the grimy row houses of Bloomsbury's cheerless squares, the trees slowly exposing their limbs in autumnal nakedness, none of this disheartening scenery providing any hint that I was the ragged neighbor of a distinguished literary company, gathering on Gordon Square, only a few steps from my own shabby domicile. If I had, would it have made any difference? At Eerde I had tried to read Virginia Woolf's *Waves* but put the book down as incomprehensible, oracular, and turned away from the reader, as London appeared— this time—turned away from me. I missed Eerde's empathetic teachers, faithful friends, and interesting classes. Although I assured my mother that "one cannot remain a child and go to school forever," I found this next stage of growing up hard to endure.

Pitman's was, of course, a school, too, but a bore. From October 1, 1937, to July 1, 1938, I spent five days a week, from 10:00 to 1:00 and

2:00 to 5:00, learning the magic symbols of its shorthand and trying to put them on paper in response to increasingly speedy dictation. Learning how to type without looking at the keys was a far cry from Billy Hilsley's Monday morning services at the altar of Polyhymnia. Taking a set of books to the climax of a balance sheet that "came out" without the furtive addition of *miscellaneous* on the debit or credit side did not compare to the thrill of seeing the words "re-markable fluency" under an English essay of mine, put there in Mr. Neuse's unmistakable, calligraphic hand. The dreary translation of humdrum textbook exercises, coupled with the inane copying of business letters in French, threatened to kill my enthusiasm for the language of the Enlightenment.

The "spirit" of the school was likewise not calculated to awaken enthusiasm for its curriculum. Besides training us to become competent clerks, it sought to foster rigorously celibate habits. The building had two student entrances, one for each sex. School regulations forbade conversation, in the classroom or in the halls, between what its authorities insisted on calling "boys" and "girls." Coeducational dialogue was punished with expulsion. To be fair, I never heard of anyone getting the sack for talking to a girl, and the rule actually gave rise to a good deal of merriment. As we passed one another in the corridor, we would silently move our lips, mouthing greetings and confidences. Teachers standing guard as we hurried from class to class would scold or look the other way. We passed notes, a practice not covered by the regulations, or—*horribile dictu*—we might use the congestion of the intermission traffic to bump into one another in ways that awakened in my consciousness an interest in aspects of coeducation I had heretofore been too innocent to explore.

My assimilation into this scene was complicated the first day by my unintentional violation of the school's dress code. I appeared wearing flannels and a short-sleeved polo shirt and was immediately lambasted by the horrified shorthand mistress, who told me we were expected to wear coats and ties. For the remainder of the morning I went through a real-life version of the common nightmare in which one finds oneself walking the streets naked. After I had endured a similar lecture in each morning class, I donned the proper uniform during the lunch break.

At Pitman's we rarely spoke to our teachers outside the classroom. We did not learn, we drilled; and the proceedings plainly bored instructors as much as students. This life offered little joy to any of us, as I discovered quite by accident later in the year during a conversation with my commerce teacher, the only prolonged personal exchange I ever had with an adult at Pitman's. I mentioned that I might become a teacher myself. "Oh, I pity you," he sighed, and added, pointing to the rows of students bent over their books, finishing the exercise I had just handed in, "Look what I have got here, Mr. Schmitt." At the time I was struck by the injustice of the remark. "What display of student brilliance does he expect," I wrote my parents, "in a school in which everybody takes the easy road, by reducing everything to rote memorization. Teaching business subjects is probably dull," I postulated, "but need it be quite as deadly as it is at Pitman's?" Personal initiative was energetically discouraged, as evidenced by a silly daily ritual. Before leaving a classroom, students were required to put books and notebooks on a shelf, divided into cubbyholes, bearing their numbers (I was 21447). Working at home to advance faster was frowned upon, and I had a terrible set-to with my French teacher when I took work to my room and brought to class written answers to an exercise not yet covered. "You are not supposed to do homework," she thundered, and threatened to send me to the principal if I repeated the offense.

In the long run, however, I benefited even from this antediluvian instruction. During my free time, I took up once again the reading of Jacques Chastenet's *Le Temps,* from whose pages I extracted a far more versatile vocabulary than that contained in the pedestrian exercises in business correspondence. In the bargain bookstalls outside Bloomsbury's bookshops, I also discovered much interesting reading, marked down to sixpence or less, including Alfred de Musset's *Confessions d'un enfant du siècle* and Roger Martin du Gard's *Jean Barois,* my first literary introduction to the Dreyfus affair and the ubiquity of anti-Semitism.

It was a measure of my self-discipline that I applied myself to my work sufficiently to derive substantial benefits from my year at Pitman's. Without the salary-producing skills acquired on Southampton Row, I would never have been able to finance a significant part of my subsequent education in the United States. Looking back, I also realize that the lock-step progress, not too slow to jeopardize the reputation of the school, or too fast to deprive it of a substantial financial return from each student, reflected the needs of a private school that could not survive without making a profit. But I chafed under these restraints, and my letters home resounded with complaints that my schedule did not permit me to advance more quickly. Still, in the end I was able to take shorthand at a rate of 120 words and to type 60 words per minute. By the time I had passed intermediate bookkeeping, I had actually finished the entire pensum of that subject by copying exercises on a sheet of paper I secretly took to my room. But when I applied to take the final examination, the management simply turned me down. Rules won out as usual. This reflected the school's ethos in yet another way. Pitman's was a school for clerks, not a training ground for executives. We were taught skills, and we were taught to obey. I wrote in one of my letters home that entering Pitman's was in some ways like going to school in Frankfurt again. On Southampton Row we were regimented, not to serve the state, but for permanent subalternity in private business. Initiative was not part of our education, nor encouraged for our future.

But London, for all its gray, dirty grubbiness, was still a city in which one could build a second life. It contained a small circle of Eerde alumni, living similarly forlorn lives. My parents' friends, now securely installed in Golders Green, issued me a standing invitation for Sunday dinner. Another German couple, the Adlers—whose two boys were in grade school at Eerde—proved equally hospitable. Sorrows already described, and others yet to come, turned me into a poet, and the absence of homework left me an excess of time to pursue my burgeoning literary ambitions. The city also offered an astounding amount of entertainment even to the near penniless: museums, free lectures, free concerts, and cheap tickets to subsidized culture of every description. My fascination with politics had not abated, and the academic year 1937–1938 certainly offered ample occasion for emotional, if not actual, involvement in issues creating an increasingly polarized world.

Closest to my daily experiences was, however, the polyglot company of my fellow boarders at Gowardene House, whose members came from every corner of Europe, a few from even more distant places. Unheated rooms, to which one repaired only when ready to go to bed, made us all convivial. Downstairs, the dining and sitting rooms were warmed by fireplaces, which—together with the accumulated body heat of the cosmopolitan company—made winter more bearable. Only one in our circle, a silent, wraithlike girl named Joyce, would drink a cup of tea after dinner and then hasten upstairs. Perhaps she had an electric heater in her room. The rest of us lingered until ten o'clock, when Elsie, the Scottish maid-of-all-work, who had been about since six in the morning, threw the last log on the fire and announced that she was going to bed.

When I arrived, the largest contingent was Scandinavian. There was Miss Larsen from Sweden, a buxom girl with coal black hair, and Miss Lund from Helsinki, often visited by a German boyfriend who claimed to be the only person in London capable of speaking both Chinese and Japanese. His knowledge of languages was indeed prodigious. He and Miss Lund alternately conversed in Swedish and Finnish; then they might disappear for a while to her room, from which they would emerge in due time, looking relaxed and pleased with themselves.

Of two Danes in our compound, one attended the London School of Economics. His English was so flawless that I first mistook him for a native. The other was a sculptor who would fill temporary silences by passing around photos of his work taken in his Copenhagen studio. The budding economist occasionally took me to his club, where we played some serious table tennis. On other evenings he would lecture me on the soundness of Nazi economic policy, until I began to be wary, suspecting—with the paranoia that sooner or later dominates all refugee milieus—that he might be a Fascist agent whom I had better keep at a distance.

A Belgian named Schevensteen, from Antwerp, was learning business English at Pitman's Tavistock Square dependency. He wore gray suits, white shirts, and conservative ties. His hair was always slicked down and neatly parted in the middle, with never a strand out of place. I took an instinctive, quite unreasoning dislike to him until one night when we happened to talk French to each other—a language, as I wrote my parents delightedly, that wrought the most astonishing transformation in his drab personality. "When he speaks Dutch or English," I reported excitedly, "he seems grouchy and arrogant, but the minute he switches to French he becomes animated, witty, and amusing."

Then there was Liese Grote, originally from Berlin, a plain, shapeless woman with stringy blond hair. Until recently she had lived in Paris with a young poet named Rudi, whose only claim to fame seemed to be that he had once exchanged letters with Rainer Maria Rilke. His visit was expected shortly before Christmas, and I was especially keen to hear at first hand of his brief contact with one of my idols. But on the appointed day I returned from school and found

Liese alone in the sitting room, her face deathly pale, her right hand holding a letter. Elsie came rushing into the room when she heard me, and motioned me outside. In a whisper she confided that the letter bore tragic news. Not only had Rilke's correspondent failed to arrive, but his epistle bade Liese good-bye forever, claiming their relationship threatened to extinguish his fragile inspiration. This incident left his rejected love adrift, without purpose in life. In the spring, she left London for the Highlands and Elsie's home, finding a new refuge not only from despair but also from immigration authorities, I suspect. I never learned what became of her.

Shortly before Liese's departure, a handsome Jewish woman from Prague, Ludmilla, joined our circle. More prescient than many of her ilk, she had come to London to find asylum for her husband and herself before the Nazi wave engulfed her country. By the standards of Gowardene House she dressed elegantly, and spent her days seeing people who might help. She would depart for these interviews carefully made up and exuding clouds of perfume. In conversation she left no doubt that she was ready to employ every means of persuasion that a generous nature had placed at her disposal. Once, when I must have looked unusually shocked as I listened to a particularly cynical description of her stratagems, she looked at me with a warm and wistful smile and asked, "How old are you?" When I told her, she laughed and said, "Of course, you are still a romantic."

The most important person in our company, so far as I was concerned, was a young woman whom I shall call Golbyshka. She was born in Taganrog on the Sea of Azov, to a German family that for generations had lived in Russia. Her clan, headed by her maternal grandfather, a Lutheran minister, had fled the Bolshevik revolution to Lithuania and settled in Kaunas, the capital. Her mother, a dentist, supported the family, consisting of Golbyshka, a younger brother, and a father whom she bitterly described as "a handsome man, and making the most of it." She had finished secondary school and spoke Russian, German, and Lithuanian equally well. Her mother had dispatched her to London to spend the better part of the academic year 1937–1938 at Pitman's Tavistock Square facility in order to add to her linguistic repertoire, not only English in general, but business English in particular. In her adopted home town, she was a sprinter of some repute, and her slim, taut figure reflected her athletic bent. Curly brown hair framed her oval, rosy face, distinguished by a small flat nose and brown eyes of fascinating luminosity.

Golbyshka roomed with a girl from Riga, Traute, also of German descent, whose sturdy peasant physique only served to accentuate the young athlete's delicate beauty. Traute must have had a matronly look long before she reached twenty-one. She was tall, with even, uninteresting features, always wearing a kindly half smile. Towards her younger, more vivacious roommate she affected the tone and bearing of a chaperone aunt. She was always treating Golbyshka to low-voiced admonitions, concerning her clothes, her openness with strangers, and her candid, often quite audible criticisms of the world around her: dust in the sitting room, a hair in the soup, and the ugliness of London. Traute was patient and long-suffering, the soul of forbearance, always speaking well of everyone and blushing when anybody paid her the most trivial compliment. My recollections of her remain vivid because of the emotional havoc she caused at least one of the boarders at Gowardene House. In early spring a Palestinian Arab moved into the room recently vacated by the Danish sculptor, and immediately professed to have been seized by a violent passion for Traute. He brought her flowers, asked her out, and also invited her to spend the night in his room. This proposal threw her into a hysterical fit, and she took to her bed, nursed and consoled by Golbyshka, while her admirer planted himself outside her door, proclaiming his love and begging her forgiveness. After a day or two of much tumult on the fourth-floor corridor, the landlady asked him to leave, and peace returned to our boardinghouse.

Golbyshka and I were the youngest inhabitants of No. 60 Torrington Square, she nineteen and I sixteen, and so it was inevitable that we had more to say to each other than to anyone else in the house. Less predictably, I became the father-confessor to whom she would pour out her homesick heart. Between these outpourings she wrote daily letters to her fiancé, a fellow athlete and the embodiment of every masculine virtue known to the annals of social grace. I was an expert on homesickness, and if I knew anything, I knew how to survive it. Christmas was approaching, and we expected it to be a particularly sad season for both of us. We prepared to suffer through it together.

As it happened, I got a reprieve from the anticipated ordeal. In the last week of November, my uncle sent the ticket that enabled me to spend the holidays with my family. Golbyshka was a good sport and pretended to rejoice with me. I am afraid that I did not return the favor. During my two weeks on the Continent, I put everybody and everything in London out of my mind.

When I returned, a few days into January, 1938, she happened to be in the hall when I rang, and answered the door. Like the applause greeting my return to Eerde three years earlier, Golbyshka's manifest pleasure at seeing me also transformed this return into a homecoming. "Welcome back," she said. "We have missed you . . ." and stopped, embarrassed. The last phrase seemed to have slipped out inadvertently. All day I had been wondering whether my uncle's generosity would not make the next months in London even harder to bear. This second separation could well turn out to be worse than the weeks following my sudden departure in September. Now it took only a few friendly words of welcome to lighten my heart. I had not expected anyone to take much notice of my temporary absence. "Happy New Year, Golbyshka," I replied, and added, more deliberately, "I have missed you, too." She laughed. "I doubt that. Celebrating Christmas with your family will have given you more important things to think about." But I was determined not to leave it there. "You'll go back to your home when school is over," I insisted, "and you'll be staying home. My returns are always temporary and to different places. I have no home and may never have one again," I concluded with pathos.

"Well, you are back and you are home now, right here," she cut off my theatrics, before they got out of hand. "Come and say hello to what is left of our fire in the sitting room. It is too cold out here." I followed her willingly, and we sat for a while gazing into the dying glow, talking of this and that, before it was time to retire. The next day, after all, school would resume.

When it came to our respective futures, I turned out to be a poor prophet. I did not become a vagrant, but soon found a home in another world. Within two years of that wet January day, on the other hand, the Bolsheviks occupied Lithuania, and whether Golbyshka and her family escaped them a second time I do not know. I also realize today that even before that catastrophe she had less of a home than I had once possessed. Her family life was unhappy, unlike mine. Lithuania was no more her homeland than England was mine, except that Germans in Kaunas probably encountered as much routine, daily hostility as my family had only recently met in

Germany. Finally, if Golbyshka and her family escaped the Soviets, it would be by going to Germany, and what boon was it to "escape" to nazism?

Both of us were driftwood on the sea of history, and after this accidental encounter at the door, we became friends. When I stood in line for hours to buy a sixpence ticket to the top gallery at the Old Vic or the Sadler's Wells Opera, I now had a companion, warmly and affectionately huddled against me. When I scoured the bookstalls or wandered through the British Museum, she was at my side. What a different place London had suddenly become!

During my first week after my return from vacation, while Traute was away visiting English relatives, I would sit with Golbyshka in their room—still decorated with a tiny Christmas tree—and read to her. One evening I had chosen Rilke's *Book of Hours*. With growing enthusiasm, I declaimed poem after poem until I ran out of breath. As I paused, she suddenly threw her arms around me and gave me a long, passionate kiss. As she clung to me, I was confused and overwhelmed. We sat for hours, close together, mindless of the cold, until dawn.

The next time we spoke to each other, Golbyshka tried to undo what had happened. Remorse had assumed command. She wept over her "weakness," the betrayal of her distant lover, and begged me to treat her with the contempt she deserved. But for me it was too late to be sensible. This effervescent, sparkling girl liked me, loved me perhaps. The passion that her sudden display of affection had aroused could not be curbed by one fit of contrition. I urged her to postpone remorse, regret, and nostalgia until our paths had separated once more. After all, our time in London was short. Besides, her mournful reaction reminded me that the magic of my company had not diminished her attachment to her absent boyfriend, and this discovery tarnished my love with jealousy. We quarreled, and the next weekend she went to church with Traute while I had dinner at the house of my family's friends in Golders Green. In the evening we rushed into each other's arms once more and went for a long walk to make up for the misspent Sunday. After that, Golbyshka decided to keep repentance to a minimum.

At Gowardene House we conducted ourselves with discretion, and no one took any particular notice of us except Elsie, the maid, a much more confirmed romantic than I, and poor Liese Grote, whose own misfortunes needed the diversion of our ephemeral romance.

She urged me repeatedly to turn my lyrical relationship with Golbyshka into a sexual conquest. Such a "great experience" would deaden the pain of our inevitable separation. I only responded each time with an embarrassed silence. In the days before contraception was readily available, one did not discuss such personal affairs with others, and besides, I knew better than to court pregnancy before marriage. Golbyshka and I sought out a variety of surrogate experiences, without the fear of catastrophic consequences. They included visits to my many friends at the National Gallery and to the glowing canvases of Turner at the Tate. I took her to see *Macbeth* at the Old Vic, with Lawrence Olivier and Judith Anderson. We shared the same theater's famous Victorian production of *A Midsummer Night's Dream*, complete with Ralph Richardson's immortal version of Bottom. One Sunday we reveled in Beethoven concertos and symphonies under Sir Henry Wood's direction at the Palladium; on Palm Sunday we climbed to the highest gallery in the Royal Albert Hall and abandoned ourselves to the *Missa Solemnis.* We stood in line for tickets to *Carmen,* to *Parsifal,* and to any Mozart opera on the repertory of the Sadler's Wells. (Covent Garden was beyond our means.) Golbyshka's Easter present to me was a ticket to the London Philharmonic, and we sat in the cheap seats of Queens Hall, behind the orchestra, facing its founder, financier, and Svengali, Sir Thomas Beecham. We watched the famed maestro stride from the wings of the podium, erect and stately like a Spanish grandee, and then fling himself with furious passion at the music of Mozart and Boccherini.

We continued to read to each other: Shakespeare's plays before we attended their performance; more Rilke, more Nietzsche, especially *Thus Spake Zarathustra* and *Twilight of the Idols;* on the other side of the spectrum, Heine's account of his travels and *The Rabbi of Bacharach.* Together we discovered Friedrich Hölderlin's *Hyperion,* in which I identified myself with the disconsolate hero and Golbyshka with the unattainable Diotima. The world offered us no end of "great experiences." No dissonance and no third presence intruded as we escaped to a common ground of happiness.

Temporarily, the magic of love even distracted me from the menacing political scene. Golbyshka was a true German, or perhaps simply a woman of her time, taking little interest in politics. Her family past had bequeathed her a natural hatred of bolshevism, which always bubbled close to the surface of her consciousness. The only time I ever saw her being rude to anyone was when there arrived at Gowardene House an Australian Communist named Parker, an importunate doctrinaire and inept evangelist of a cause that he himself understood only imperfectly. One Sunday afternoon at teatime, when Parker insisted that Napoleon would undoubtedly be a Communist were he alive today, she put down her cup with a clatter, rose, screamed at me, "How can you sit there and listen to that idiot?" and stalked out of the room. Otherwise, the affairs of the world seemed not to touch her. The Spanish civil war and events in Germany were not her business; even the border quarrels between Poland and Lithuania left her indifferent; and although I had earlier in the year resumed, on occasion, the habits of the summer of 1936 and attended rallies at which Chinese generals denounced the Japanese, and members of the new, left-wing leadership of the Labour party deplored the government's indifference to the fate of the Spanish republic, I ceased making those rounds after I fell in love with Golbyshka. But then came a Saturday in March when we emerged from one of our long forays into Hyde Park and Kensington Gardens to hear the newspaper vendors at Marble Arch hawk extras: Germany had invaded Austria.

This event struck close to me and stirred more than the moral indignation distant wars randomly arouse in cosmopolitan readers. At once I thought of my uncle and his family. What had happened to them? I also realized that if nazism was spilling over the borders of Germany, it would be wise for me to consider moving on. My desire to emigrate to the United States leaped back to life. A tide was rising in which I did not propose to drown. Shortly thereafter, the German government ordered all its citizens abroad, including those who had until recently been Austrians, to register at the nearest embassy. In London we actually reported to the former Austrian legation, whose mournful Viennese porter, gracious, resigned, and seemingly forever on the verge of tears, made a deep impression on Golbyshka, who accompanied me.

The annexation of Austria aroused in me anguished feelings of another kind. In many ways Golbyshka had helped turn me back into a German. Except for Shakespeare, the poets whose reading had brought us together were German. Most of the music we enjoyed came from the same source. The language we used to describe our feelings to each other was German. Now I tried to explain to her how Germany's new masters degraded this heritage, and she listened to me patiently, like a mother to the capricious whining of a child.

143

Never having lived in the homeland of her distant ancestors, how could she understand how much it had changed in her own lifetime? But I do retain one touching souvenir of these conversations: a token which may indicate that my mournful reflections about the homeland I had lost found more of an echo in her heart than she was able to express. As a farewell present, she gave me a copy of Richard Wagner's *Beethoven*. This was a more appropriate gift than may at first appear, and I like to think that she chose it, not only because it was a reminder of shared discoveries, but also because she had read the book and understood its relevance to the loss I had suffered. The work was, after all, a reflection on the first German conquest of France and the centennial of Beethoven's birth, both occurring in 1870. The last page ended with a thought that would have fallen dissonantly on the ears of Austria's recent conqueror, who professed such admiration for Wagner: "We celebrate the great pathbreaker [Beethoven] in the [cultural] wilderness of the degenerate paradise [France]. But let us celebrate him with dignity—with the same dignity with which we celebrate the victories of German courage: For the benefactor of the world still ranks above the conqueror of the world."

Amidst these joys and sorrows our time was running out. The day of Golbyshka's departure came, and in cruel disregard of my feelings, it was April 20, Hitler's birthday. I did not want to accompany her to the train, but she pleaded for my company on the trip to Victoria Station, and I was only too willing to postpone the inevitable by the span of one taxi ride. The longer the walk to the scaffold, the later the execution. At the station I struggled gallantly with her huge suitcase, bulging with a year's wardrobe and an assortment of souvenirs. She offered to hire a porter, but I knew that she could no more afford such a luxury than I. Besides, our laborious progress to the platform and her train was another short reprieve.

The train was waiting, the engine steaming. In minutes the schedule of the Great Southern Railway would sever us far more quickly than we had grown together. From the platform I saw her standing at the compartment window, already gone, turned into a picture, fainter even than a photograph behind the grimy glass. The train began to move. The picture moved, a gloved hand raised to her mouth as if to stifle a cry. A gust of steam crossed my vision, and after it had passed, the world I gazed at was empty.

Luckily, care for my own future kept me occupied during the

ensuing weeks. Following the Austrian crisis, I had asked my parents for permission to see the American consul in London to determine how I might qualify as an emigrant to the United States. Shortly after I had made these inquiries, a cousin of my mother's offered to sponsor my immigration. Since 1914 this relative had been an engineer with Carl Zeiss, the famous manufacturer of cameras and lenses. After Hitler's advent to power, his employer had been pressed to dismiss him, but the firm decided, instead, to transfer this trusted and experienced senior employee to New York to head its sales office there. This move proved to be my salvation. When his offer arrived, my parents dropped their objections and instructed me to go at once to Grosvenor Square to learn what documents were needed to admit me to this distant haven. For once the bureaucratic mills worked fairly swiftly, and by the end of May, I carried a hefty folder with the required credentials back to the United States consulate general.

In order to explain how easy this process turned out to be, I must again point to my almost habitual luck and to the absence of lines at American consulates in those days. Thanks, in part at least, to the quota laws of 1921 and 1924, the flood of westward immigrants had since World War I been reduced to a trickle. Then came the depression, which actually reversed the current for a while. At the time I sought admission to the United States, the German quota had not been filled for several years. If I nevertheless speak of luck when recalling the ease with which my emigration was negotiated, it is because a few weeks after my application this situation changed very suddenly. The lessons of Austria began to sink in. The subsequent threat to Czechoslovakia and, in November, the pillaging of German synagogues, homes, and stores—the *Kristallnacht*—suddenly produced a flash flood of applicants. A lucky few finally reached their American destination after years of waiting; most never escaped the wartime machinery of extermination.

I got in just under the wire. Less than two months after my first visit to the consular office of the United States, I was invited for the crucial interview. The day was June 23, 1938, and my recollection of the most important date after my birth has been jogged by the perusal of a letter I wrote to my mother that evening. I reported:

At first it appeared as if nothing would go right. When examining the police record from Frankfurt, a lady vice-consul could not understand how I managed to go to school in Holland, and, at the same time, remain a legal resident of Germany. Then she asked suspiciously why my passport was issued to "Hans Adolf," while my birth certificate identified me as "Johann Adolf." Finally I had to explain to her that Uncle Franz' [the cousin in New York] mother was the sister of your father. I hope that's right. What added to the difficulty was that the woman talked awfully fast, and I was constrained to interrupt her with a string of stupid "Beg your pardons." At last I was asked to sign a long document and then was led to the doctor.

Here I was taken over by another severe lady who evidently believed that foreigners understand better if you shout at them. "Stand against the wall for the vision test," she commanded. Having determined that I was sighted in both eyes, she ordered me to go into a small cubicle, strip to my waist, and wait for the physician. After a few minutes a friendly old gentleman entered the room, bade me sit down, and asked me about childhood diseases. I was only too willing to oblige with my dramatic medical history, but he never let me finish, so that we never got to my diphtheria, but stopped halfway through my middle-ear operation. Then he listened to my heart and had me cough a couple of times. That was all there was to it.

Finally, they led me to the vice-consul, who told me in a cordial and *very soft* voice that everything was okay, and that in return for two pounds, one shilling and eight pence, he would stamp my passport with the immigration visa. He also informed me, in the same affable tone, that this stamp did not, however, oblige the immigration officials in New York, or wherever, to admit me if they determined that I was insane, lunatic, psychopathic, or a prostitute. I think that I shall be able to establish my innocence on all four of these counts.

I walked out of the consulate a free, happy, and very luck young man. On subsequent visits to London, the sounds and sights of Grosvenor Square never failed to exhilarate me, for this is where my life began all over again.

Life in London, however, continued to be full of complications to the end. In the last week of May, all denizens of Gowardene House had to move. Our section of Torrington Square was about to be torn down to make room for a new wing of the university's Senate House. Less than a month before I planned to leave England, I had to look for another room. I found shelter in the attic of another boarding-house on nearby Taviton Street, whose inhabitants were almost all English. I occupied these quarters too short a time to remember much about the tenants, except for a Polish veteran of the Spanish civil war. He was a physical wreck, with a painful limp and a nervous facial tick, a melancholy chain smoker whose condition made me grateful that my parents had scotched earlier ill-considered requests of mine to volunteer for the republic.

During these last weeks, I also ran into a contemporary from an English Quaker school, Leighton Park, with whom I had become friends years earlier when he had visited Eerde. Robin was the son of the well-known Liberal journalist John Langdon-Davies, and when we hailed each other he was on his way home from a day's work at the nearby offices of the Spanish Relief Organization. Much of his spare time was devoted to the Young Communist League. Had I not left England soon after our reunion, I am sure that we would have renewed our friendship; as it turned out, we never saw each other again. When I think of Robin and my other English acquaintances in the Communist camp, and then ponder recent revelations of Communist infiltration of the highest level of British intelligence, I am struck by an extraordinary paradox. My young friends John Smith, Leslie Wolf, and Robin were no traitors when I knew them, and I am confident that this remained true. They were decent, ordinary young people. Their penchant for political extremes was a symptom of youth of which, I imagine, age has long cured them. The real traitors, as we know now, came from the ranks of the privileged, men who went to Oxford or Cambridge and who rose rapidly in the bureaucracy. Their impeccable respectability was the decisive prerequisite for careers of disloyalty. Declared true believers, on the other hand, were generally harmless, as were visible nonconformists.

I left Britain on July 1 to spend a last summer with my family, and passed another channel crossing in animated conversation with a young German Nazi. He had just spent a year as an exchange student at Columbia University, but this prolonged contact with a free society had failed to shake his loyalties. Everything he had read in American papers and everything he had heard in the classroom he dismissed as lies or manifestations of ignorance. The annexation of Austria thrilled him, and he prophesied the same fate for Czechoslovakia. I had never met anyone quite so devoted to national socialism as this young world traveler. I concluded that if he was a typical product of contemporary German education, it was high time for me to go west, far west.

I wished that I could have paraded my travel companion before some of the British audiences I had observed during various political rallies in the course of the past year. It might have jolted the pacifists among them. This is not the hindsight of old age. As my letters at the time confirm, I viewed appeasement with far less tolerance than I do today. The Quaker influence had not taken root in my mind. On the contrary, I was convinced that these lovely people, to whom I owed so much, were doing their unwitting best to inaugurate an epoch of terrifying bloodshed.

Not that I was without illusions of my own. I was wrapped up in my literary interests and, in my letters home, speculated not about what business I would enter but whether I would ultimately become a poet or a playwright. I wonder what feelings of consternation such senseless dreams must have created in the hearts of my poor, beleaguered parents. They said nothing and probably consoled themselves with the package of diplomas I brought home from Pitman's College. I had done something besides writing paeans to Golbyshka.

VIII   BEGINNINGS OF AN AMERICAN EDUCATION

It is now time to turn to my last major migration and my transition from homelessness to a new citizenship. A flood of letters, most of them preserved by my mother, documents each stage of this metamorphosis. I was a prodigious chronicler; indeed, I wonder today how I made time for anything besides providing my family in Europe with a blow-by-blow account of my daily life in the United States, or how there could have been anything to report about a life that seems to have consisted only of writing letters.

But I am getting, once again, ahead of myself. After my return from England, my family and I spent six weeks in a *pension* on the Dutch heath near Apeldoorn, in a quiet resort called Hoog-Soeren. It was a lugubrious reunion since we did not know when we would see one another again. My mother was now persuaded that the whole clan must eventually follow me. My father, knowing no English, and therefore presumably unable to support us in the English-speaking world, was equally convinced that he would not join our exodus. Many hours were spent in futile debate over this difference of opinion. My mother, unyielding, nagged until my father agreed to go wherever the rest of us went. I call this dialogue futile because I sensed that his eventual, weary acquiescence signified no change of mind, but merely a desire to have some peace. For the moment, both parents had achieved what they wanted: my mother the feeling that her eloquence had preserved the family, my father the boon of having our collective future struck from the agenda of daily conversation. For the rest of the holidays all of us put on a brave front, as if convinced that my departure was the mere prelude to happier days to be enjoyed in safety and liberty.

We returned to Eerde at the beginning of the last week of August. This time extensive farewells could not be avoided. At times it seemed to me as if I had paid parting visits to every family in the immediate neighborhood, including the domiciles of local dignitaries, ranging from the baron to the school physician in the nearby town of Ommen.

On the morning of the last day, my mother discovered with indignation that I had not finished packing. Given my few belongings, it took less than an hour to arrange everything in a splendid leather suitcase, one of my father's farewell presents. (The other, a tennis racket, was his touching way of giving me the means to pursue my athletic interest in a world then without soccer. As it turned out, I had little opportunity to use it.) Then I "dressed up" in one of my better hand-me-downs and an elegant new striped shirt with a detachable collar. Unaccustomed to so grown up a garment, I had trouble manipulating the collar button. My little brother finally climbed on a chair and installed the vexatious gadget for me, worrying aloud all the time how I would manage to dress in the future without his help.

My father was to accompany me as far as Zwolle, where we would spend the night. After lunch the old Ommen taxi lumbered into the manorial yard to take us to the train, me for the last time. A small crowd of teachers and summer students gathered to watch my departure. When I turned to say good-bye, my brother broke into a heart-rending wail, and these bystanders silently stole away, realizing they had intruded on a family sorrow. My parents and I tried to console him. But time was pressing, and after hugging my mother I had to leave him still weeping helplessly. If only my going away had been the worst he would have to endure!

An hour or two later, my father and I were installed in a hotel across from the Zwolle railway station. We took a stroll through the familiar town, sad and also uneasy, because after six weeks all that was left unsaid was thoughts we wanted to keep to ourselves. Both of us had a troubled conscience: I, because I was escaping once again, more or less at his expense. He, because he was once again sending me off alone, to shift for myself in a strange land. My unease was compounded by the fact that the impending trip was too much of an adventure to arouse, momentarily at least, much grief in me. I cannot but wonder whether my father asked himself what our eventual reunion would be like. I would stand at the dock and welcome him; I would know, and therefore decide, what to do next. In fact, I would by then have become the head of the family.

A gargantuan breakfast the next morning cheered us somewhat— good food is a marvelous antidote to anxiety and fear—and prompted him to say with a wistful smile that he was at least sending me out with a full stomach. But his brave front collapsed before we parted. As he jogged beside the slowly moving train, waving as I gained on him, he wept unashamedly. It was the only time I saw my father cry. Would he have shown this emotion if he had expected to see me again?

My next stop was Nijmegen, where I was scheduled to spend the afternoon and night with my uncle. I found him and his family living in a pleasant house, and they spent most of our time together telling me about their latest flight. When the Germans invaded Austria, my uncle fortunately was visiting clients in Switzerland. Instead of returning, he made straight for the home office of his firm in Holland, leaving the rest to my aunt. She kept her head. Calmly she went to the local mover to arrange for the shipment of their furniture. Then she packed their portable belongings, put them and the two children in the family car, and resolutely drove the same snappy convertible that had taken me on a memorable ride to Zurich the year before through the ranks of advancing columns into Germany, and thence to Holland. No one stopped her. On the contrary, the blue-eyed, fair-haired mother and her two children were waved on graciously wherever a bottleneck threatened, and the entire journey went without hitch or unpleasantness. Now the family was set again. My uncle continued his work, and my eleven-year-old cousin Dorothea was already enrolled in the local school.

The next morning I rolled on to Antwerp. At the first and only stop after crossing the Belgian border, a group of farmwives crowded into the compartment, most of them carrying butter and eggs to the city market. When they learned my destination, they wanted to press some of their produce on me—to feed me on the long voyage—and I had some difficulty convincing them that their gifts would spoil before they could be consumed. As we disembarked, they clapped me on the back, shook my hand, and promised me their prayers. Since I knew Antwerp from my bicycle trip in 1935, I had no difficulty finding my way to the shipping line's booking office, where I checked my suitcase and confirmed my reservation. Having a few hours to wander about, I paid a visit to the cathedral and then took one of those luxurious taxis, which earlier had made so deep an impression on me, to the pier. I was ready to turn my back on Europe.

My conveyance to the New World, a ten-thousand-ton steamer, the *Geroldstein,* belonged to the Red Star Line: a German, Jewish-owned, small transatlantic carrier, pioneering inexpensive, class-less travel. Because of its proprietor, it traveled from a foreign port, but flew the swastika. The ship seemed awfully small and filled me with misgivings about its seaworthiness. This concern, unfounded as it happened, was minor compared to the mounting political crisis engulfing Europe during the last days of a smooth, comfortable trip. Daily news bulletins kept us passengers apprised of Germany's concern for the welfare of Czechoslovakia's German minority, a situation that threatened to explode into war. On the very day of our arrival in New York, September 7, 1938, France began to call up her reservists. On our last evening aboard, already within sight of the Manhattan skyline, the ship's commanding officer told us at the captain's dinner that had war broken out before the ship reached American waters, he would have had to follow orders, turn around, and race for a friendly, presumably German port. That was the last place passengers such as myself wanted to go, and this announcement prompted some of us to bless the appeaser Neville Chamberlain, until then not one of my heroes. He had at least delayed disaster until we had friendly soil under our feet.

As usual, I had managed to put the real world behind me during most of the trip. A large number of cheerful young Americans, returning from a summer in Europe, turned the journey into a carefree holiday for me. It was on board, amidst these citizens of my future homeland, that the next chapter of my education began. It opened on the second day out when I stood by a table in the bar, kibitzing two chess players. My interest in the game had always been minimal, but one of the players was a very pretty girl. Suddenly she turned to me and said, "I'm Jill, what's your name?" Having been accustomed to more formal introductions—with full names, bows, handshakes, and heel clicking—this friendly simplicity left me at a loss for words. Somewhat haltingly, I sputtered my first name, and she bade me sit down. Before long, other members of her ebullient circle joined us, and I was swept up in a new and carefree world of shipboard games and the most innocent flirtations. If these young people had any worries, they were not apparent. The social tone was friendly, easygoing, invariably gracious and relaxed. A more experienced traveler today, I realize that the uniqueness of shipboard life may have had a good deal to do with this camaraderie. Whatever the reason, this passage during which worries were suspended, and trouble was kept at a safe distance, convinced me, if I needed convincing, that my destination was indeed the promised land.

This encouraging contrast between Europe and America was enhanced by my dinner-table company. A charming graduate student of Germanic languages, returning from a year at the University of Frankfurt, represented the brighter future. Disturbed by what she had seen and heard during her year abroad, she reassured me that I would find the atmosphere on American campuses more open and hospitable. I also mingled with older people, among them a retired Brooklyn schoolteacher, Mr. Margon, himself the son of German parents. His description of life and learning in America still retained an immigrant's perspective but also encouraged me to pursue a career in education. More to the point, he concluded one of our evening conversations on deck with this simple observation: "You know, Hans, you will do well in America." I blushed at a remark I mistook for a compliment. "Really?" I countered, "How can you tell?" He replied: "You are a bright fellow, and besides, you have no choice. Immigrants with your aspirations can't make it by just getting by." This was as sound a maxim as anyone could have offered me at this point in my life. Mr. Margon's view of my future was fully in tune with the Eerde precepts that excluded failure from the list of our options. It applies to all immigrants and explains why so many of them, from German bourgeois intellectuals of the 1930s to boat people almost fifty years later, succeeded so conspicuously in turning adversity into success. If we could now persuade more young native Americans to adopt the same view of life, our society would come closer to the greatness a generous environment has placed within its grasp.

When we docked at the Red Star pier in Hoboken, our classless society scattered, of course. My shipboard companions joined the line of privileged natives who faced nothing more than customs inspection. I should add that I was impressed by the obvious emotion with which, the previous night, they had greeted the appearance on the horizon of the American shore. Many assured me that their travels abroad had made them appreciate their country more. Someday I, too, would be among the fortunate who could experience their euphoria. For the moment, however, I returned to the company of "refugees," as people like us were known then, many of whom had envied me my English and the resultant ability to mix with these American children of the sun.

I positioned myself as closely as possible to the tail end of the American line, in order to face my examiners as soon as possible. The first of these functionaries appeared as malevolent and unaccommodating as my tormentors in Harwich a year earlier. He looked suspiciously at my passport, as if doubting its authenticity, and inquired gruffly what business I had in the United States, how long I intended to stay, and so forth. I was taken aback by these queries. After all, my passport displayed an immigrant's visa and seemed to make most of these inquiries unnecessary. The next questioner was more friendly. He asked for a succession of routine, likewise superfluous bits of information, transferring my answers to another long form. When I finally signed on the bottom line, I was once more declaring myself, under oath, free from a host of loathsome diseases and innocent of a variety of immoral and criminal habits. Then I waited while my relatives were paged on the pier. During that time I was accosted by a representative of the Jewish Women's Association, for whom I unraveled my complex religious antecedents. Unlike my previous interrogators, she tried to make me feel comfortable by confessing that she did not observe Jewish holidays either. After this relaxing exchange, she shook my hand and welcomed me to America. She was the first citizen of this strange country to show any pleasure at my arrival, and I am sorry to say that I lacked the presence of mind to express my gratitude to her.

Soon my aunt Gladys appeared, the English wife of my mother's cousin, and after she had reassured the immigration officers, once again, that she and her husband were both willing and able to look after me, I was permitted to leave the ship. After some waiting, the customs men gave my sparse belongings short shrift; my suitcase was entrusted to Railway Express, and we took the subway home. I use the word *home* advisedly, because the relatives I joined were no strangers. I had spent several holidays with them in Germany; their son was my age, about to enter his sophomore year at New York University, their daughter only a year younger. Arriving at the apartment, we simply celebrated a reunion under unusually pleasant circumstances. In the afternoon my cousin Mathilde took me sightseeing in Manhattan, up Rockefeller Center by express elevator, and down Fifth Avenue on its famous, open doubledecker buses.

When I awoke to full consciousness the following morning, the sudden realization that I was now three thousand miles from Europe, beyond the reach of German armies and airplanes, flooded my being with a warm, ecstatic rush of happiness. I was secure and free at last, not for a month or a year, but for an indefinite time.

But practical decisions had once again to be made quickly. At my relatives' apartment in Jackson Heights, enough mail had accumulated to make me feel more like a visiting celebrity than an anonymous immigrant. It was apparent that I had allies other than kinfolk in the New World. Foremost among these was the refugee counselor of the American Friends' Service Committee, Herta Kraus, a professor of sociology at Bryn Mawr College and a former social worker in Konrad Adenauer's city administration of Cologne. She and my mother were old acquaintances, and it was she who had advised us before my departure that I would need a college degree to compete in the tight American labor market. She had, meanwhile, brought me to the attention of a number of American colleges willing to assist a deserving newcomer.

Given my total ignorance about America, the names of these institutions meant nothing to me, and I was faced with choices for which I was truly unprepared. The fall semester had started at most colleges, so I had to move at once. I had already decided to resist the temptation of remaining in New York, where I would be sheltered by members of my family and, at the same time, kept from coming to personal terms with new surroundings. I wanted to meet this new country head on and on my own. My relatives seemed disappointed by my eagerness to leave, but they did not interfere.

But where would I go? A letter to Herta Kraus from Washington and Lee University in Lexington, Virginia, immediately attracted my attention. Here is what it said:

President [Francis Pendleton] Gaines has expressed genuine interest in . . . admitting H.S. to our student body next September. We think that Mr. Schmitt's presence among students would afford a valuable opportunity for firsthand acquaintance with political policies as now practised in Europe.

If you decide to recommend us to Mr. Schmitt and he wishes to make application, we assure you that we shall undertake to give him every reasonable consideration. If he should enter our student body, we shall give him as much credit for previous work in college as we can. We shall take a personal interest in his studies, in his social relations, in his financial needs, and in his college life in general.

This sounded almost too good to be true. The administration of Washington and Lee, one of the oldest schools in the country, actually suggested that I might do them a favor by enrolling. They offered the prospect of advanced standing, saving me valuable time and money. Washington and Lee further documented its serious intent by sending a member of the class of 1939, Arthur Basile, to interview me. Art was one of four sons of Italian immigrants, all of whom graduated from Washington and Lee. His later career as a Baptist minister does not indicate that we had much in common, but our meeting was pleasant and his report must have been favorable, for two days later I received a telegram offering me a scholarship no other college matched. The fact that the other institutions on my list appeared to have close denominational connections, whereas Washington and Lee did not, added to the persuasiveness of this financial advantage. As a result, I did not even unpack my trunk, but decided on Lexington, Virginia, as my first American domicile.

Getting from New York to my destination proved unexpectedly difficult for the greenhorn that I was. Unaware of the many Lexingtons in the United States, I purchased a ticket that would have taken me to Lexington, Kentucky, had not my aunt produced a map showing conclusively how far from my actual destination this particular university town was. A second visit to Grand Central Station elicited that the Lexington I wanted had no railway station, but a helpful agent of the Baltimore and Ohio railroad discovered that I could disembark at Buena Vista, only a few miles off course. My relatives generously staked me to a Pullman berth, so that I would arrive rested and ready, instead of disheveled and groggy. As it turned out, I did not sleep much on the train. I arrived on Virginia soil on September 10, at six o'clock in the morning. A taxi brought me to Lexington and left me, less than an hour later, standing on the sidewalk at the edge of the campus.

There was not a human being in sight. Suitcase in hand, I began my desultory inspection of the deserted grounds. I passed the president's house, on whose garage I discovered a plaque reminding the passerby that it had once been the stable of Robert E. Lee's horse Traveler. I was amazed. Where I came from, the habitats of emperors, statesmen, and other national heroes often bore such memorial reminders. Palaces, castles, the birthplaces of great men—the Continent was replete with shrines of this kind—but the stall of a defeated general's horse had never figured among the revered places I had visited in my childhood. I was perplexed, and wondered what uncommon virtues had entitled this humble beast to such distinction.

I sauntered on until I reached the main buildings, the skyline of red-bricked, white-columned temples clustered on the modest elevation at the edge of town, then as now. In front of Washington Hall I decided to plant myself and wait until someone would appear to take notice of me.

In due time faculty, and some students, drifted by. Several descried the unusual spectacle of a shabby young man sitting on a suitcase in front of—as I soon found out—the registrar's office. Washington and Lee gentlemen, as I likewise discovered before long, generally came to town in automobiles ranging in magnificence from second-hand Chevrolets to Cadillacs and Duesenbergs. To find a lonely pedestrian at the gates was bound to attract attention. A couple of young men whom I mistook for students, because of not only their youth but their informal demeanor, asked whether they could help me and then, realizing that I was a new student, and a foreign one at that, lingered to chat and discuss the affairs of Europe. As our conversation continued, new faces would appear in the widening circle, each requiring new introductions and eliciting an increasingly predictable repetition of standard inquiries.

At last my floating seminar was joined by Rupert N. Latture, the gentleman with whom I had been corresponding, who took me away from this Socratic exercise to attend to more serious business. He became my fatherly friend, as he has been to thousands of students in Lexington. When I last visited my alma mater, he had just celebrated his ninetieth birthday, still serving the university as an assistant to its current president.

Under Mr. Latture's guidance I worked out my program, including the question of advanced standing. After examination of my prior school records, it became clear that I had already satisfied numerous requirements for graduation. I spoke four languages; my secondary education had included four years of biology, three of physics, and one of chemistry. My sufferings with mathematics also paid off now, since they included what was then the equivalent of the introductory college version of that subject. I even received credit—and quite properly, I must say—for such freshman subjects as Western civilization and English composition. This consideration would save me and my family a great deal of money. By taking six courses, instead of five, at least during the first semester, I would most likely be able to graduate in two years. I was more than satisfied and accepted these privileges without comment, but I began to wonder then, and have never ceased wondering, what American students learn in high school if so much of the first two years of college is taken up by high-school subjects.

Thus it became clear to me from the beginning that my decision to enter America full tilt, to see the hinterland and live among the indigenous, was going to pay dividends. It had also deposited me in a small, hospitable school community, whose guides received me with the warmth with which Mrs. Petersen had welcomed me to Eerde—was it only four years ago?

Later in the morning Mr. Latture handed me over to an amiable recent graduate in the student-affairs office, who began making calls to find me a room. At that time dormitories housed only freshmen, and since I had already been promoted to higher rank, I was permitted to live in town. Harry, my temporary custodian, who lived to rise to the presidency of one of the South's finest state universities, found me a large room on a quiet, tree-lined avenue for twelve dollars a month. I inscribed myself in the rolls of the University dining hall, entitling me to three square meals a day for twenty-five dollars per month.

I soon learned that the majority of students at Washington and Lee belonged to fraternities and came from affluent backgrounds. The circle I entered at the dining hall consisted of young men in humbler circumstances. Most of them held scholarships, as did I, and were outsiders in the sense that they did not participate in the elaborate, noisy, and digressive social life for which the school was known. In no sense did we constitute a separate clique, however. Differences in material fortunes did not become personal barriers in any fixed sense, and in everyday school life there existed no visible distinction between lords and commoners. At one time during my two years at the "Beanery," as the dining hall was irreverently called, one of the football players tried to found a "non-fraternity association." He even urged me to stand for the secretaryship in this club of the barefoot nobility, but I saw no sense in the undertaking and declined. My indifference seems to have been typical of the group, for the organization collapsed after one meeting.

During my first weeks in Lexington, I attracted a certain amount of extra attention as the campus' resident European. I was quite unprepared for the eagerness with which all generations sought my opinion on the European crises of 1938. Dignified professors would cross the street to converse with me about Chamberlain's visits to Berchtesgaden and Godesberg. I remember evening gatherings at which I was asked to prophesy German intentions, as if I were coming fresh from a briefing by the führer himself. Men of mature years saw nothing unusual about asking a seventeen-year-old for information. American adults constituted such a pleasant contrast to their European counterparts. I cannot vouch that they learned much from me or that my presence on campus taught students or faculty much about "political policies as now practised in Europe," but I am sure that none will blame me for enjoying my brief career as local oracle. Fewer perhaps can understand how startled and then taken I was by this first contact with a society in which persons of authority felt sufficiently secure to admit that they did not know everything. Not even my three years in Eerde had prepared me for such an easy relationship between teachers and students.

At the beginning of my American school career, I was even rushed by one or two fraternities without realizing it, of course, since I was completely unfamiliar with that ritual. One Jewish house invited me over repeatedly during these opening weeks, and its president finally asked me to join. When I explained that membership in a fraternity was simply not part of my $40-a-month budget, he waved my protest aside with the observation that the financial side "would be taken care of" so that membership would cost me no more than the daily feeding at the dining hall. All I was expected to do was to commit myself to Judaism. That comment took me back to my brief career as a Jewish Boy Scout in Germany. I had to explain, once again, that I had not been raised a Jew and, although I treasured this part of my origins quite as much as the other elements of my heritage, I simply could not make such a religious commitment.

My fraternity friends were not all Jews. Charlie Hobson, a Kentuckian and a Lambda Phi Alpha, also brought me to his house frequently. His housemother, Mrs. Lucius P. Dillon, a warm-hearted, hospitable Virginian, did not try to negotiate my admission to her establishment, but became my surrogate mother on a less formal basis. She had me regularly for Sunday afternoon tea throughout my two years in Lexington, and became a good and faithful friend with whom I corresponded for the next quarter century, until long after my wedding and the birth of my children.

The fundamental reason for my unwillingness to join any of the social institutions of college life, even those that are sometimes viewed as rivaling learning in importance, was of course quite simple. I had come to study—to make the grades needed to justify advanced standing and keep my scholarship. I was a solitary newcomer, ignorant of the ways of the New World, and I needed the irrefutable credentials of competence, not only for myself, but to help my family and to persuade my benefactors that I had been worthy of their help. I did not expect to have much spare time.

My choice of a major subject had to be made at once. At the time of my arrival in Lexington, I had not entirely abandoned the idea of studying Oriental languages and becoming an interpreter. But Washington and Lee offered only French, German, Spanish, and the classics: commonplace subjects leading someone like me to a career as language teacher. I had no interest in such a future. Several students whom I subsequently tutored in German, with frustratingly little success, confirmed both my aversion to and my lack of talent for this calling. I therefore returned to my first love, history. After having endured for a year the uncongenial curriculum of Pitman's College, I decided to mitigate prospects of serious study in strange surroundings with a course of intellectual self-indulgence.

There is, however, no reason to dwell on my academic progress and day-by-day college life. I shall confine myself to a chronicle of my gradual and sometimes painful Americanization. Let me begin with one bizarre interlude. On my first class day, I was seated in my introductory psychology class, awaiting the arrival of the instructor, when a tall, sturdy young man asked me whether the chair next to mine was taken. To my surprise he spoke with a heavy German accent. I invited him to sit down and discovered during the ensuing conversation that, for the moment at least, I was not the only German at Washington and Lee. The beginning of the class prevented my neighbor from going into details, but after the lecture he followed me to my room, where he launched into a prolonged confessional that suddenly transported me back into the world from which I had just escaped.

My compatriot was a reserve lieutenant in the Wehrmacht, only recently demobilized after doing his compulsory military service, which had included liberating Austria from its burdensome independence. His mother belonged to a famous American family whose members included major benefactors of the university. She had married a Munich businessman and now wanted her son's education to be rounded out by a year or two at an American college. To avoid any misunderstandings, I told him who I was and why I was at Washington and Lee. He scarcely listened to what I said, except to assure me he disapproved of anti-Semitism. Then he resumed his own autobiographical recital and dwelt on his current sufferings in a strange, hostile land, far from home. This was his first contact with a milieu in which admirers of Hitler were in the minority, if they existed at all—a situation he found intolerable.

Barely having come to terms with my position as Lexington's resident expert on European affairs, I did not consider it my duty to reconcile a Nazi with the surprises and frustrations of voluntary and temporary exile. Instead, I tried to buck him up, urging him to be patient and learn to understand his unfamiliar surroundings. My advice availed little, and for a while I was forced to provide daily therapy for this specimen of Aryan superiority who seemed to choke on the air of freedom. As I have thought back on this unusual encounter, I have wondered what made him overlook the fact that I was as far from home as he, and suffering from the same pains. Did his Nazi upbringing assume that I, half Jewish, was no German or that Jews were not entitled to national identity and, unlike "true" German, were incapable of feeling homesick? Most likely, thought processes much less complicated drew him to me. *Judenstämmling* or not, I was the only young person in Lexington with whom he could speak German.

At the beginning of my second week, our precarious symbiosis abruptly ended when I found the seat next to mine in psychology empty; that afternoon my patient did not knock on my door. Over the weekend he had packed up and returned home. Mr. Latture subsequently confessed that the college administration had hoped to keep us out of each other's way, fearing that any meeting between us might become ugly and possibly alienate members of a family that had been, and continues to be, one of the most conspicuous benefactors of Washington and Lee. Although these fears turned out to be groundless, and I did not cost this generous institution more than it had chosen to invest in me, the powers in Washington Hall may have been relieved when Superman decamped.

My immediate reaction to the episode speaks from a letter to my mother: "I have little pity for him. Today thousands share his fate, without being asked whether they want to leave or where they want to go. It is good for him to get a taste of our lot." But why had I not told him openly what I thought? Was it because he would someday go back to Germany, and any hostility on my part might result in denunciation of my father? This explanation may strike readers as paranoid, but I could not take the chance. My own safety did not give me the right to endanger members of my family.

Once this improbable companion was gone, I actually missed him for a while. Although I had done everything I could to avoid a prolonged stay in New York's refugee milieu, talking German once more to someone my own age had warmed my soul and quickened remembrance of my origins. On the one hand, the contradictions between the martial pretensions of this whining conquistador and his psychological vulnerability gave me added cause to rejoice in my own liberation. On the other hand, they also laid bare other contradictory feelings that would not leave me for years. They rekindled my sorrow stemming from Germany's progressive degradation, a feeling I had tried to share with Golbyshka. The Anglophile atmosphere of Virginia, especially evident after the outbreak of war in 1939, did little to render my own cultural transition less hurtful, and there were times when the friendly, hospitable bustle around me failed to compensate for my feelings of isolation between a homeland lost and one not yet attained.

I began to avoid political discussions. Incapable of defending Germany, I preferred to remain silent. Only the passion roused by the study of history led me occasionally to drop this reserve. One such lapse occurred in a class on contemporary Europe wherein I volunteered to debate with another student the controversies surrounding the Treaty of Versailles. When the instructor suggested that it would render the proceedings more titillating were I to defend the treaty, I heatedly refused. Instead, I immersed myself in a two-volume work published ten years after the treaty's signing, which detailed the Weimar Republic's grievances against the peace settlement.[1] I

1. Heinrich Schnee and Hans Draeger (eds.), *Zehn Jahre Versailles* (2 vols.; Berlin, 1929).

pointed out that law-abiding, liberty-loving Germans rejected its provisions as categorically as did the present government. Otherwise, the debate did not amount to much. My vis-à-vis was not sufficiently at home in the subject to test my slender argumentative skills, and I became so immersed in arcane detail that my presentation resembled more a filibuster than an effective summary of my case.

My opinions on the nature and meaning of the Versailles treaty have since changed in a number of respects, but during the summer holidays of 1939, I was ready to take my fixed and angry views on the road. Finding myself in Scranton, Pennsylvania, and as usual with meager finances, I accepted an offer from the editor of the local *Times* to speak to the Rotary Club for the munificent honorarium of ten dollars. After consumption of the obligatory chicken, peas, and mashed potatoes, and the singing of a few songs (once again, nothing in my German upbringing had prepared me for the sight of solid citizens rising and intoning, *vivace* and *con brio*, "Little Sir Echo, how do you do?"), I took up my verbal carving knife and embarrassed my sponsor and offended my audience by insisting that Allied policy had been the chief gravedigger of German democracy. I told the gathering that "we Social Democrats" had been forced to pay for the sins of the kaiser, adding that this injustice was now being compounded by governments that conceded to Hitler what they had denied the Weimar Republic. My outraged sense of justice was further intensified when Mr. Goodman, the editor, buttonholed me a few days later and reported that some of the members had complained because club funds had been paid to a speaker who "posed as a refugee, but who was obviously a Nazi agent!" This was my first audience that would not listen to what it did not want to hear.

Other trivial incidents added to the psychological dissonances of my youthful position. The day after Hitler's march into Prague, on March 15, 1939, a faculty member, with whom I do not remember having had any social or intellectual contact otherwise, stopped me on the street and sneered, "A charming man, your Mr. Hitler." My Mr. Hitler! I felt like spitting in his face. In the spring of 1940, I heard from friends that a meeting of the local chapter of the United Daughters of the Confederacy had been taken up with speculations about the real, and no doubt sinister, reasons for my presence in Lexington. Here, too, the consensus seemed to be that I was an agent of the German government. When my growing frustrations over the course of the war prompted me to tell my professor in English history that taking Britain's side in the war seemed a prescription for national suicide, this pronouncement likewise made the rounds as rapidly as if it had appeared on the editorial page of the New York *Times.* Perhaps I would have fared better had my adolescent opinions been taken less seriously.

However, the day before graduation, when I said good-bye to my academic adviser, William Gleason Bean, he assured me that he would always be available as a reference and, more important, that I should not hesitate to call on him if during the difficult years ahead my outspokenness should get me into trouble. Whatever happened, he would always try to bail me out. I never had to call on him. Views that had reportedly caused such scandal in a small town caused no ripple in the big city to which I would move after receiving my bachelor of arts.

Most of my days at Washington and Lee were outwardly more placid than the preceding pages indicate, and more rewarding. Among my unforgettable educational experiences there, my introduction to American literature ranks first. Apart from an accidental initiation into Mark Twain as a child, and my reading of Upton Sinclair under Jan Boost's tutelage, I had never knowingly read an American author. I had heard of Edgar Allan Poe and Longfellow but assumed them to be English. Now an unknown universe, from the alpha of Jonathan Edwards to the omega of Thomas Wolfe, revealed its countless constellations. I took to it greedily; my faith in poets made the effort to learn what true America was saying all the more important. I sampled not only what my teacher required but whatever else I could get my hands on. Soon another personal gallery of house gods surrounded me, turning a staid, academic survey course into a private voyage of exploration, during which I reserved the right to make an unlimited number of unscheduled stops.

The compulsory reading of *The Scarlet Letter* was a tedious imposition for many of my classmates. I, to the contrary, went out and bought the Modern Library Giant containing all of Hawthorne's major novels. While my peers grumbled at the assignment of *The Education of Henry Adams,* I was not content until I had also read *Mont-St.-Michel and Chartres* and several volumes of the *History of the United States.* Adams' pessimism was a congenial surprise. It soothed the pains of my self-centered adolescence, for I naturally considered myself to be as much at odds with the world as did the New England aristocrat in whom I have never ceased to sense a kindred spirit. He made the new country less of an alien land to me.

Our second semester was devoted to younger stars such as Sinclair Lewis, whose influence and credibility I later questioned when I discovered, first hand, that the Midwest was far removed from the bigoted wasteland depicted in *Main Street.* I think I read every play Eugene O'Neill had then published and admired most some of the most discredited: *Dynamo,* with its baiting of the industrial age, so fashionable in all industrial regions; *The Great God Brown,* portraying the bourgeois beating up the bourgeoisie; and *Marco Millions,* transferring an arbitrary version of distant history to the present. Reverently I grappled with the heavenly lengths of Thomas Wolfe, finding that a slow, chapter-by-chapter reading of *Look Homeward Angel* turned this ungainly chronicle into a string of narrative pearls. Although a graduate student in English at the University of Chicago later denigrated this enthusiasm as sophomoric and a common childhood disease of my generation, I have not been able to change my mind on Wolfe to this day.

My fourth favorite writer probably illustrates even more forcefully the caprice and utter inexpertness of my literary opinions. I suppose that Edwin Arlington Robinson is both gone and forgotten. What I admired in his poems was a quality certainly absent from Wolfe's prose, the ability to create characters in a few formal, rhymed lines: the "man Flamonde"; the raging, drinking Miniver Cheevy; Richard Cory, who abruptly "one summer night, went home and put a bullet through his head"; and Tristram, "a mystery more to be felt than seen among the shadows."

I realize that my predilections comprehend some large misses. I recall no comparable thrill attending the reading of Hemingway, and I may never become sufficiently Americanized to understand the fuss over F. Scott Fitzgerald. Carl Sandburg paled quickly—"too much like Whitman" I reported disapprovingly to my parents—and I do not remember even hearing the name William Faulkner.

My civic education was less headlong and less of a startling experience. Here, too, I started from zero, but since Lexington was not London, I learned less (and more slowly) than I had in the summer of 1936. What took a particularly long time to sink in was the realization that American politics was more decentralized than that of any jurisdiction I had hitherto observed. The well-known separation of powers was compounded by a separation of national issues from regional and local ones. The complexity of the system dawned on me bit by bit as I came to know different sections of the country, and I grew even more familiar with it after I became a citizen and an active participant.

First came the cursory impressions of Virginia's one-party politics, coupled with an Anglophilia that struck me as inappropriate for the home state of George Washington and Thomas Jefferson. One election day, for example, in November, 1938, I ran into a professor who, incidentally, has since made his reputation as historian of the Byrd machine and who was on his way downtown to cast his ballot. He hailed me and asked, "Do you know where I am going, Hans?" I replied, "No sir, I have no idea." He laughed. "I am going to the polling place to vote 'Ja.'" Seeing me nonplussed, he gave me a short but helpful lecture on the difference between primaries and elections, from which I gathered that in this case all state issues had been decided well before the first Tuesday in November. Still, it shocked me to hear my mentor compare, even if facetiously, the actual election to a phony Hitlerian plebiscite. I was reassured, however, when the nationwide returns in next day's New York *Times* revealed that voters in many other states were presented with more choices.

After the war broke out in 1939, Virginia seemed ready to join the Allied cause almost at once. Three years later, when I lived in Chicago, the congressional elections in Illinois brought victory to an isolationist slate, and that almost a year after the attack on Pearl Harbor. The two positions were difficult to reconcile. Who could head such a country and speak for it? In the East, belligerence surged and strained against the bonds of neutrality; in the Midwest, opponents of intervention still spoke for the majority, both at the state and the federal level, even after the country had been forced to enter the war.

Some of these regional differences affected me in immediate, disconcerting ways. On the East Coast, I had met hospitality and sympathy for Germany's persecuted. As I penetrated the interior of America, I encountered open anti-Semitism for the first time since leaving Germany. After spending part of my first summer in a work camp run by the Church of the Brethren in a small mining community near Scranton, 90 percent of whose working population was unemployed, I decided to take to the road, hitchhiking, and to visit a newly acquired college friend, Paul Morrison, in Chicago. I saw much of the Midwest—its monotonous scenery, the sameness of its towns and cities, and a certain uniformity of views that emerged from conversations with the friendly drivers who picked me up. Many were salesmen glad to have somebody to talk to, usually good for several hours of uninterrupted, free transportation. But each discourse moved in what became depressing and predictable channels. After the pickup, my charitable host would volunteer his name and I would tell him mine. "German are you?" the driver would say. "I thought I detected an accent. How long have you been in this country?" I would then give a brief account of my recent peregrinations. "Terrible guy, that Hitler," was the usual response. "But you've got to admit, he's right about the Jews." This nettlesome pronouncement challenged me to disclose my maternal ancestors, which produced an even more bewildering response. Far from stopping the car and telling me to take my contaminating presence elsewhere, the chauffeur-of-the-moment would suddenly turn solicitous: "Now don't get me wrong. Some of my best friends are Jews."

Back in camp after one of these excursions, I was just in time for a community open house. Here is what I wrote my parents about that occasion:

> One of the most unpleasant discoveries I have made this summer is the apparent increase of anti-Semitism. Everyone seems to have a grievance against some Jew, just as everyone knows at least one "very fine Jewish gentleman." It is like the old joke back home: "How many good Jews are there in Germany?" "Sixty-three million; every German knows one." Here business competition seems to be the invariable reason. Isaac Cohen does better than I; *ergo* he must be a fraud. Besides, we know that most Jews are dishonest. I talked last night to a Scranton pharmacist who complained about "Jewish business methods" (some branch of their religion, no doubt), and concluded with resignation that one could do nothing about their deceitful ways because "they" controlled the country's finances. I asked him 1) whether Rockefeller, Morgan, Carnegie or Frick made their money more honestly than John Jacob Astor. 2) whether he ever observed the thousands of "rich" Jews in the East End of New York. To what distinctive character defect did he ascribe their condition? "Don't get me wrong," he said. "Some of my best friends are Jews." "That is very forgiving of you," I replied.

My letter concluded with the outraged exclamation: "A bigoted ignoramus such as this is unworthy of freedom."

Fortunately, my stay in Scranton was short. By the time I left, I had certainly given enough offense. What I learned from these encounters was, however, not wholly disillusioning. If prejudice ran rampant in the United States, one could at least oppose it with the same openness. If a teacher here had commented in class that *Jew* and *scoundrel* fitted together nicely, that teacher most certainly would be called on the carpet.

In Europe, meanwhile, the options for the persecuted steadily decreased. On the evening of August 23, 1939, I wearily stepped from the car of one of my Samaritans-in-transit onto Chicago's Michigan Avenue. It was drizzling, and the newsboys were hawking extras announcing the signing of the Hitler-Stalin pact. I read the early (that is, late-evening) edition of the *Tribune* while sitting on the steps leading up to the Art Institute, my mind in tune with the weather, and seeing enemies everywhere. I had never admired the Soviet Union, but this news came as a blow. What hope was there? The Spanish republic had just collapsed; now the USSR had deserted what was left of an international front against fascism. France was isolated; no other country on the Continent had sufficient political power to contain German expansionism. I was staring at the fabled Hog Butcher of the World, but I was thinking about the butchering of men, women, and children that was about to commence.

By the end of my first year in college, my knowledge of American politics rested on more than random impressions. I had completed one year-long introductory course in United States government and a comparable survey in American history. Neither inspired the enthusiasm or generated the excitement that accompanied my discoveries of American writers. These courses were simply quick and comprehensive remedies for another aspect of my total ignorance. When I arrived in Lexington, I had heard of George Washington and knew that Abraham Lincoln had freed the slaves and been assassinated. I was also aware that Franklin D. Roosevelt was the current president. On my first day in history class, the instructor had asked me my opinion of Patrick Henry. I was speechless, having never heard of him. (I remembered Tom Sawyer's mortifying experience with the "Give me liberty or give me death" oration. But Mark Twain had seen no need to remind his American readers of its author.) Our first test in government asked us to identify the members of the cabinet. I knew only Cordell Hull and had to leave the rest blank. Ten years later, in the course of my own teaching debut, I tried the same question on forty-five native American students in Alabama, who turned out to be equally ignorant. One member of that class actually mistook Henry A. Wallace for the presidential candidate of the Dixiecrats.

Slowly I dug my way out of this slough of nescience. But I do not remember many details about my discovery of America's secular side. What does remain in my mind is the critical view my history teachers took of America's past, particularly the cynical perception my amiable, alcoholic instructor in government purveyed about American politics. From him I learned that corruption was the norm at all levels: it took the form of hypocrisy when people spoke and outright venality when they acted. Such practices would have worried me more had I been a citizen. Since I was not, I took in what he said, wondering the while why if wrongdoing in a free society was well known, and extensively documented as it seemed to be, nobody did anything about it.

In history the negativism emanating from the lectern made a deeper impression. Coming from Georg Friedrich Hegel's soil, where historians considered their discipline to be a cult of the unique, I had been conditioned to view history as drama: tragedy when divine purpose was frustrated, and fulfillment when it triumphed, but never comedy. The discipline recorded a succession of great achievements and of villainies avenged. History was grandeur to be cherished as part of the culture's monotheist beliefs—the manifestation of the Creator and of his greatest achievement, man. By the time I came to America, doubt had, of course, touched my soul, and some images had become tarnished. In my homeland I had seen criminals elevated to high office. In Holland and England I had watched amiable mediocrity (Queen Wilhelmina and King George VI) routinely enthroned, assisted by prime ministers (Neville Chamberlain and Hendrikus Colijn) who looked suspiciously like my older *Gymnasium* teachers. Reading newspaper accounts of French cabinet crises, I had discovered that nation and state could pass through times that neither produced great men nor set in motion inspiring or epic enterprises. Still, public life retained the ceremonial magnificence associated with a more glorious past. The president of France might be a powerless simpleton, but what a colorfully attired praetorian guard attended his arrivals and departures! Even in its darkest hours, Germany could on patriotic holidays muster a goose-stepping spectacle moving to the rhythm of thunderous bands and surrounded by a forest of regimental standards.

America's past and present, in contrast, seemed to lack such display, and more recent attempts to invest it with pomp have often foundered on public ridicule. Thus it had been from the country's beginning, when the American War of Independence owed much of its outcome to French assistance. As a child I had read how the king of Prussia called "his people" to arms against Napoleon and how "everyone" responded to his summons. No such unanimity seemed to have supported the war against George III (it was also absent from Prussian history, to tell the truth), and with the coming of each winter, George Washington's heterodox contingents threatened to disintegrate. It seemed as if Valley Forge symbolized not so much patriotism as the widespread lack of it.

I found such candor impressive. In my eyes, it increased the stature of the founding fathers, because the risks they had taken had been shared by so few. Despite what many self-appointed guardians of American virtue tell us today, cutting the past down to size is a wholesome labor; it deflates the egotism of subsequent generations. Germany had taught me that an uncritical view of the national past generated an equally subservient acceptance of the present. Americans, on the other hand, seemed to have felt free to follow their leaders or stay home. They made decisions and mistakes independently, and at all levels.

Clearly, my first brush with American history had accustomed me to ask questions. I also learned to view the past as the work of ordinary men, and as fact rather than myth. Only later did I come to understand that these critical approaches contained their own distortions and were often shaped by needs of the present rather than by an abstract quest for absolute truth. Most Americans between 1938 and 1940 did not want to go to war. This was certainly true of my peers—many of whom joined the Veterans of Future Wars, founded to oppose as well as poke fun at their flag-waving elders. Their pacific spirit projected a postwar attitude into a prewar setting and reflected a larger past in which men had never been prone to abandon the pursuit of material and spiritual happiness for some cosmic call to arms. To me groups of this sort presented a people whose feet were firmly planted on the ground, wholesomely different from the ugly ambitions of my German compatriots.

My first intimate contact with the contemporary American political system occurred in the spring of my second college year, when Washington and Lee observed the impending presidential election with its own famous mock convention. It was, and remains, the practice to hold such a gathering on behalf of the party out of office, in this case the Republicans. The entire student body was organized into forty-eight state and additional territorial delegations, ranging in size from seventy-nine delegates (New York) to one (Virgin Islands). Students served so far as possible in the contingent of their home states, whose ranks were brought up to strength from the large reservoir of supernumerary Virginians, northeasterners, and me. I became an interested backbencher in Utah's delegation.

Each group sought instructions from the Republican organization of the state it represented and then conducted itself accordingly. The resulting facsimile generated much cigar smoke and the consumption of many cases of beer (campus prohibition was temporarily suspended), and featured such authentic attractions as gun-totin', blank-firing delegations from Texas, New Mexico, and Oklahoma, in cowboy dress, whose barrages drowned out many a resonant speech from the platform. Congressman James W. Wadsworth, Jr., of New York, a key participant in the back-room intrigues that led to the Republican nomination of Warren G. Harding in 1920, gave the keynote address and provided us the opportunity to hear and see a professional up close.

The convention ritual was painstakingly reenacted: chairmen, secretaries, and other functionaries wordily nominated and noisily elected. Then came the rambunctious report of the credentials committee, culminating in a quarrel over the admission of the lone delegate from the Virgin Islands. The reading of the platform that— as I explained to my distant family— "promised everything to everybody" filled the hall, while delegates opened still another bottle and recovered from the credentials battle.

In 1940 the balloting of our mock convention lasted much longer than the real event. The numerous supporters of Robert Taft, Arthur Vandenberg, and Thomas Dewey fought one another to a standstill, and after more than twenty ballots, the deadlock was broken by a sudden westward surge toward Senator Charles McNary from Oregon, whom we finally nominated. Balancing a Republican ticket in those days did not involve southerners since the delegations from below the Mason-Dixon line often represented such small electorates. In 1940, therefore, we arrived at a relatively quick verdict:

Senator Styles Bridges of New Hampshire after a mere three ballots. Wendell L. Willkie's star had not begun to rise when we convened, which explains the absence of his name from our proceedings. It was two days of glorious fun: no classes, plenty of beer, no home-work—all for the sake of our civic education.

The mock-convention ritual capped an academic year marked by personal anxieties. When I returned to the campus in September, 1939, this time directly by bus, the first person I encountered was Dean Robert Tucker, who poked me in the ribs and guffawed, "I see that you haven't gone back to fight the Poles." There was no chance of that, but the German advance on Warsaw increased my worries for my less fortunate family. When I had last heard from them, my father was still unemployed. Several job offers during the preceding year had been contingent on his divorcing his Jewish wife. Although my mother encouraged him to take that step—their personal rela-tionship would not have changed—he would not hear of it. One reward for his steadfastness was an unusually long summer vaca-tion in Holland. But once the war broke out, his Dutch residence permit was abruptly withdrawn, and he had to return to Germany. At the American consulate in Rotterdam, my mother and brother were on a long waiting list. Would their number come up in time? The answer arrived on May 10, 1940, less than two weeks after the mock convention, when German forces invaded the Low Countries. For weeks contact with all members of my family was suspended. Just before graduation I wrote my father about my future plans, wonder-ing whether the letter would ever reach him. Decisions had to be mine alone. All the adults who had heretofore charted my career were cut off from me. I was on my own, without parental supervision for the first time in my life.

Friends stepped into the vacuum: the parents of Paul Morrison, whom I had met at my table in the "Beanery." A native of Texas, but a later transplant to the Midwest, he was attending Washington and Lee on a four-year scholarship and was a young man of awesome scholarly attainments. For four years he ground out a monotonous succession of A's in everything from advanced courses in philoso-phy to physical education (then listed in the catalog as "Hygiene"). Paul's many endowments included not only a retentive mind but a flawless ear as well. He was an accomplished flutist, knew entire symphonic scores by heart, and could mimic accents to perfection. His German and self-taught Russian were passable, his French sparkling. Most Sundays he and I relaxed by his little radio, listening to the New York Philharmonic; many evenings we monopolized the college's record collection and its fine record player.

Paul set me a good example as a student and convinced me that the European cliché of America as civilized but not cultured was hopelessly wide of the mark. In his life, work came first. After the philharmonic broadcasts, for instance, he would politely show me the door and resume his studies, leaving me little choice but to do likewise. Paul's determination to excel in every subject turned him, too, into an alien of sorts in Washington and Lee's hedonistic atmosphere, and we two outsiders took to each other, becoming the odd couple of the class of 1940. When music did not absorb us, we sometimes roamed the streets, speaking French, arguing about the existence of God, which I might question and he denied. In a way, his presence at Washington and Lee comforted his southern-born parents in their midwestern exile, but it made no southern gentleman of him any more than it did me.

Paul became my first and most important American friend. His restless, inquisitive mind and his ceaseless preoccupation with academic achievement awakened my own slumbering ambitions. In the shadow of his eminence I, too, began to strive for scholarly success, though it would be much later, in graduate school after World War II, that I would gain recognition as a prize student.

A few weeks before graduation, Paul knocked on my door one evening to hand me a letter. Puzzled, I opened the envelope. It was from his mother. She wrote that since her son and I had become such good friends, it was both his wish and that of her and her husband that I share their home as long as I chose to and continue my studies at the University of Chicago.

This generous, completely unanticipated offer came at the perfect moment. For some time I had worried about what I would do after graduation. I could, of course, return to New York, where my relatives always treated me as a member of the family. But that would mean returning to an environment I was anxious to avoid. My quest for a fellowship at Columbia University had ended in disappointment after the formidable Carlton Hayes had informed me gruffly, if accurately, that I was not the only bright student knocking at the university's door. Chicago offered similar attractions in the fields of history in which I wanted to specialize: Bernadotte Schmitt, the diplomatic historian; Albert Mathiez' brilliant American protégé,

Louis Gottschalk; the medievalist Jacob Larsen; and the pioneer in Latin American studies, J. Fred Rippy. Robert Maynard Hutchins' fief, Chicago was a young, unconventional institution, willing to experiment, in the process of creating traditions rather than following well-trodden paths. To be given the opportunity to become part of its exciting life was like finding gold. Gratefully and enthusiastically, I accepted.

The Morrisons' first good deed, however, was to salvage what might have been for me a sad graduation. Tradition has made the last day of college into an occasion of unutterable boredom. Attired in the unaccustomed medieval disguise of caps and gowns, students and faculty move in slovenly procession to a meeting place where all sit captive until a generally witless commencement address, followed by a monotonous parade to the rostrum for the distribution of diplomas, finally endows the students with written confirmation of academic approval. Everybody is sleepy and worn out from a night of drinking. The occasion is unleavened by any semblance of drama or suspense, because one has known for months that one will graduate, and reaching that goal is by no standard a breath-taking accomplishment.

Fortunately, the weather is generally sunny, and then there are one's relatives, whose pleasure and pride invest the occasion with a joy the graduate could never summon up unassisted. Anticlimax from beginning to end: that is the way I remember June 7, 1940. It was the day after my nineteenth birthday. The Germans were threatening Paris, as Alaric and his marauding Goths had Rome more than fifteen hundred years earlier. And as for family, not only was mine not present, but I had not heard from any of them for weeks.

The Morrisons, however, made it an occasion for Paul, and I was warmed by the pride they took in their son and the goodness of their hospitable hearts that also embraced me. We celebrated and then we packed; my surrogate family and I said good-bye to Lexington, that quiet and faceless little town through whose main street I had entered America. Twenty-three years would elapse before I would see town and campus again, in happier circumstances—accompanied by my wife and our three children. I introduced them to my former professors, now my colleagues, whose first questions were about Paul Morrison. . . .

IX   MY AMERICAN EDUCATION, CONTINUED

And so the Hog Butcher of the World became my next domicile. Chicago in my time was a city with many handicaps, besides its reputation for crime and corruption. The cold of its winters lacerated the flesh, and the heat of its summers melted the asphalt on the streets. Before the closing of the stockyards, their odors, driven across town by ceaseless, captious winds, conjured up a potter's field of unburied corpses. Soot from the city's chimneys fell like black snow through all seasons and settled as a dark frost on every window sill. My Sunday strolls to the corner newsstand led through an unkempt street where paper and refuse performed a grimy ballet on the wind-swept sidewalk. These memories of an unwashed city, set in the boundless reaches of the Midwest, are joined to the recollections of penny pinching, of minimum-wage (35¢ an hour) jobs and 19¢ milkshakes in lieu of lunch. When I started dating a young woman on the South Shore, her family was shocked to discover that my plans for entertaining their daughter consisted chiefly of walks in Jackson Park, then a thoroughly safe place, and included only occasionally the extravagance of a movie.

Without the hospitality of Paul, Sr., and Marian Morrison, life would have been even grimmer. Financially, they treated me like their son. When young Paul and I worked, we paid 25 percent of our weekly wage into the household treasury. If and when either of us attended school, we lived free. Despite his superlative college record, Paul opted for a business career. (After the war, however, he returned to graduate school and eventually became an academic, as did I.) He found employment as a pricing clerk with Inland Steel, while I spent the summer quarter of 1940 beginning graduate work at the University of Chicago.

I discovered at once what a fortunate choice this institution had been. The unorthodox, quarterly schedule allowed some students to work all year and study a full term in the summer: a timetable no other graduate school provided at that time. My first quarter in the Midway classrooms and in the stacks of Harper Library kept every promise of the reputation the university had acquired since opening its doors in 1892. William S. Halperin, a young assistant professor who would ultimately become my doctoral mentor, introduced me to the history of modern Italy, and I began exploring the terra incognita of Latin America under the guidance of the willful and ebullient J. Fred Rippy.

By September, however, full tuition at Robert Maynard Hutchins' academy had reduced my residual capital to such a level that I had to look for a job. I began reading the Chicago *Tribune* want ads daily. (I disagreed with Colonel Robert McCormick's isolationist politics but recognized that the back pages of his daily were every job hunter's indispensable guide.) As I pursued leads, the Loop and its adjacent western and southern industrial precincts soon became as familiar to me as the suburb of Frankfurt where I had lived as a child. The depression still lingered; even with a college degree, I remained a nineteen-year-old without job experience. Some prospective employers, furthermore, did not hire sons of Jewish women. One large insurance company put me through a battery of tests, informed me that I had scored at the top of the group, but never offered me a position. (After the war, when I spent two years in the insurance business, I learned that this particular industry was rigorously divided between gentile and Jewish firms.) Other employers had qualms about hiring me because I was still a German citizen. They expected their share of impending military contracts and could not allow my suspicious person to jeopardize those prospects.

The Morrisons, however, kept up my courage in adversity and prevented me from making desperate and ill-considered choices. A trucking firm offered me a job but would not tell me at what pay until they had a chance "to look me over." Next, I was offered a position as rent collector in the black ghetto west of Cottage Grove Avenue. Both times Paul's mother insisted that I keep looking for a less uncertain or hazardous living.

After a couple of weeks the clouds parted. An importer of "interior decorative accessories" in the Merchandise Mart advertised for a male stenographer, a relatively rare commodity of which I represented a decent facsimile, thanks to Pitman's College, and I applied for the job. My new employer even considered my foreign birth an asset, though, in fact, it was just as irrelevant as my mother's antecedents. My clerical duties enlisted neither my mastery of languages nor my knowledge of history. For one and a half years, I pounded on my typewriter amidst such objets d'art as Staffordshire dogs and birds, Chinese figurines and vases, tole lamps, Audubon and Currier and Ives Prints, and mass-produced Rubensian portraits from Italy on which the paint still glistened when they reached our shipping room. In the summer of 1941, I was ready to leave this employ to absolve my second quarter at the university, but my employer proposed that I continue working half time, an arrangement enabling me to mix graduate school and work so that I had completed my master of arts by the time I entered the army.

A year later, however, the economic upswing, and its attendant reversal of the labor market, led me to exchange the elegant surroundings of what was then the world's largest business complex for a more lucrative position in the office of a small metal plater, busy with war work, in one of Chicago's dreariest sections. The owner of this factory was likewise attracted by my foreign origins, naïvely assuming that enemy aliens were exempt from the draft. I pointed out that the law made no such distinction, but he waved aside my concerns. "What about my security clearance?" I finally asked. "The FBI will clear you," he responded nonchalantly. So I went to work, exchanging my $20-per-week position in chic surroundings for twice that amount in a run-down neighborhood off Lake Street. In due time, two well-dressed gentlemen called on me, identified themselves as members of J. Edgar Hoover's forces, and carried on a brief and relaxed interrogation in the office of my boss, who obligingly departed for a prolonged lunch. They decided then and there that my presence on the premises posed no threat to American security.

For a better part of the year that followed, I rose at six o'clock and rode a rickety elevated train past ghetto, Loop, and the slummiest part of the West Side. At five in the afternoon I locked my desk and went, three or four evenings a week, to the Newberry Library, where, until closing, I worked on a master's thesis that investigated what artists and intellectuals thought of mad Ludwig of Bavaria as king and Maecenas. This privately endowed temple of knowledge occupying the north side of Walton Place was also surrounded by blocks of the most appalling squalor. It was another example of the cheek-by-jowl existence of heaven and hell characterizing Chicago and explaining why I—like so many newcomers before and after me—succumbed to the fascination of this corrupt, pock-marked metropolis.

Ugly and foul-smelling, teeming with a variety of ethnic and racial communities and seething with tribal hatreds, this urban compost heap fertilized a cultural landscape of surprising abundance. To me, the university was, of course, the vital center. Apart from my own department, the faculty included the physiologist Anton Carlson—a vocal opponent of America's entry into World War II—and the chemist Harold Urey. The Oriental Institute, with its formidable contingent of German refugee scholars, was world renowned. The anthropologist Robert Redfield, political scientists like Charles Merriam and Quincy Wright, and economists of Paul Douglas' and Oscar Lange's fame pioneered a variety of new methods in societal investigation. At the neo-Gothic, nondenominational chapel, named after the university's patron saint, John D. Rockefeller, the theologian Paul Tillich, another German exile, preached on Sunday, and masters like John Power-Biggs and Marcel Dupré played the organ. At the apex of the communal hierarchy, Hutchins, just approaching middle age as he entered the second decade of his stewardship, was recruiting his round table of the knights of general education. Their major field of action, the undergraduate college, admitted high-school juniors to a prescribed four-year college curriculum, preceding a three-year course of specialized study leading to the master of arts.

Little did it trouble me that this assemblage of stars and innovators was widely distrusted by many good Illinois citizens, who believed the university to be a breeding place of subversion. For several years Hutchins made annual trips to the state legislature in Springfield, where a special committee, devoted to the preservation of American virtues, tried to extract from him the admission that he presided over an enterprise dedicated to the uprooting of traditional values. Hutchins treated his interrogators to a display of wit and arrogant sarcasm. He probably did not make any converts, but his tormentors eventually wearied of a game they saw no chance of winning and left him and the university alone. We students took this victory and the intellectual freedom that went with it for granted; after all, ours was not a state institution. We also appreciated something else about the University of Chicago of that day: the institution's indifference to conventional academic record keeping. One signed up for courses, attended lectures if and when one liked, and, whenever one thought one was ready, took the requisite examinations and prepared one's thesis. Degrees were duly conferred. On the road to such formal fulfillment, Chicago students basked in the greatness of their teachers as if it were their own, aped their professional jargon, and confidently accepted their teachings as revealed truth.

If the great academy fulfilled expectations I had formulated before my arrival, the city as a center of the creative arts came as a happy surprise. Both public and private cultural opportunities abounded. The magnate in whose employ my friend Paul learned to price steel chaired the board of benefactors that kept alive and in fighting trim one of the world's great symphony orchestras, whose concerts I began to enjoy (top balcony, as always) once my income began to rise above the minimum level. At Orchestra Hall I heard the cellist Gregor Piatigorsky and the pianist Artur Schnabel, and witnessed Sergei Rachmaninoff's last public appearance a few weeks before his sudden death in 1943. I watched Bruno Walter conduct the Mozart Requiem and pay homage to his own revered mentor, Gustav Mahler. In the summer I took the North Shore Railroad to Ravinia Park to admire the great conductors Pierre Monteux and—in surroundings radically different from Queens Hall—the indestructible Sir Thomas Beecham. A few blocks south of Orchestra Hall, in an abandoned theater, Izler Solomon led the Illinois WPA orchestra through music not found in the more staid repertory of the symphony. On winter Sundays the Fine Arts Quartet, consisting of the symphony's first-desk men, played to capacity audiences in the auditorium of the Art Institute. Chicago was also one of a handful of American cities to maintain an opera company, though at prices my budget could not afford.

The Art Institute was a godsend in other ways for a penniless lover of beauty such as me; here I received my belated introduction to the French impressionists (They were well represented in the Tate Gallery, but somehow Turner's overpowering presence had prompted me to walk past them with hardly a glance.) The father of the young woman with whom I kept frequent company in Jackson Park, who was a member of the Art Institute, put at our disposal his season ticket to the institute's Goodman Theater. Not only did his gratuitous offering provide him peace of mind as to his daughter's whereabouts, but it also opened another world to me: that of the modern theater. It turned me into the insatiable playgoer I have been ever since. This teaching stage was peopled by students, not stars, enthusiastic rather than jaded and skilled, who learned their craft by performing Pirandello, Molnár, and O'Neill, Shaw, and Oscar Wilde, as well as countless other interesting, if more transient, products of the contemporary stage. At the Actors Company of Chicago, I attended the unforgettable unveiling of John Steinbeck's *The Moon Is Down,* the most evenhanded, humane, and moving play about the war, at least until Jean-Paul Sartre's *Les Mains sales,* written while wartime frenzy was at its height.

A cultural historian's chronicle of Chicago's civilization would add a great deal to these sketchy observations. He would, no doubt, write about the university's famous alumni of my generation, ranging from David Rockefeller to Studs Terkel. He would pay tribute to Marianne Moore's *Poetry* magazine, then edited by Karl Shapiro, and to Nelson Algren and James T. Farrell. (Less parochial than I, he would certainly have a kind word or two for Northwestern University.) But my own limited experience was a sufficient revelation of a great American city. Chicago continued my Americanization through pain and happiness. While I lived there, I lost my father and met my future wife.

After the invasion of the Low Countries in the spring of 1940, my father in Germany became for a time my only link with family. Until then I had written to my mother, who would forward to Germany suitable versions of my letters, expurgated for the Nazi censor. Now I wrote to him instead and became my own censor. This was the first direct, serious exchange between father and son since my leaving Germany, and it brought me closer to him than I had been for many years. I reported my move to Chicago and my courses at the university—I even sent him some of my papers. We discovered common intellectual interests and decided to read certain authors and then exchange our reactions to them. In November I suggested that we tackle Schopenhauer's *On the Fourfold Root of the Principle of Sufficient Reason* and then *On Vision and Color,* before plunging into *The World as Will and Idea.* For me these were somewhat reckless choices. I had struggled with *On the Fourfold Root* during my summer in Austria and done no more systematic reading in philosophy since, Nietzsche excepted. But I knew that my father liked Schopenhauer, and I was further attracted to this philosopher because he had spent the last thirty years of his life in Frankfurt, a lonely and embittered solitary like my father (though for totally different reasons).

My last contribution to this correspondence bears the date of December 6, 1940. This letter reminds me of the degree to which I had quickly learned to confide in my father and speaks of my gradual acquisition of English as first language: "For two years now I have spoken hardly any German, and English becomes more and more my new mother tongue." In the letter I enclosed six poems of mine, written in German, the last I wrote in that language. They reflected a young man's doubts about established beliefs, established values, and the purpose of life—in short, a typically adolescent negation of all certitude. This last letter also reminds me that we had been corresponding about religion. I had reported my surprise encounter on campus with an Eerde classmate, Peter Kaufmann, who was attending the seminary of the Church of the Brethren on Chicago's West Side. I criticized vigorously and intolerantly his decision to become a clergyman, viewing it as a betrayal of our boardingschool's enlightened teachings. My father upbraided me for such disrespect of another person's conviction, and I defended myself by insisting that it was not my classmate's commitment but the clergy's preoccupation with dogma at the expense of ethics that repelled me. "God ceases to be God once preachers get their hands on him," I wrote. "In my opinion nothing we can grasp can be divine. We can neither know nor comprehend God, which also means that our notions of right and wrong must be our own. My maxim, therefore, is not fear God, do right and shame the devil, but do right and fear no one, neither man nor God." And I added these parting words: "We suffer for our convictions perhaps not only at the hands of man but also at the hands of God."

My father accepted my reading program and agreed to the Schopenhauer assignment. This was his last message to me. Cheerful and responsive, this last epistle also reported that he had prepared several talks on Nietzsche to be delivered before a circle of friends whose nature and composition I have never learned. Its core undoubtedly consisted of Frankfurt's diminutive Quaker meeting, among whose members my father had found friendship and solace during the years of separation from my mother. The darker, truer side of his last years survives in his letters to her. In them he dropped the smiling mask and recorded a tale of temporal damnation. Their contents reveal that there can be more to suffering than confinement and physical torture. Tyranny knows how to deal out large measures of misery to every refractory member of society.

The last chapter of my father's agony began on August 2, 1940. "I have work," he announced to my mother, "real work, and a reasonably decent salary to go with it." He continued: "The responses which I had to give [my new employer], in respect to the two of us, [and] concerning Aryan descent, of which I assumed that they would at once torpedo the entire transaction, still leave some matters up in the air. The firm itself (defense plant) does not seem to care, because they suffer from a tremendous shortage of staff and because I am a specialist with extensive experience. At any rate, they have taken me on."

My father was fifty-six years old, physically young, but emotionally worn by struggle and disappointment. His new job meant a fifty- to sixty-hour work week. He rose at five-thirty in the morning, returned home around seven o'clock, prepared his meal, and afterwards washed and put away his dishes. Special and routine errands, complicated by war, not for him alone of course, added to the pressures of daily life. After his death, his landlady wrote to my mother: "The *Herr Doktor* was often very tired and said, 'I want to do nothing but sleep,' which one can understand in view of his long working hours. Perhaps it was too much, because he had so much to take care of, always on the run."

Hundreds of details in his letters recount how his life began to wear him down. His only consolation was that this hard existence helped him resume financial responsibility for the education of his younger son. If he had any idle moments, they were absorbed by efforts to enable wife and child to follow me to America as soon as possible. The uncertainty of this prospect added sleepless nights to exhausting days. My father's letters to all of us pleaded unceasingly that we mobilize heaven and earth to save everyone in the family but him. My mother wondered at times whether it would not be easier to dispatch my brother alone across the Atlantic while she returned to Germany, but he fought single-mindedly for her berth to safety. After knocking on many official and private doors, he prevailed on the north German Lloyd to send me a top-alarm telegram in November, 1940, requesting a new set of affidavits for my mother and brother. (This, after confirmation arrived that all documents previously submitted to the United States consulate had been destroyed on May 14, 1940, during the German air raid on Rotterdam.) I was fortunate in being able to secure these guarantees from the Morrisons and other friends. (My mother's cousin, who had cleared my passage to the United States, was unable to assist us. Carl Zeiss had closed its American office in 1940, and our relative was looking for a new job himself.) Whether these assurances from virtual strangers would move the American consul in Rotterdam, whether they would have *any* effect in view of the desperate, lengthening waiting lines for the promised land, one had no way of knowing. After both my father and I had done all we could, only waiting remained. Whether or not my father realized by then what fate awaited Europe's Jews I do not know. The desperate tone of his last letters to my mother leads me to believe that he did, if not from concrete knowledge, then from rumors and the intuitive understanding given to souls who are practiced in the endurance of the worst.

A letter to my mother, written on December 2, culminates in a categorical confession, underlined in my father's own hand: *"Life holds no joy any more.* In past years we could at least look forward to each other's Christmas presents . . . this year I have nothing to give. That is dreadful. What if this is the last Christmas you will spend on this side?" Perhaps he understood for the first time the true horror of his position. If Nazi vengeance should overtake my mother, he would be bereaved; if she—and my brother—should be rescued, he would be forsaken. Although he prayed for their escape, and I think that he was praying again, he knew that the granting of this wish would leave him forever separated from his family, especially in case of German victory—so close at hand, it seemed, after the fall of France.

These prospects were rendered even less tolerable by the humiliations that the world randomly inflicted on my father. On December 8, the day before his fifty-seventh birthday, he reported receiving a Christmas bonus. As his letter explained, his employer doled out eighty marks to each married staff member, but because the husband of a Jewish woman was considered to be single, he received only half that amount, plus an additional one mark and seventy five pfennigs for each of his sons. "It isn't much, considering that many firms now add a month's pay at Christmas, but it is still better than having the farmer run after you with a shotgun," he added wryly. "Besides, a person in the know told me Wednesday that I can count on being kept in my position. That pleases me very much. I rejoice to be able to work in the service of the fatherland, and, more important, earning means eating. I am disappointed that today's mail brought no birthday greetings, because tomorrow, Monday, I shall get it only late in the evening."

Three weeks later, just after the New Year, the mail brought me a letter from my uncle in Amsterdam. I had not heard from him in years, and I opened with the utmost eagerness what I expected to be a rare and welcome, if delayed, Christmas greeting. As I read it, my joy quickly turned to puzzlement, and then cold grief. Instead of wishing me a merry Christmas, my uncle explained how much he had always respected my father, even though their relationship had been full of conflict. He wrote in the past tense, and I realized that my father had died. Thanks to the vagaries of wartime mail service, an earlier letter from my mother bearing this news arrived several days later (a routine lapse nowadays). It conveyed what little she knew. On the evening of his birthday, December 9, my father had chatted with his landlady and bidden her good night around eight to retire to his rooms. The next day no one saw him, and when no one heard or saw him depart for work on December 11, the landlady used her keys to enter his quarters. The well-meaning intruder found him "lying on his bed, one hand on his heart, but looking peaceful. Apparently death overcame him unexpectedly. But who knows what his last thoughts were," she had added in her report to my mother, "for the *Herr Doktor* died alone." She concluded, "It is awful when a human being has to bear as much spiritual suffering as the *Herr Doktor*." The physician whom the landlady called confirmed her account. "It will be consolation to you," he wrote my mother, "that your husband died peacefully, without knowing what was happening. All attending circumstances, and the peaceful expression on his face, confirm it."

A week later, the Quaker community and some former neighbors gathered for my father's funeral. One member of the congregation played Händel and Bach. The elder of the meeting, Rudolf Schlosser, subsequently killed in an air raid on Frankfurt, read my father's favorite passage from the New Testament: 1 Cor. 13. Then the mourners followed his remains to the grave site of his Jewish in-laws, Adolf and Jenny Hamburger, next to whom he was laid to rest, in accordance with his own instructions. Even in death he defied the powers of this world. Nazi retribution could, however, still reach the living, and German authorities denied my mother permission to attend her husband's funeral. Instead, she and my brother spent these days of mourning with her brother and his family in Amsterdam, where they passed the hour of his entombment in a small catholic chapel at the *Begijnenhof*.

What then appeared to be my last link with Germany was broken. To safeguard our property, which included the house in Frohnau, my mother relinquished the inheritance to her sons, and I paid my last visit to a German official at the consulate general on Michigan Avenue. There, beneath the Nazi flag and a picture of Hitler, I signed and had notarized a power of attorney authorizing our lawyer in Frankfurt, Franz Calvelli-Adorno, to settle the estate. I included the request that my half be added to my brother's inheritance. This, too, was turned down by the authorities, who, strange to say, did not use this opportunity to confiscate my share as enemy alien property.

Life went on, but after my father's death my separation from the family was all but complete. My mother's letters could not convey much about the reality of existence in occupied Holland. After Pearl Harbor that correspondence declined to a trickle of 25-word messages, exchanged through the medium of the International Red Cross, and occasional letters transmitted by third persons. The mother of my Eerde music teacher, Billy Hilsley, living near Bern in Switzerland, and an Eerde alumnus in Stockholm, Kurt Weingarten, intermittently served as channels between me and my mother. What her life was really like during that time I would not discover until 1945.

December 7, 1941, two days before the first anniversary of my father's death, found me, as well as millions of American citizens, before the radio, listening to the New York Philharmonic. Until that day I had often wondered why men and women in all the belligerent capitals of Europe had cheered the outbreak of war in 1914. What perversity of spirit could prompt mankind to hail the advent of death and destruction? Now I was guilty of the same irrational behavior. The news of the Japanese bombing of Pearl Harbor did not primarily elicit from me sympathy for the thousands who had died in the treacherous assault (so terrifyingly avenged at Hiroshima and Nagasaki). My *sacro egoismo* only responded to its liberating effect. We were at war. The time of passive suffering was over. Now I could *do* something. The next day, during my lunch hour, I hastened to the recruiting office in the civic opera building. There was a line, but it moved swiftly. Soon my turn came, but not to enlist. The noncommissioned officer who spoke to me was civil but firm. I was an enemy alien and could not volunteer. I must wait until my draft number was called. Crestfallen, I went back to my typewriter, to the porcelain birds and the English hunting prints. For the time being, I would have to continue to help decorate the elegant homes of Chicago's North Shore and leave the epic struggle against evil to those of more fortunate birth.

I waited and waited. My frustration grew when Paul, who was not nearly as keen as I, received his precious presidential greetings. Enviously I watched him depart, whiz through basic training at Fort Devens, Massachusetts, then the officer candidate school for the military police. Enviously I escorted him through some of our favorite Chicago haunts on his first leave as a gleaming second lieutenant. The year wore on. The second anniversary of my father's death came and went; the North African campaign became history, and I was still a civilian. The father of my friend Joan, an architect in his forties with six children, volunteered and was accepted. Her only brother got his call and eventually departed for the South Pacific. Soon the entire family left for California, where its head became base camouflage officer at Hamilton Field. In despair I asked him to write a letter to the 6th Corps command to remind them of my existence. He complied promptly, testifying that I was "anxious to be in the military service" and that my "exceptional knowledge of European languages and customs would make [me] particularly valuable to the military forces." I have no way of knowing what effect his letter had, but early in April, 1943, after I had completed my master's thesis at the University of Chicago, the president of the United States finally took formal notice of me, and I marched off to war at last.

Entering military service, like going to college, was an experience shared by millions, and I shall spare the reader an account of my initiation as a warrior. I became a serious and conscientious soldier, and a reasonably successful one. Once in uniform I was eligible to apply for citizenship, and I did so at once. Because of an inopportune transfer to Camp Ellis, Illinois, I did not receive my final papers, first drawn up in Cheyenne, Wyoming, until autumn. It was, therefore, almost exactly five years since my immigration that I appeared before the district judge in Peoria, in the company of a dozen or so other eager aliens and accompanied by the required "two witnesses of the rank of Corporal or higher, both of whom must be able to testify to [my] character, loyalty, and other qualifications for citizenship." His Honor welcomed us to the charmed circle of United

States citizens and declared that our uniform was proof enough of our worthiness. Back at Company E, 371st Engineer General Service Regiment, where I had recently become company clerk, my mates welcomed me with cheers, and the officers addressed me as "citizen" instead of "corporal."

I was now in uniform and a full-fledged citizen, but still stuck behind a typewriter. I had learned how to shoot a rifle and charge with a bayonet but was not called upon to do either. Meanwhile, the North African campaign had ended in German surrender. Mussolini had been overthrown, and Allied armies were marching up the Italian boot. Everyone was expecting the opening of new Continental fronts.

I decided to apply for OCS, and because it was part of my job to know the bureaucratic procedure as well as the time and place of the selection board's convening, I chose the moment well, applied for training in a branch short of officers, and learned in due time that I had been chosen to attend Engineer OCS at Fort Belvoir, Virginia. Once graduated, I hoped that the magic of commissioned status would somehow transform me into a combatant.

How wrong I was! As it happened, the 371st Engineers arrived in Europe before I did. I had been at Fort Belvoir hardly a month when Allied forces landed in Normandy. The news so distracted me that I cut myself shaving and received five demerits for arriving in formation with a bloody shirt collar. OCS became uncongenial for other reasons. My foreign background and limited experience in traditional American ways soon proved a severe handicap. I was "different," and that could prove fatal to one aspiring to attain a commission in the United States Army. I was, for example, the only member of my platoon who had never owned or driven a car. Two instructors were detailed at once to remedy this defect in my education as well as my character. It was also soon discovered that I was deficient in another area, namely, that all-American sport, softball. Every Friday afternoon the schedule required that we play this native game. Our tactical officer, Lieutenant Kennedy, who treated me with particular malevolence after discovering that I had a master of arts ("Degrees don't cut no ice with me, Schmitt"), simply refused to believe that there was alive on this earth a human being who had never pursued this commonplace pastime. He suspected some subterfuge on my part to obtain an unscheduled half holiday. All these failings he interpreted to reflect an uncooperative attitude, which prompted him to put me on "check"; that is, I was marched with two other delinquents to the battalion commander to discuss "our troubles." A paternal major asked each of us, in turn, what we thought the source of our difficulties to be and what he might do to help. To me this solicitude did not ring true. I knew what he would do to help: kick us out. My two companions-in-disgrace took him at his word, however, and poured out their hearts. I, on the other hand, returned to the mendacious ways of my childhood, looked him brazenly in the eye, and professed utter surprise at standing before him. So far as I could fathom, everything was going well, and if there was any trouble, I could not identify it for him. My instincts proved sound. In this instance dishonesty proved to be the best policy. The next afternoon, the other two candidates were packing and saying good-bye while I stayed on.

On another occasion, even my special talents added to my trouble and aroused more malevolence in Lieutenant Kennedy. Every Friday night one of the officers in our company was required to bring us up to date on current events, especially the campaigns of the war. This was one time of the week when we could nap with impunity in the classroom. Our lecturers, mostly engineers in civilian life, ill at ease with unfamiliar subjects, seemed not to mind since they had only the haziest notion of the matter under discussion. After the Normandy invasion, however, one of the members of my platoon asked Lieutenant Kennedy if he would let me take a turn next Friday night. Since I came from Europe, some of my classmates thought, my personal experiences might enliven the weekly information hour. My tormentor agreed, and I gave the first class lecture of my life. This time nobody slept; there were even questions—the whole occasion became so lively that someone suggested I give the information talk every week.

This favorable reaction did not sit well with Lieutenant Kennedy, for I was not asked to repeat. Instead, he called me into his office to tell me that I was still "in plenty of trouble." My only eventual consolation was that he did not succeed in getting rid of me. A few weeks later he had to watch me graduate.

That was a grand day for the survivors, less than half the class that had entered Engineer OCS in May. I was both relieved and surprised by the happy outcome of seventeen strenuous weeks—surprised, because I had succeeded without having in any sense acquired the skills of an army engineer. In the final analysis, Lieutenant Kennedy's suspicions had rested on sound instincts; I did not belong in that graduating class. Fleetingly, I worried what would happen to my career if in the near future I had to take to the field with a platoon and participate in a bridge-building exercise. But only fleetingly, as I packed my new officer's wardrobe and hastened to catch a train that would carry me to a special vacation.

During the last months of stress and conflict, I had gained from the ordeal of OCS more than two gold bars. The trip to Fort Belvoir had begun one of the most important friendships of my life, and two days after commissioning I was married. To explain the first of these events, I must go back to May 1, 1944, when I set out from Camp Ellis on the journey to OCS in the company of three others who had been selected. By some bureaucratic accident, I had been put in charge of this group: two corporals and that rarest of birds among the fauna of the World War II army, a technician third grade. Two of us were foreign born, a Czech Jew from Prague and I; of the two American natives one was black, Corporal James E. Hall.

Before emigrating to the United States, I had heard a great deal about American racial segregation. My uncle and Mrs. Petersen, as well as Mr. Neuse, had returned from their forays across the Atlantic puzzled by the paradox of a democratic society whose Caucasian majority, Quakers included, accepted a separation of races. None of them had ever been south, but before I left New York for Lexington in 1938, my relatives, as well as Herta Kraus at the American Friends' Service Committee, warned me that this was a region where the separation was enforced with particular rigor and where an alien visitor had best avoid commenting on the status quo.

I needed little coaching. I had come to America to save myself and to establish a bridgehead for my family, not to solve the national dilemma. I was a guest, not a missionary. During the ensuing years I only met blacks, north and south, in faceless, subaltern roles. Only once, during my first semester at Washington and Lee, when I upbraided one of my table companions in the dining hall for referring to blacks as "niggers," did I overstep the bounds of prudence. (As I recall, my crony was genuinely puzzled by this outburst. But being a well-mannered southern gentleman, he courteously deferred to my eccentricity and—so far as I can recollect—never again used the word in my presence.) The rest of the time I rarely pondered the question.

The Morrisons were southerners, and in their home my isolation from the other America continued. They had a black part-time maid, Mamie, a hard, reliable worker, to whom they were devoted as a guardian might be to his ward. My surrogate parents took it for granted that Mamie could function reliably so long as their demands on her were tailored to what they believed to be the limited capacities of her race.

By the time I took the memorable train ride to Fort Belvoir, sitting next to Jim Hall, I was ready to come out of this shell of caution and ignorance. I was of age, a citizen, and in uniform. I had long ceased to look to my elders, no matter how well intentioned, for day-to-day guidance. This was 1944, and we four officer candidates had a train ride of almost twenty-four hours ahead of us. It would provide ample time to get acquainted.

At first the racial composition of our expedition had no effect on its conduct or internal harmony. We stowed our gear and took our seats; at lunchtime and dinnertime we carried our meal tickets to the dining car and consumed the *prix fixe* menu, agreeing afterwards that the portions fell short of our appetites. But the army provided not only food but berths as well. Only one proviso set us apart from ordinary civilian occupants of a Pullman car: We had to sleep two to a lower berth. As the sky darkened outside, a certain tension seemed to grip our group. With the approach of bedtime, I noticed that my two white companions were beginning to sweat a little at the prospect of sharing their rest with a dark-skinned comrade. Embarrassed by this visible uneasiness, I assigned them one berth and took the other one with Jim. I did not understand their feelings but thought it best to avoid a disconcerting and humiliating scene. Our black companion was obviously our equal: In the ensuing months, I barely cleared the hurdles of officer training, whereas the other two washed out after four weeks; Jim alone breezed through the course. We should all have been proud of his company, instead of threatening him with an ostracism born of racist superstitions. In the end, we all slept well; Jim's skin turned out to be colorfast, and the next morning we met at breakfast as if nothing had happened.

We reached Washington, D.C., where we had to change to a local train for Accotink, Virginia: the railhead of Fort Belvoir, south of the Mason-Dixon line. As soon as we boarded, the conductor directed Jim to the car reserved for blacks. I should have foreseen this—I do not know whether Jim had—but I had not. I made a dreadful row. I refused to let Jim leave us, explaining to the conductor that we were traveling on one ticket, that we were all wearing the same uniform and preparing to fight the same war (if given half a chance), and that we would stay together. Without consulting my fellow travelers, I gave the rattled man but one choice: Let us stay where we were, or send all four of us to the Jim Crow car. The conductor obviously was as unprepared for this confrontation as I had been for the conditions that gave rise to it; he was outnumbered and gave in. I savored my triumph for the remainder of the short trip. If we were at war with bigotry, then we could not tolerate it in our own ranks. It was that simple.

We reached camp without further incident and were assigned to barracks in the OCS area. As soon as I saw where Jim had put his bag, I picked the bunk next to him. After placing his belongings in his footlocker, he sat down on my bed and said, "I know you meant well, but I wish you hadn't done what you did on the train."

"Why on earth not?" I exclaimed, jolted out of my self-satisfaction.

"I don't want to be where I am not wanted. The people in the Jim Crow car are good enough for me," he answered.

"But they shouldn't be there either," I protested.

"But they are, and you have no idea what a miserable ride I had to Fort Belvoir, with everybody staring and smirking at me. It may have pleased you to get your way, but it was no picnic for me."

I could see his point and apologized, halfheartedly, for exposing him to an ordeal he then considered more painful than segregation. Indeed, it had not occurred to me to ask him what *he* wanted. Still, what should one do? "Should I just accept that you be treated the way my mother is being treated by the Germans?" I asked. "I am afraid that would be asking too much of me."

We talked on until lights out. The fact was, of course, that riding separately was the least of Jim's troubles. In Chicago, where he had been born and raised, he was not forced to go to the back of the bus but was still subject to heartbreaking injustice. He had graduated from college with a degree in engineering, yet when he applied for employment commensurate with his education, the answer inevitably was, "Sorry, boy, that's a white man's job." He might acquire all the degrees in academe; he would still end up sweeping the floor. At last I had met a black man on equal terms, not the maid or the shoeshine boy, and it began to dawn on me what it meant to be black in the land of the free. I had found something new to fight for, but not on the beaches of Normandy.

In the months that ensued, Jim and I were too busy to continue our dialogue. I seem to recall that we once had a beer together in the OCS PX. According to regulations, he should have tramped to the other end of camp to the only exchange facility reserved for "colored" troops, but no one bothered us. I planned to get married after graduation and wanted to invite Jim to my wedding, but I had learned my lesson on the Accotink train. If he accepted my invitation, he would probably be a wallflower at the white reception, where nobody would know or want to know him. Although I was confident that the Morrisons would not turn him away, I was equally certain that he would sense their discomfort at his presence. So I suppressed my impulse to invite him.

After the commissioning ceremony, Jim and I went our separate ways. Seven years later we passed each other on the campus of the University of Chicago (my favorite place for retrieving past friendships). We both started, stopped, and confirmed the other's identity. Then we took up where we had left off. He was on his way to a brilliant career. But that is a story he must tell. We, and our families, became friends for life, and that is all that remains to be said.

The chain of events leading to my wedding began several months before the army sent me to OCS. Since Camp Ellis, where I was stationed after basic training, was only two hundred miles from Chicago, I was able to spend many weekends with the Morrisons in the windy city. On Saturday afternoons I would cadge a ride with a hospitable noncommissioned officer who lived in Peoria, board an express train—the Rock Island "Rocket"—and reach Union Station before nightfall. Sunday evening, a Greyhound bus returned me to camp in time for Monday reveille.

On one of these weekends, as I finished lacing my freshly shined boots and was sitting back, watching the hands of the living-room clock approach the moment of departure, the door opened and Florence entered the room. She was a tall, slim girl with brown curly hair, hazel eyes, and a firm chin. We had barely time to introduce ourselves before I had to leave. After Paul and I had entered the military service, this lovely young woman, Florence Brandow, a third-year undergraduate at the University of Chicago, had replaced me as the object of the Morrisons' penchant for good works. Marian was her supervisor on the night shift at *Time-Life*'s subscription department, and Florence accepted the invitation to cut her expenses and mitigate the pressures of a crowded working life by moving into Paul's and my abandoned quarters. This arrangement had relegated me to the living-room sofa during my weekend visits, but since Florence usually spent her free time with a married sister, we had never met.

Two weeks later, I came home on my first two-week furlough and found that Florence's work schedule was not conducive to further acquaintance. She had classes to attend, and at four in the afternoon went to work, returning at midnight. I roamed the city in the daytime and was usually asleep when she came home. On one of my excursions, however, I bought two tickets to an afternoon concert of the Chicago symphony. I waited for her that evening and invited her to go with me. After expressing what I remember as minimal reservations about cutting classes—no cardinal sin at Chicago, as I have already indicated—she agreed. The orchestra, then under the somewhat uninspired and short-lived stewardship of Désiré Defauw, led off with the Benvenuto Cellini Overture by Berlioz. Then Piatigorsky played the Saint-Saëns First Cello concerto, a war horse he rode with easy grace. I have forgotten the rest of the program because during its second half I was completely absorbed by my companion. After the performance we went to a bar on Randolph Street—Gimbel's—and then I took Florence to work. My heart's rapture transcended Chicago's sodden air; the bus became a magic carpet, and dreary Cermak Road, where we alighted, a province of heaven.

Two days later I asked Florence to marry me. I was twenty-two and she was twenty. Neither of us owned much besides the clothes on our backs, and I could not even truly claim them. She was the youngest child of Swedish immigrants who had come to America at the turn of the century for reasons as compelling and desperate as my own. Her father had grown up on a tenant farm whose exhausted acres provided an excess of back-breaking work and too little food to sustain a large family. When he was eighteen he, too, ran for his life. I had escaped from terror, he from hunger.

Florence very sensibly resisted my proposal. She objected that we barely knew each other, which was of course true, but she did not squelch my hopes. Instead, she skipped more classes, and I was never asleep when she returned from work. On our last evening before my return to camp, we dined in a cozy French restaurant on North Michigan Avenue. It was November 1, 1943. Afterwards we ambled past elegant shop windows to the water tower, and there, in the biting wind of approaching winter, she met me halfway and agreed to our engagement. Years later, she confessed she was too cold for further resistance.

I returned to Camp Ellis, to my morning reports and my service records. Each day, after I closed my office, I stayed at the company typewriter to give vent to my love and my happiness. Florence's responses to my letters matched my efforts. I also communicated my honorable intentions to her mother, who answered promptly and kindly. She warned me that we came from different worlds, but left the decision to her daughter.

After my successful visit to the selection board for OCS, we decided to get married following my graduation. On September 6, after being dubbed an officer at Fort Belvoir's Post Theater No. 2, I returned to Chicago, where on September 8 Florence and I took our vows. Although neither of us had any strong religious attachment, we shared a craving for ceremony and a respect for the feelings of Florence's pious Swedish-Lutheran mother. On a golden autumn day, we were married in the university's Hilton Chapel by a clergyman of her family's denomination. Paul's father substituted as best man for his son, who was already in England with the 8th Air Force. My American family and Florence's, as well as a few friends, helped us eat our wedding cake in the cloisters surrounding the chapel.

After a week's honeymoon, I departed for my first commissioned assignment, Camp Rucker, Alabama. Florence followed a few weeks later, and we established our first household in a one-room kitchenette apartment in Ozark, just outside the camp, where the owner's wife confessed to Florence that my "cute accent" sent pleasant shivers down her spine. But my life became so unpredictable, and special assignments and transfers followed in such rapid succession, that we decided in December, 1944, that it would be best for Florence to return to Chicago and her job. Months later, in March, 1945, I joined her on my last leave before going overseas, in another one-room apartment, the place I would now think of as home while being stationed in Europe. Sixteen months would elapse before we would be reunited. This was the most miserable time of our lives; yet we were more fortunate than many war couples, who suffered longer separations—for some, permanent ones.

But we came out of it together. At the outset, our marriage violated every commonsense prescription for success. We were of different nationalities, came from different social origins, and were raised according to different religious precepts. Finally, ours was a hasty wartime decision, followed by a long separation. On the surface it might appear that a checking account, which usually ran dry before the next payday, was all we had in common—our only worldly possession for years to come.

Actually, we were drawn together by important common experiences. Even if she had not gone through it herself, my wife easily entered the emotional world of the uprooted, in which so much of her parents' life had been spent. She had been raised in a small, western Pennsylvania town in which class distinctions were, in part at least, determined by nationality. The town was run by an indigenous petty patriciate—the insurance agents, physicians, politicians, and store managers—while emigrant families toiled and spun in relative obscurity. Florence was also troubled by dim memories, supplemented by parental accounts, of cross burnings on the lawns of Catholics and some foreign-born families in her neighborhood. As in my case, these experiences had rendered her intolerant of intolerance.

There was, therefore, more than enough fight in both of us to rise above the predictable liabilities threatening our relationship. We were each on our own when we met, and, in a way, marriage began our adult life. What followed belonged to us; with every passing year we had more at stake, even before our children were born, so that giving up was unthinkable. At the outset of our marriage we hardly knew each other, but each of us turned out as the other had hoped. As we grew older, we continued to change in unison. Quarrels never assumed critical importance; the interference of third persons could not lessen our devotion. In retrospect it looks easy. So long as one understands how empty life would be without it, marriage will work.

X   MY RETURN TO EUROPE

My first orders after graduation from OCS sent me and eight classmates to the 1298th Engineer Combat Battalion, a unit as new as our gold bars. The commanding officer, a Major Landry from New Orleans, took one look at my record and appointed me battalion adjutant. I still wielded no deathly weapon, merely a fountain pen to sign what others had typed. But I was satisfied with this assignment. It gave me time to adjust to my new rank; running headquarters and keeping its records was a familiar task. In time I even convinced my sergeant major, a grizzled, thirty-year veteran named Volz, that I understood what I was signing and that I knew the rules as well as he did. My job also gave me the unexpected opportunity to cut short my association with the Army Corps of Engineers, where a person with my background hardly belonged.

The course of my army service dramatically changed one day when a request came across my desk to list all officers of the command who could speak German. The answer was brief: I was the only one. At the time I attached no significance to the inquiry. Throughout the war the army attempted to establish an adequate inventory of its rapidly increasing resources in numbers and skills. It might commission a manually inept individual like me in the Army Corps of Engineers, but it never gave up finding better ways of using my talents. Just after Christmas, at the height of the Battle of the Bulge, a telegram arrived telling me to report to the military intelligence training center at Camp Ritchie, Maryland. These orders, delivered without security classification by Western Union messenger, included instructions to keep my destination secret.

My new station seemed more like a resort than a military post. The wooded hills north of Hagerstown inclined one to sit back and enjoy the scenery rather than ponder matters of life and death. But the large and unusually literate and competent teaching staff kept one's mind on the grim business at hand. The inmates of the installation formed a fairly select company. Master's degrees cut no ice here either; they were commonplace. Many of my contemporaries at Camp Ritchie subsequently became brilliant academics and conspicuous public servants. Henry Kissinger figures among Ritchie alumni, and as recently as 1984, I discovered that one of our instructors, Lieutenant Dollibois, a Luxembourger, had become Ronald Reagan's ambassador to the country of his birth. For a time we were once again students, learning everything possible about the German army, regularly viewing captured German training films and newsreels, analyzing the intelligence value of German newspapers and other current publications, and—in my case—training in the interrogation of prisoners. Curiously, however, the curriculum included neither European nor German history, nor the analysis of Continental economic or political institutions. Our aptitudes were harnessed to contribute to military operations, not to decide Germany's long-term fate.

At the end of the two-month course, I was put in charge of the Interrogation of Prisoners of War (IPW) Team 221, consisting of one warrant officer and four noncommissioned officers, and sent to Europe. Most of our transport consisted of the 17th Airborne Division, which, like us, arrived too late to engage the enemy. Because of the disproportionate percentage of officers among us, the majority on board christened us the "Hollywood Battalion"; it would have been more fitting to call us the "battalion of accents." Even my little contingent displayed a colorful diversity: two Germans, one Romanian, one Frenchman—all with brogues to match—and one linguistic whiz from Philadelphia, who, besides other languages, spoke Italian so flawlessly (without ever having visited Italy) that natives of that country invariably mistook him for a Milanese.

After a week at sea, we docked at Greenock in the Firth of Clyde, famous as the birthplace of James Watt, and a free French naval base during World War II. We were not given time to explore this historic port but were rushed to a waiting train. How different from my last entry to the British Isles! No passport inspection, no suspicious official inquiring about my means of support. As soon as the train was full, the whistle blew, and we were off on a journey spanning the length of the United Kingdom. Night fell as we reached the southern border of Scotland. Soldiers learn to take their rest anywhere, and I snoozed long and deeply. When I awoke, it was light and the train had stopped. Bleary-eyed, I looked out the window. The station sign read "Highbury." Before realizing the time, the day, and the circumstance, I jumped out of my seat and rushed to the compartment door. Highbury is the section of London where the Arsenal Football Stadium stands, where eight years before I had occasionally watched the home games of England's finest soccer team. Fortunately, I recovered full consciousness before I made an unscheduled, unauthorized descent from the troop train. This time there was no noisy crowd pressing toward the stadium entrance, only the silent desolation wrought by countless German air raids.

The train moved, through more London ruins, back into the countryside until we reached our destination: Southampton. Here we spent two days encamped on the outskirts of the city. Spring was rampant, and English gardens were beginning to unfold their annual glory. From our tent doors we watched endless processions of Flying Fortresses on their way to and from Germany. The skyways were never empty.

I spent much of the time walking the streets of the Southampton suburb near our tent city, talking to its cordial inhabitants. Back "home" (this is how I thought of America by then), most civilians near military bases tended to be cool, if not downright unfriendly, and for good reason: too many soldiers, too many bars, too many prostitutes. Here I saw only smiling faces. I asked one woman, whose gardening I had interrupted with a request for directions, "Aren't you tired of all this military traffic around here?" She responded cheerfully, "Oh, no, we're glad to have you," and went back to her work.

That same evening we were marched to another boat that was to carry us to France. Most of the Channel ports on the other side were still in German hands, and we received extensive instructions on how to respond should a submarine attack. The enemy, though nearing collapse, was still taken seriously. Excitement, not fear, kept me awake, and I spent the night on deck, watching Europe coming closer. Instead of the enthusiastic Nazi youth with whom I had passed my last crossing in 1937, a French lieutenant, an Algerian named Abdessalam, shared my vigil. We exchanged life stories and recounted to each other the events that had brought us to this same spot. Finally, we watched Le Havre appear through the morning mist.

We docked and in the ensuing hubbub did not even have time to say good-bye.

Shortly, the "Hollywood Battalion" claimed another train, this one in much worse condition than the tidy conveyance on which we had traveled through Scotland and England. Broken seats, broken windows, and toilets *hors concours* bore witness to France's pitiful condition in 1945. Although our English journey had given the impression that there were still schedules and ways of meeting them, the trip from Le Havre to Paris took thirty-six hours. During frequent stops curious civilians crowded the tracks, usually to buy cigarettes. We talked to children, many of whom looked stunted, appearing years younger than their actual age. At night we pulled black-out blinds over glassless windows, although it must have been several months since a hostile aircraft had attacked any objective, stationary or moving, in any part of France. It was surprisingly cold, and we huddled in blankets. Protracted idleness cast out sleep, and I remember crouching in the dark reading a succession of Georges Simenon detective novels by the surreptitious gleam of a flashlight. It was my first acquaintance with the work of this Belgian Balzac, who not only wrote *romans policiers* populated by credible characters but turned the spirit and substance of any environment into a compelling tale. (I am thinking particularly of *The Bottom of the Bottle,* a saga of alcoholism and death on the banks of the Rio Grande.)

Eventually we reached Paris, entering the city of light through one of its darkest gates: the Gare St. Lazare. Fortunately, the depression evoked by this smoke-soiled antechamber of Hades was quickly dispelled as our olive drab buses rolled through Baron Haussmann's avenues to the elegant suburb of Le Vesinet, where the military intelligence service had established its Continental headquarters. Paris in the spring compensated for all the battles I had missed. My team and I were assigned rooms in a villa on a quiet street lined with majestic chestnut trees and already expeditiously renamed in honor of General De Gaulle. Our stay turned out to be brief, but long enough to allow me some days on the town, inhaling its atmosphere, rubbing shoulders with its people, and drinking watery aperitifs and cups of pungent chicory at a succession of sidewalk cafés. In the evening I joined the line before a *guichet* at the opera, where reduced tickets were offered to members of the Allied armies. Behind me waited a middle-aged French captain with his motherly looking wife, and after a while I realized they were talking about me and my uniform. When the man explained to his spouse that the towers on my lapels stood for the same branch of service as that to which he belonged, I summoned my courage and introduced myself. A pleasant exchange ensued, and by the time our turn at the window came, we decided to try to purchase seats together. We succeeded and shared a corner in the same box.

As the lights dimmed in this enchanted palace, I felt transported into the nineteenth century and would not have been surprised to see the door open once more to admit Napoleon III, surrounded by the false glitter of his entourage of parvenus. The day's attraction suited the eve of German surrender: Berlioz' *Damnation of Faust,* symbolic reenactment of the consequences of a Teutonic prototype's pact with the devil. Although the composer had been the laureate music maker of the July Monarchy, he had died a year before the Second Empire was overthrown. His music harmonized, therefore, with the time of this performance and the gilded splendors of the emperor's own musical theater.

The orchestra under Louis Fourestier attacked the score with patriotic enthusiasm, and the crowd frequently interrupted the performance with explosive applause. (Years later I learned from Jacques Barzun's annotated translation of Berlioz' memoirs that the composer had all but given up on hearing the work competently performed, until he attended its German premiere in Weimar under the direction of Franz Liszt.) The voices that evening faltered on occasion, and so did the lighting, but no one minded. The music orchestrated the history of the moment; a great Frenchman spoke to his liberated countrymen and made them forget their recent humiliation.

My companions, Captain and Mme Mayer, were delighted by my enthusiasm and after the performance invited me to their apartment in Montparnasse. The arrival of an American created a stir in the neighborhood and resulted in an *ad hoc* open house, lasting until well after midnight. People quizzed me endlessly about "my country," and I was in the mood to satisfy their curiosity. I remember one young man in particular, a tenor at the Opéra Comique, who could not hear enough about America's musical life. When I finally took my leave, quite sober, but completely exhausted from hours of conversation in a language I had until then only known from the classroom, I asked the Mayers to have dinner with me the next evening, at the officer's mess in Le Vesinet. I apologized for the plain GI cuisine, but they dug enthusiastically into the hearty fare; no doubt the education in austerity provided by the past five years had taught them to appreciate quantity at the expense of culinary sophistication.

After dessert, Madame rummaged in her purse and emerged with a present for my wife: a bottle of genuine Chanel No. 5. As we lingered over another cup of coffee, she suddenly looked me squarely in the eye, blushed, and finally asked, "Are you really an American?" Although I thought I knew the source of her curiosity, I responded, "Why do you ask?" Frenchmen are often perplexed by my accent, not exactly German—I have learned to avoid the customary Teutonic errors of pronunciation—but hardly Anglo-Saxon. Her query sprang from a different source, however. "Americans either laugh or smile all the time," she said. "You never do." This had never occurred to me, and since I felt that I was among friends, I told her who I was and why I possibly had less cause for incessant merriment than my countrymen. I walked the Mayers back to the train, and as we strolled through the quiet suburban avenues, I brought my chronicle to its present state of suspension. Like the story I am now telling, it was unfinished, and would remain so until I knew how my mother and brother had survived the war.

I saw these French friends once more during a subsequent visit to Paris. The captain invited me to inspect his company, and then brought his wife and me to a delightful restaurant in the country where time seemed to have stood still or—more likely—the black market had helped preserve the splendors of the local cuisine. For a while Mme Mayer and I exchanged letters, but then we lost contact—largely because I had less and less to write as the protracted separation from my wife numbed and depressed me.

Before I could become addicted to the pleasures and treasures of Paris, my team and I were sent to report to the 12th Army Group in Wiesbaden. It was early May when we left Paris, driving north through Reims and the French Ardennes into Belgium. Peace was in the air, and in every town we were greeted with cheers and pelted with flowers. Since our little group had played absolutely no part in the recent liberation of the region, we considered ourselves unworthy of these tributes and never halted to savor them. It was almost with relief that we crossed the borders of Germany and entered the silent melancholy of a defeated land. Here the spring sun shone just as brightly, but the people merely stared: Only the children waved, briefly, before angry mothers slapped their hands.

The intelligence section in Wiesbaden sent us on to the 106th Infantry Division, whose command post was at Bad Ems, an idyllic location. This quiet resort with its healing springs, said to cure respiratory and digestive complaints, as well as female infertility, had been discovered by the Romans and operated continuously since the fourteenth century. It was here that Bismarck drafted and sent the famous telegram whose provocative text prompted the people of Prussia in July, 1870, to clamor for war against the insolent French. Now, seventy-five years later, we saw the end of another war about to undo the work of Germany's founding father. Bad Ems was a German town the war had passed by. In this pleasant, untroubled setting we set to work, playing our own infinitesimal part in the liquidation of Hitler's empire.

According to a yellowed separation qualification record in my files, my military duties during the next fifteen months consisted of three related activities. First, I "supervised and participated in the collection of military intelligence through interrogation of prisoners of war." Second, I "screened prisoners to find out their political affiliations and segregated those who could not be released," and I also "investigated war crimes and questioned prisoners in an effort to find participants in [such] crimes." Finally, I "investigated black-market activities among prisoners."

My training had only prepared me for the first of these chores. The rest I learned by doing, since the course of history proved too swift for the curriculum planners of the War Department. Not only was the war all but over when I finally reported for duty with the 424th Infantry Regiment of the 106th Division, but that unit had months before taken such a beating on the battlefields of Belgium that it was moved out of the line and assigned to the care and feeding of a rising tide of prisoners of war.

Before my unit went to work, however, I was authorized to requisition living quarters for my men and myself. This task led me to my first face-to-face encounter with the enemy. At the city hall, an intimidated and obsequious German official promptly offered me a house owned, he told me, by a local party functionary who had disappeared. He phoned the man's daughter to tell her that she and her mother would have to evacuate their home at once. But the intended evictee turned out to be less compliant than either of us had anticipated. The young woman appeared almost at once and explained that her invalid mother could not be moved. While directing this protest at her fellow townsman, she glared at me. I soon wearied of this unproductive quarrel and joined the conversation. That put a stop to the lady's harangue. Challenging authority in a uniform required more courage than she could muster. Actually, I was in no conquering mood. I merely wanted to look at the house and its aged inhabitant and then decide her fate. Subdued and silent, the recalcitrant occupant led us to her residence, where her mother presented, indeed, a rather pathetic sight, frightened and wizened, and I decided not to press my claim. Next we were sent to the dwelling of a former mayor. The inhabitants presented a similar problem: the husband's whereabouts unknown, his wife and mother this time meeting the threat of expulsion with tears. Anxious to end my search, but unwilling to become a scourge of women and children—this household also included a three-year-old boy—I told the family they could live in a large carriage house in the courtyard and look after the premises during our daily absence. The city official objected that this was against regulations, and indeed it was, since troops at that time were not allowed to "fraternize" with German civilians. But I told him to let me assume responsibility for the enforcement of army regulations, and my men and I moved in that afternoon. We intended to live there, not strike up a friendship with the owner's family.

I allowed myself but one indulgence: before nightfall I had my men paint and affix a sign to the front of the house. It read, "Das wir hier arbeiten verdanken wir dem Führer" ("That we work here, we owe to the führer"). This inscription had surmounted countless construction sites after 1933, to remind Germans of the speedy inroads Nazi public works and rearmament projects were making on unemployment. Sitting in the evening by an open window, I heard passersby stop and read the placard. Nobody was amused. "But the Führer is dead," one of them commented in a puzzled voice. "What do they mean?" said another. "Hitler did not ask them to come here." One white-haired old man looked at the ironic statement a long time, shook his head, said with a voice of infinite resignation, "Ja, das ist schon wahr" ("To be sure, that is true"), and hobbled on.

The next day we began screening tens of thousands of Germans of all ages and ranks. This unkempt swarm of defeated enemy, confined to an open field surrounded by barbed wire—between the town of Ingelheim on the Rhine and the village of Sprendlingen—had been put to digging their latrine trenches, which, apart from a gaggle of soup kitchens, constituted the only "camp facilities." Here we toiled day and night to separate the innocent sheep from the Nazi wolves. Our goal was not only to keep the predators entrapped but to reduce as speedily as possible the number of mouths to be fed. It was especially urgent to return as many of this pathetic multitude to their former homes in what was to become the Russian zone of occupation.

This proved more difficult than we had anticipated. We discovered that the average German soldier's home address was not always easy to determine. Families had been evacuated or bombed out, or had simply disappeared. Although our advance units were still encamped on the banks of the Elbe, and the boundaries of the zones of occupation had not been made public, every German seemed to know how his country was to be divided among the victors, and most would not admit that they lived in the region assigned to the Red Army. Then there were the inhabitants of regions annexed to Germany since 1938 and now about to be separated again, as well as of those provinces east of the Oder, already claimed and occupied by Poland. Most men who passed my desk claimed Bavaria as home, making that southern state easily the most populous in Germany. Many prisoners from the eastern borderlands, Polonized or re-Polonized, suddenly decided to opt for Polish citizenship. This preference required the endorsement of a mobile Polish repatriation commission before we could discharge such individuals to the jurisdiction of Germany's eastern neighbor. We managed, nevertheless, to thin these ranks rapidly. Two-and-a-half-ton army trucks carted load after load of Germans to discharge centers or, if their rank and background placed them in one of the automatic arrest categories, to more permanent and, we hoped, secure detention camps. Those under arrest included officers of all services and paramilitary party formations above the rank of lieutenant colonel, party officials, and all ranks of the SS, as well as individuals whom we had reason to suspect of subversive intentions. Given the speed at which we had to work, this last became an extremely flexible category, including everyone we suspected of lying but could not grill long enough to determine the truth.

We found few admitted supporters of national socialism. Even so high a party functionary as the deputy *Gauleiter* of the Nazi party in

Saxony attempted to convince us that his political rise was entirely due to circumstances beyond his control. Everyone, whatever his role in the regime, claimed to have been the victim of irresistible coercion. The participle *gezwungen* ("forced") and the noun *Zwang* ("duress") became the buzzwords of the moment, while the coercers seemed to have disappeared from the face of the earth.

In long, almost daily letters to my wife, I described my feelings resulting from this encounter with a homeless nation. I had been trained to look for manifest villainy. Instead, I found a spectacle of pathos and disaster on a bewildering scale. I vacillated between hostility and pity. In May, 1945, I reported:

> Only slowly can I gain a coherent picture of the German soldiery that we have gathered in such astronomical quantities during the last few weeks. Ages vary from 16 to 60. Some boys have barely changed voices; some men are grizzled and seamed by age as well as by many years of suffering. The kids are generally on the verge of tears; some are ill from exposure. Yesterday I was called to one corner of the camp where I found a fourteen-year-old boy, unconscious, and sweating with fever, whom I had at once taken to a field hospital. Another was so unspeakably filthy that I took him to our house for his first bath since God knows when, so that we could at least see what he looked like.

At the beginning of a day's work, I often stopped by the small tent near the camp's improvised medical station that sheltered the remains of those who had not survived through the night. Ironically, it was a German *Oberstarzt* (a colonel in the Luftwaffe's medical service) who attempted to cheer me by pointing out that any normal town our camp's size (more than twenty thousand) would have to bury some dead every day and that our mortality rate, especially under prevailing conditions, was unbelievably low. This medicine man was in high spirits for other reasons. A specialist in venereal diseases, he had found the war a godsend for his research interests. "In peacetime," he explained, "we had hardly any cases of syphilis. But since 1940, I have seen the most interesting varieties, and, for the first time, in significant numbers. Believe me, it has been an extraordinarily interesting time." I had never had much acquaintance with death; the pain I felt when I saw the tent with its shrouded, lifeless forms was not allayed by the assertion that the war had been a boon to science.

Yet, as one of my letters recalls, "pity [was] replaced by contempt" as the day wore on. "The Germans are mighty poor losers. They lack dignity in defeat." That observation reflected another confusion. I had expected unregenerate hatred, and was not prepared for the tide of self-pity and self-abasement surrounding me. Few of our captives would assume any responsibility for their participation in recent events. Almost everyone denied the past. "The führer is dead, lead us to a new führer," seemed to be the prevalent attitude. Countless German air-force officers inquired where they could enlist in the United States Air Force; members of other services likewise asked after new careers with the Allied armies. Even worse was the alacrity with which prisoners ratted on one another. Many an arrest of ours resulted, not from our modest inquisitorial skill, but from revelations volunteered by prisoners anxious to ingratiate themselves. I thought back to 1933, when denunciation likewise flourished but served a different master.

Since we were stationed little more than twenty-five miles from my birthplace, I used my first free day to drive to Frankfurt. The excursion deepened my muddled state of mind. Physical destruction made much of the city unrecognizable, and I lost my way again and again. Finally, like other disoriented soldiers, I followed the signs leading to Allied headquarters in the former administration building of the I.G. Farben combine, one of my father's previous employers. Here the levels of ruination subsided, and I was able to make my way northwestward to the neighborhood where I spent my childhood. Little had changed. Only one house on my street had suffered bomb damage. It belonged to the parents of my friend (and fellow Aryan) Fritz Ewald, less deserving of such misfortune than almost anyone else in the block. What a symbol of the injustice wrought by the cruel randomness of modern weaponry! I walked from house to house, inspecting the names on each door. They had not changed. But what of their occupants? I was overwhelmed by a desire to see a friendly face. On a neighboring street I rang the bell at the house of Professor Hillmann, an old Social Democrat. His married daughter, Ille, answering my ring, appeared startled at the sight of a uniformed stranger but then, recognizing me, engulfed me in her arms. I was invited in and asked to join the family for afternoon-*Ersatz*—coffee. The ensuing conversation, however, did not give me the mental respite I sought, even though other members of the family bade me welcome with equal warmth. They asked about my mother and brother, about whom I could tell them little. Ille's husband and her son, who was about my age, were both missing. Her spouse had written so recently that she could, with good reason, assume him to be with the German forces that had just recently surrendered in Italy. Their son had disappeared in Normandy. After these revelations there was silence. Then the professor, who was old enough to remember Bismarck, raised his voice in solemn protest against Germany's occupation. As he saw it, Hitler had come close to destroying Germany; now the Allies were about to finish the job, instead of providing conditions for a meaningful revival of self-government.

Hillmann's children seemed less inclined to mourn the passing of a Germany they knew largely from the failures of both democracy and dictatorship. Closest to sharing the father's hostile attitude toward the Allies was his oldest daughter, later to become a Communist city councillor in Frankfurt. She accused the victors of suppressing the inevitable social revolution by restoring, or perpetuating, Germany's authoritarian capitalism. As I prepared to leave, Ille, the most optimistic of the three, put her hand on my shoulder and said: "You know, you have to come back. We need you now." It was a measure of my own transformation since leaving college that this possibility had never occurred to me. To anyone else I would have said honestly: "Never. That is out of the question." I might even have added, "I could never ask my American wife to live among Germans." But face to face with these decent, forthright people who had stood by their convictions while I enjoyed the safety of an American haven, I felt it was my turn to hide my feelings behind an enigmatic silence. I did point out that it would not do for a collection of carpetbaggers from overseas to guide Germany's future (making sure that they understood what a carpetbagger was), and took my leave. I did not have the courage to visit them again, wanting no further discussion of my mission to save Germany.

At the Hillmanns I learned that the bombed-out Ewald family had occupied, since the destruction of their home, an apartment nearby and that their two sons, both fighting on the eastern front, had likewise not been heard from. However, I had had enough neighborhood reunion for one day and, rather than visit the Ewalds, returned to my own GI world.

In my childhood Frankfurt, with its landmarks, its dialect, and its distinctive foods, had been my universe. It came as a shock to me now that the sight of this battered world of my youth did not evoke more sorrow or sympathy in my heart. It was as if I had been awakened from a long sleep amidst surroundings I could at first not connect with my previous state of consciousness. I was watching something familiar but beyond the ken of the present.

Or so it seemed on that particular afternoon. A need still persisted, however, to close the gap between past and present that this visit had generated. In the ensuing months I seized every opportunity to retrace my steps and seek out former friends. One Sunday I called at the home of Rainer, my old classmate who had given me the biography of Frederick the Great when I left Germany for the first time. A maid ushered me into the drawing room, where I was welcomed by his father. There followed the now-customary chronicle of tragedy. Rainer's older brother, Wolfgang, had been killed on the eastern front. Of his two sisters, the older was happily married and apparently well. The younger, and the most promising intellect among the four children, had married a Jew with whom she had emigrated to Brazil. There she had died while giving birth to her second child. Nor had my host's Austrian-born wife been spared from persecution. After the German invasion of Yugoslavia, she had sent to a friend a letter decrying the "barbaric bombardment" of Belgrade. The missive was read by the censors, and she was arrested and imprisoned. Only after prolonged and desperate efforts had her husband succeeded in getting her free, and then taken her to a family cottage in the Alps, where she presently lived. Rainer had escaped military service because of a residual limp following a childhood bout with infantile paralysis and now lived in Weimar; his father hoped he would return to Frankfurt before the Russians claimed that city as part of their zone of occupation.

The home I was visiting still exuded the affluence that had so impressed me as a child. It was still managed by a housekeeper and two maids. Dinner, which the father insisted I share, likewise revealed a bountiful kitchen. As we sat over coffee—real coffee this time—Rainer's father must have sensed my wonderment at a household so untouched by more than a decade of rationing, for he haltingly offered an explanation for his continued material well-being. (He knew, of course, that my father had died, and must have had some idea of what might have befallen my mother). He hinted that his pest-control firm, Institut für Schädlingsbekämpfung, had been busy during the war. This was understandable since war heightened the danger of disease. But at this point the conversation took a terrifying turn. "It is true, by the way," my host continued, "what many people tell you. We, too, did our work without knowing what went on behind the scene. Why I actually visited Auschwitz, without ever realizing what was happening there."

"My God," I exclaimed, "what were you doing in Auschwitz?"

"Disease control," he replied in a businesslike tone. "We constructed some hygienic facilities. We provided delousing apparatus for the prisoners. An exemplary installation, believe me."

The ground seemed to shake under me. I do not remember how I made my sudden, confused departure. The family of my closest childhood friend, devoted neighbors whose treatment of my parents the advent of Hitler had not affected, were at that moment, when I was speaking to the father, subsisting on the profits from the sale of Zyklon-B, a gas, as we know today, used for more than killing lice!

Only my third reunion with Frankfurt friends was an unclouded renewal of friendship. On my next visit I ran into my missing friend Fritz on the street. "Jesus Christ," he called out, "look what we have here." Then he added with a chuckle, "Let's go down to the meadow, where you won't get caught fraternizing." We descended a staircase from the street to the green open space still separating, in 1945, my native suburb of Eschersheim from Ginnheim—a section known in my childhood for the excellence of its hard cider. We sat by the brook, whose newts had annually replenished the decimated population of our aquariums, and relived our respective military careers. His turned out to have been a great deal more interesting and harrowing than mine. As a graduate of an academic preparatory school, he had been tagged for officer's training, but—so he believed quite reasonably—because he was also a good Catholic and no member of the Hitler Youth, his devotion to führer and country had been tested by three-and-one-half years of continuous service on the Russian front. At the end of the war he had found himself in Czechoslovakia, the commander of a company of semi-invalids. To obtain maximum benefit from the near-disabled, the German army in its dying days had grouped men with identical afflictions into infantry units, whose service limitations were uniform and therefore manageable. Fritz's last command was a *Magen Kompanie* (an outfit made up of men with stomach complaints). He and his men had finally surrendered to Czech partisans. As bad luck would have it, his tattered, bedraggled troop, just before its capture, had plundered an SS warehouse. There his men drew an overdue change of shirts, alas, all party brown rather than Wehrmacht gray. As a result, their captors believed them to be members of the hated Waffen-SS and decided to begin retribution by shooting the officers. Only the intervention of a Red Army major stopped the execution. Fritz was spared. The officer examined my friend, issued him a piece of paper indicating that he was a prisoner of war released from Russian captivity, and with a friendly kick in the behind sent him on his way home. Fritz had walked from the Czech border to Frankfurt. His older brother Herbert was less fortunate. Also a captive of the Russians, he would not return home until 1955.

I also learned from my old friend that many of our *Gymnasium* classmates had perished on various battlefields. Fritz verbally crossed off one after another from the register of the living. Then he wanted to hear about America and about officer training on our side; we sat for a couple of hours, talking as if we had never been separated, totally at ease, both glad to be alive, to have beaten the odds and, by our very survival, gotten the better of "them" once more.

Fritz, in turn, helped me locate other former family friends. He put me in touch with someone who knew our lawyer, Franz Calvelli-Adorno, for whom I had searched unsuccessfully since my first return to Frankfurt. Descended from Corsican immigrants, and son of a Jewish woman whose death preceded the rise of Hitler by many years, he had married Helene Mommsen, my mother's closest friend from her days at the University of Berlin. In 1933 Adorno had lost his judgeship and thereafter supported his family with violin lessons and such occasional legal work as came his way, including the stewardship of our inconsequential family fortune. Just before the war, he had succeeded in placing his oldest daughter and his only son with English families. Since our brief business correspondence after my father's death, I had lost contact with him.

I had gone to the Feldbergstrasse on Frankfurt's west side in search of the Adorno apartment only to find the entire block destroyed. The city hall and its records had suffered the same fate, and there was at the time no way of locating missing persons in this city of half a million. Fritz suggested that a neighbor, Count Lanskuronski, like Adorno a former judge, might know our lawyer's whereabouts. I remembered the countess from childhood: a strange, ungainly woman, always bundled in a long coat, regardless of the season, and invariably wearing a broad-brimmed, floppy hat. We children snickered when this strange apparition passed; we called her a witch, often—I am afraid—within her hearing. Now I was ushered into her husband's presence. She did not appear, much to my relief, and the dignified, bearded aristocrat listened to my concern. He, too, had lost touch with our friend but went to the phone immediately to make inquiries. He obviously assumed my search to be official, for I heard myself and Fritz—whom the count failed to recognize—referred to, respectfully, as "two American gentlemen" who wished to consult Dr. Calvelli-Adorno on urgent business. Whether the allusion to a nonexistent, weighty official purpose was a factor I do not know, but the call produced results. After he put down the receiver, the count informed us that the Adorno family was believed to be living in the town of Bensheim, near Heidelberg. Fritz, who had reacted to his own misidentification with mock solemnity, thanked his neighbor formally in both of our names.

With this information in hand, I proceeded to Heidelberg. Since my time for such expeditions was limited, I decided to combine the further search for the Adornos with a visit to my mother's *Doktorvater*, Gerhard Anschütz, for many years professor of constitutional law at the university. By now I had heard from my mother and received from her a letter with the request that it be delivered to her former mentor. They had remained friends long after she had received her doctorate in 1916, and I remembered him well from frequent visits to our home, in both Frankfurt and Berlin. This friendship had not suffered during the Nazi era; Anschütz' loyalty to his Jewish students was unflinching, and my mother was anxious for a renewal of this warm relationship.

Heidelberg, like Bad Ems, showed few marks of combat; only its bridges had been destroyed by retreating German troops. I found the professor's house with ease. I knew by now, of course, that the "Uncle Gerhard" of my childhood was a man of national as well as international eminence. I also knew that the events of decades just past had been as destructive of his work as they had been of the fortunes of his nation. The first volume of his classic commentary on the Prussian constitution had been published on the eve of World War I. The second volume never appeared. The revolution of 1918 had destroyed the political order it described. Subsequently, Anschütz had become the academic authority on the Weimar Constitution, the definitive version of his commentary appearing in February, 1933, one month after Hitler's accession to power. Once again, the pace of events had turned a monument to living law into a gravestone.

I had other, less personal reasons for wanting to visit my mother's teacher. I had not forgotten the letter in which Anschütz had, twelve years earlier, drawn a line between himself and the new order. On March 31, 1933, just a week after the Reichstag's passage of the enabling law that turned Germany into a dictatorship, he had petitioned the minister of education of the state of Baden to permit him to retire. This remarkable document found its way into the columns of the Frankfurt *Zeitung*; I have also found a carbon copy in the papers of my mother. It includes the following candid passage:

> My teaching assignment has primarily dealt with German Constitutional Law. I hope you will agree that this subject . . . demands of the instructor services which are both scholarly and political. It is the task of the teacher of constitutional law not only to transmit *knowledge* of Germany's fundamental law, but also to educate the student in accordance with the spirit and substance of the existing political order. This requires a high degree of intrinsic identification with that order. It is my duty . . . to confess that I cannot presently muster this [necessary degree of] regard for the new political laws emerging in Germany.

Anschütz' request was readily granted. No doubt Germany's new masters would sooner or later have rid themselves of this nettlesome critic. But one cannot help wondering whether a flood of such resignations, addressed to German state ministries of education in 1933, particularly in a society so respectful of academic authority, might not have slowed the tide of tyranny.

After what I had seen of Germany and the Germans in recent months, this memory inspired in me both reverence and diffidence as I entered the presence of the aged scholar. Nor was my respect for him diminished by what was a rather chilly, if not hostile, exchange. For a moment he stared grimly at my uniform—he obviously did not recognize me—and then asked curtly for the purpose of my visit. After I told him who I was and had given him my mother's letter, his countenance cleared a trifle, and he asked me to sit down. With some difficulty his arthritic hands opened the envelope and unfolded the letter it contained. During his perusal of the letter he nodded often, and an occasional rueful smile would briefly light up his seamed, ascetic countenance. The silence was punctuated by his intermittent growls of assent: "Well put . . . a beautiful thought . . . how true . . . yes, indeed," and so on.

When he finished reading and looked up, he seemed surprised to find me still in the room. He asked if I could wait while he wrote a brief answer he hoped I might forward to my mother, and I agreed, of course. After he enclosed his reply, once again painfully and laboriously, in an envelope, he did not, however, dismiss me. He asked me point-blank how it felt to stand shoulder to shoulder with the Soviet Union. How long would this alliance, so at cross-purposes with professed Anglo-Saxon war aims, last?

It was a familiar question, not only asked by Germans, and I had prepared not so much a reply as an admonition: He and his countrymen should not expect to capitalize on future conflicts between present allies. "Do you really think that I pray for such a terrifying eventuality?" he shot back indignantly. "How do you imagine Germany could profit from becoming the battlefield of the next war? What is there left for a country to capitalize on after it has ceased to exist?" He went on to repeat, with bitter eloquence, the sorrows that Professor Hillmann had voiced at the family coffee table some weeks earlier. Anschütz, however, transformed them into a history lesson unlike any I had ever received.

Anschütz was born in 1867. The unification of Germany coincided with his childhood; the dismissal of Bismarck in 1890 took place the year he completed his university education. He went on to become a critical but loyal citizen of the empire and rose to a professorship at the University of Berlin. In 1914 he was forty-seven years old—too old to join a war that did, however, claim the life of his firstborn. Five years later, Heidelberg colleagues, like the Weber brothers, Max and Alfred, enlisted him in the founding of the German Democratic party. Although he soon turned his back on party politics, his commitment to the republic was unreserved, expressed not only in the lecture hall but through service on numerous commissions charged to draft proposals for constitutional reform. The Nazi revolution ended his career, while the fraternal meeting of the United States and Red Army soldiers at Torgau on the Elbe spelled the end of his fatherland's existence. The family friend whom I was visiting had, according to his lights, become a man without a country. His world lay in ruins, and all he asked of the future was that it be brief.

We faced each other across his sturdy oak desk—denizens of different centuries. What he said was true, but what did it mean to me? I had talked to a latter-day Marius, contemplating not the ruins of Carthage but those of Rome. This patriarchal survivor had witnessed both birth and death of the Bismarckian state. I remembered the summer of my graduation from Washington and Lee, when Hitler seemed about to cap German unity with the conquest of the Continent. Within five years the meaning of the threescore and ten years preceding the fall of France had been turned upside down. The era of German preponderance had not materialized; Hitler had not succeeded Phillip II, Ludwig XIV, Metternich, or Disraeli as the arbiter of Europe's fate.

Anschütz also helped me see that my escape had saved me from sharing the fate of the Germans as well as the Jews of Europe. I had eluded another extermination—legal and political rather than physical, but no less final. There was nothing more to be said. Politely, we took leave of each other, and—needless to say—I was not invited to come back.

My search proceeded from Heidelberg to Bensheim, a short drive on the scenic road to Frankfurt known as the Bergstrasse. It was familiar territory, but I tracked down the Adornos only after seemingly endless inquiries. Franz, his wife Helene, and his father Louis welcomed me much more warmly than had my mother's old professor, and they asked me to stay as long as I liked. I felt a need to relax among friends and decided to remain the weekend. My companion on this trip was the oldest and most congenial member of my team, the Egyptologist Bernard von Bothmer, who was eager to push on to Marburg and a reunion with his mother and two sisters. We agreed that he would return for me Sunday evening.

Peace had released the Adorno household from some, but not all, strictures. The father's second wife, Jewish like Franz's mother, had just returned from Theresienstadt concentration camp. Outwardly, she seemed to have survived surprisingly well, but was found to be suffering from an inoperable cancer and died a few months after my visit. Franz had only recently emerged from hiding to be reunited with his wife and youngest daughter. They had heard from their two older children in England but probably would not see them soon. Visits in either direction were out of the question. German parents could not travel abroad at the time, and their children could not visit the American zone, whose occupiers had their hands full feeding the indigenous population. The English foster parents of the Adornos' children, furthermore, had come to love and regard these adopted youngsters as their own and were reluctant even to think about giving them up. Would there be a bitter legal confrontation with these good people who otherwise had a substantial claim to the family's gratitude? The parents' own future was up in the air.

Should they leave Germany or stay? Helene was embittered by her wartime experiences and felt alienated from a homeland that had ostracized her husband. She told me that one of their neighbors still listened at their door, incapable of understanding that the time for denouncing them to the authorities was past. Yet where would they go? Franz could not resume his legal career in the Anglo-Saxon realms of common law. As a musician he was not eminent enough to compete against the army of distinguished professionals who had preceded him into exile.

Nevertheless, I remember this weekend as a happy occasion. Years of separation had not lessened mutual attachments, and after my hosts had unburdened themselves, they wanted to hear about my mother and my own experiences. Time flew, and all too soon Bernard returned. (He was then a sergeant first class, but my friends addressed him formally and somewhat incongruously promoted him to "Herr Graf.")

These reunions with good friends softened my earlier hard, vindictive stance toward the long lines of "enemies" waiting to be "processed" into civilians or political prisoners. On the following Monday, I resumed my duties with more forbearance and charity. Tragedy was often the lot of the good and the wicked alike, and I tried harder to make distinctions and do more to lighten the burden of the former. I recall one episode in which these impulses rewarded me with another lifelong friendship.

One afternoon I was examining a dark-haired, swarthy young man of nineteen, whom I shall call Dieter Moeller. Among his effects were numerous photographs, not the usual mementos of girlfriends or family, but pictures of paintings, rather old-fashioned in subject matter and technique, mostly portraits. I asked about their provenance and learned they were his own work. Rummaging in his kit bag, he produced a series of pencil sketches, partly the result of imagination, partly scenes of camp life, with whose production he had whiled away the boredom of internment. His tools were primitive: a hard pencil worn with repeated whittlings to a thumb sized stub and sheets of toilet paper. I pulled up a chair and asked him to sit down and tell me more about the origins and development of his vocation. He spoke of his childhood in the Hessian village of Wittelsberg near Marburg, where his father was principal and his mother the only teacher of the village school. He had drawn and painted ever since he could remember, his only teacher being an old

215

man occupying a small studio nearby, a painter of landscapes, especially hunting scenes so popular in Wilhelm II's Germany and still sufficiently in fashion to earn him a decent living. Dieter's military service had put an end to this association and to his life's ambition until an air force general had become aware of his talents and saved him from further risk and frustration by creating for him the position of division painter. I had not realized how totally national socialism not only enslaved and regimented but isolated the German artist. Only my subsequent study of history revealed the wasting of German civilization under a regime that placed the artist at the mercy of the failed novelist Joseph Goebbels. Dieter had lived in a spiritual vacuum. Impressionists, expressionists, cubists, fauves, and dadaists were at most names: he had never seen any of their work. Albrecht Dürer was his idol; the painter and engraver's glory survived the barbarous interlude undimmed. Dieter was a prodigy, but painting as if art had not changed since the sixteenth century. Burning to return home and to his easel, he looked forward to a more open world and the opportunity to resume his arrested education.

I wanted to help him. Instead of merely giving him a clean bill of health and leaving him to languish in the prison compound, awaiting his bureaucratic turn for the next outgoing truck, I brought him to the prison headquarters tent, where I secured his immediate release. Then we left camp, and he spent the night at our house. The next morning, Saturday, Bernard and I went AWOL to take the young genius home. It was satisfying to surprise an ordinary German family by delivering its only son, from whereabouts unknown, to the front door. Dieter's mother begged me to stay, and her friendly insistence overcame my uneasiness about intruding upon the family reunion. (Bernard was only too willing to drop me and spend the weekend in Marburg with his family.)

Amidst the household's rejoicing, my new, liberated friend shed his uniform at once and took stock of the contents of his studio. This sanctum was off limits to everyone; only I had a temporary pass. Dieter assigned me a camp bed behind his easel, where he ordinarily slept, and I spent the rest of the afternoon sitting for my portrait. Frequent calls from downstairs, asking the local prodigy so unexpectedly returned to greet various village dignitaries arriving in rapid succession to welcome the neighborhood genius, went unanswered until I prevailed on him to descend, at least to shake hands with the mayor and the pastor. In his own home, the melancholy prisoner had turned into an autocrat. On Sunday the two of us climbed a hill towering over the village, and I got a rest from posing as my friend pointed out to me the landmarks in the vicinity.

From this encounter sprang a stubborn belief in Dieter's mind that I had saved his life. A rumor, totally unfounded, that a typhus epidemic was ravaging our improvised camps on the Rhine convinced him and his folks that I had torn him from the clutches of certain death. Years later, when my family and I visited Dieter in his home on the Swiss side of Lake Constance, he regaled my wife and children with the same fable.

My growing awareness of and responsiveness to the misery around me met with increasing disapproval among the veteran foot soldiers managing the enclosure. They called my men and me "Kraut lovers." These toughened infantrymen needed our help to reduce the large prison population, but they resented our painstaking pace and what they considered to be unduly lenient methods of investigation. All of us operated under the same orders—to return as many Germans as possible to civilian life as quickly as possible. This was one of the many paradoxes of victory. Far away from our homes and loved ones, we were toiling day and night to return our enemies to theirs. To compensate for this injustice, many a GI made sure no prisoner forgot who was in charge. The defeated were forced to run, rather than march, to the waiting trucks, and hearty cuffs and kicks prodded anyone who fell behind. To a new American, whose country must and could countenance no wrong, this constituted an unworthy spectacle, and I finally complained to the battalion commander. My men and I were new on the scene and had been spared the rigors of combat, but what we were witnessing violated the rules and had to be stopped. The commanding officer agreed wholeheartedly. "You should have seen some of these heroes in my outfit under fire," he scoffed. "They were not so tough during the Battle of the Bulge." All physical abuse was prohibited forthwith. I might add that this excellent officer, whose name I have unfortunately forgotten, also kept an eagle eye on his troops' conduct outside the camp and would tolerate no discourtesies toward the civilian population. After all, life in Germany was punishing enough.

Later in the summer, as I drove through towns, especially industrial communities on the lower Rhine, all but leveled and depopulated, I saw hundreds of returning men in field gray, searching the ruins, often hailing our jeeps and asking us, the omniscient and all-powerful victors, for news about families who, for the moment, had disappeared without a trace and of whose whereabouts we, of course, knew nothing.

As autumn approached, my letters home reflected my rising compassion. To my wife I wrote: "Without you I am about to enter the worst winter of my life. But our captured enemies are facing even worse. Not knowing where their wives and children are, not knowing whether they are alive and, if so, whether they are provided with food and shelter. Being tortured by rumors and, who knows, more than rumors of rape, plunder, and expulsion. That is the fate of the German behind barbed wire.

"How justified their worries are can be seen in any German town. Curfew finds scores and scores of transient fugitives without a place to go, women with babies in their arms, invalids and old men." I also asked myself whether we, the conquerors, possessed the moral strength to deal with total victory. I observed the deterioration that triumph spread in our own ranks. "Our army should have been trained to carry out an honorable, disciplined occupation. Instead, we are turning into a band of petty racketeers. Many GIs spend more time buying and selling than doing their assigned work: PX rations, including cigarettes, gas, clothing, equipment, currency, cameras and watches, are the chief commodities traded by the burgeoning barter system." Most of western Europe was turning into a bazaar. Eisenhower's crusaders had turned into an army of black marketeers.

Fortunately, in September the army saved the remnants of my morale by sending me back to France. Here corruption abounded, too, but in surroundings dominated by the heartening symptoms of national reconstruction. A prisoner-of-war enclosure built around an abandoned Maginot line *caserne* near Metz was the next setting in which we continued the work of purging Germany of the Nazi virus. My team's task was to speed toward release, detention, or punishment 35,000 officers of all ranks. Amidst a prison population whose members had heretofore given the orders, my men and I soon regained a certain hard balance of spirit. We had by now become more seasoned inquisitors, and pursued with dogged enthusiasm that facet of our mission consisting of tracking men whose names appeared on a long Allied rogues' gallery of war criminals.

Bernard, the star intellect in our group, proposed that we systematize our inquiry by having each prisoner fill out a personal-history questionnaire, detailing, in particular, his service to party, state, and Wehrmacht. Bernard pointed out to me that by June, 1945, prisoners had had ample time to destroy incriminating personal records and to concoct sanitized versions of their past. This circumstance prompted us to add to each questionnaire a declaration affirming on the signer's "honor as a German officer" that he had told the truth and omitted nothing. Although we could never know who slipped through this homemade net, we were encouraged daily by some spectacular catches, largely the result of this Machiavellian procedure. Some replies included confessions of guilt, earning their authors death sentences.

The most extreme cases I remember were those of two SS officers, who instead of filling out this paper, committed suicide by cutting their wrists with penknives and slowly bleeding to death on their cots the night before their scheduled interrogation. Others confirmed their written confessions with verbal corroboration. I recall a conversation with an SS colonel who had, in 1944, given the order to burn down the Marseilles waterfront. High on our wanted list, he embodied all that was corrupt in Germany's recent past. But if I expected to meet an individual exhibiting marked physical attributes of villainy, I was to be disappointed. Before me stood a handsome, slim, dark-haired officer, straight but not stiff of bearing, articulate, cultured, not without dignity, and obviously resigned to his fate. Unlike many other members of his branch of service, he did not advance youthful idealism as an extenuating explanation of his crimes. He had studied romance languages at the University of Marburg, receiving his degree in 1933. The surplus of academics had reached its high point then, and he admitted to having joined the SS for lack of other prospects. This move quickly paid off. By 1939 he had risen to the rank of major and headed the archives of Himmler's Reich Main Security Office. After the fall of France, his knowledge of French had resulted in his transfer to Vichy, where he became German liaison officer with the French police. Following the occupation of the entire country in 1942, he became *SS und höherer Polizei Führer* for the Marseilles region. It was here that he had given the order for the waterfront destruction, in retribution for the rising resistance in his command to the German presence. When I spoke to him, he knew what awaited him, insisting that he assumed full responsibility for his action. We turned him over to the French, who, no doubt, have long since exacted their own just vengeance. I have often wondered, however, why this man confessed so readily. Was it conscience? Was it fear of denunciation by fellow prisoners or fellow civilians after his release? Or was it the hope that somehow he would be saved before he reached his executioner, an expectation not entirely unfounded, as the case of Klaus Barbie, the "Butcher of Lyons," shows.

Many of the older, senior officers in the camp were veterans of the imperial army who had survived two world wars; in many cases their sons had been less lucky. When I asked them how they felt now about serving the man who had sent these sons to death, they wept. I remember another encounter with an Austrian air-force major, the well-known child psychologist Anton Tesarek, leading to tears of a different kind. He was in his forties, a silver-haired, rubicund gentleman, with exceedingly ingratiating ways. His fawning manner put me off at once, for experience had taught me to associate such behavior with men who had a great deal to hide. When he added the likewise familiar claim of political persecution, and of devotion to the memory of Sigmund Freud and a longstanding friendship with the late sage's daughter Anna, my doubts increased. Throughout all this palaver I also had the uneasy feeling I was swimming out of my depth. One of the two American medical officers attached to the camp was a psychologist, and I asked him to join the interrogation. Tesarek was taken to a small room in the headquarters building, where we grilled him unmercifully about every detail of his life. After a prolonged and hostile examination, which forced him to relive at length his degrading treatment at the hands of the invading Germans in 1938, the man broke down and sobbed uncontrollably. At last we were convinced that he was telling the truth. I know today that his rank and position in an air-force construction battalion should have been enough to make his tale plausible. Both officers and men in these units were normally recruited from the ranks of the suspect. In any case, we relented and tagged him for prompt release. But this was not an interrogation I remember with pride.

The search for villains also had its nonsensical aspects. In November, 1945, someone in higher headquarters decided the employment of stool pigeons would facilitate our mission. We were encouraged to select prisoners whom we considered suited for this purpose, especially "persons formerly connected with [German Intelligence who] had proven to be particularly adaptable for this type of work." Since I gave no response to this foolish suggestion, the army decided to send me an informer of its own choice. Before long a truck delivered to my office door a Dutch SS officer, ostensibly an escapee from another prison enclosure. For appearance's sake, I spent some time in the interrogation room with the man and then placed him in one of the "cages." Within two days the entire prison population was aware of his true function, and he was speedily evacuated for his own protection.

Another absurd incident followed a series of visits by an elderly colleague (a category to which I then assigned everyone over thirty), a member of the intelligence section for which we were doing field-work, Captain Evans. Evans was screening German junior officers considered competent to take charge of prisoner-of-war labor com-panies, whose supervising quartermaster units had been reduced to mere skeleton crews by redeployment. The news of the availability of this kind of semiliberation spread like wildfire, and I received many requests for recommendations to Evans. One young first lieu-tenant struck me as being particularly worthy, and I endorsed him with warm words. But Evans turned him down just as emphatically. "You see," he told me stentoriously, "I use psychology. You can't be a good intelligence officer without psychology. Did you look at the information he gave about his family?" Evans asked me.

"Yes, I did, what about it?"

"Did you notice the name of his son?" he went on.

"I may have, but I have forgotten what it was."

"Ah, there you are," Evans roared. "His son's name is Siegfried. That man is a Nazi, and he can't pull the wool over my eyes."

"But Captain Evans," I remonstrated. "Many parents in the 1920s and 1930s named their sons Siegfried. You should have seen all the friends I had in the Jewish Boy Scouts who bore that name. It simply means that their family wanted to give them a good German name, or that they revered Richard Wagner, that's all." But Captain Evans would not be persuaded. My protégé had to spend the rest of his internment sitting on his duff, no doubt reflecting on what name, other than Siegfried, to give any sons he might beget, if and when he was released by his suspicious captors.

Finally emptying the camp, we went on to another enclosure at Stenay—a dreary little town where the German crown prince had established his headquarters during the Battle of Verdun in World War I, and where a more motley collection of ranks awaited us, including the first of those returned from prisoner-of-war camps in the United States. The last component, showing all the marks of good treatment—among them, a healthy tan acquired under a southern sun—and bearing copious luggage and such nonmilitary implements as tennis rackets, tended to revive scattered excesses of GI hostility toward an enemy blooming in defeat. Once again I had to call on a commanding officer to remind his men of the rules governing the treatment of prisoners; this time the malefactors were not only called to order but, in some instances, reduced to the rank of private.

Winter came, and as redeployment quickened, I began to lose the members of my team one by one. Finally, only I was left. I liquidated my operation at Prisoner of War Enclosure No. 17 in Stenay and this time drove my jeep myself across France to my last overseas station: the counterintelligence detachment in Le Havre, of which I had become the nominal commander. Here my troops consisted of a group of agents each of whom had his own secret mission, so highly classified that even I must not learn of its nature. This left me little to do except compare notes with my bored vis-à-vis at MP headquarters downtown and maintain friendly contacts with the local police.

Occasionally I wrote reports documenting the scruffy last chapter of the great crusade as malfeasance increased, by victors and vanquished alike. Once my group apprehended a crew of German prisoner-of-war drivers who had for months been selling American supplies off the quartermaster trucks they were operating. The culprits were caught *in flagrante delicto,* buying a small waterfront hotel with their profits. On another occasion, we uncovered evidence that the commanding officer of a service unit had whiled away his time, and supplemented his pay, by importing English prostitutes from across the Channel, using a speedboat that was part of his organizational equipment. It seems that Frenchmen preferred the services of these foreigners to those of local ladies. The officer in question had already departed for home but was arrested on the gangplank in New York and returned to France for trial. These are chapters of the war no historian has heretofore troubled to write; they revolted and depressed me, and even now I recall them with reluctance and sorrow.

At last, in the late summer of 1946, my number was also up. I moved to the other side of town into an evacuation camp from which I finally boarded ship for my second trip to America, just as happy to be leaving Europe as I had been in 1938. To keep me occupied and out of mischief during the crossing, I was appointed commanding officer of an MP company whose only task on board was to dispose of the vessel's garbage—a fitting sequel to the unsavory work of the previous months. Before the departure, one last screening job fell to my lot before the company was cleared for home: supervising the medical examination of the unit and transferring to the port's American field hospital all men found to be infected with venereal diseases. These victims of all-too-human indiscretions became the last automatic-arrest category I encountered during my military service. They were forced to stay abroad until cured.

After I and other troops embarked, only the trucks and their prisoner-of-war drivers who had transported us to the ship remained on the docks. Our German auxiliaries waved and shouted sarcastic farewells. We replied in kind. One GI standing next to me at the railing shouted, "Behave yourself, you bastards, or we'll be back." Then we pushed off for home.

XI OVERDUE REUNIONS

Finding the surviving members of my family was the most important general mission during my military service in Europe. Once found, I wanted to bring them to the United States, and the preparations for this permanent family reunion continued after my return to civilian life. I have therefore chosen to account separately for the last episode in this memoir of the Hitler years.

On a hazy summer day in July, 1945, I pointed my jeep northwestward from my regimental headquarters in Ingelheim toward Holland, where I hoped to find my mother and brother. My leave had been granted reluctantly by the commanding officer of the 424th Infantry Regiment. "I haven't seen my family in two years," he grumbled. "You've only been with the outfit for three months." I retorted that I had not seen my mother for seven years, but he seemed unmoved. I also reminded him that the prison enclosure where my team had been working had just been emptied and that I would be back in ample time to proceed to my next assignment. Grudgingly, he gave me three days.

Military regulations did not allow officers to drive, so I had to take one of my men along as chauffeur. Bernard was more than willing; not only was he an excellent driver and a first-class mechanic—an asset in this ravaged land without service stations—but he was also intelligent company. I have already mentioned that he was an Egyptologist. From 1932 until 1938 he was an assistant in the Egyptian department of the Berlin State Museums. On the eve of the war, he and his younger brother, the classical archaeologist Dietrich von Bothmer, had slipped across the German border into Switzerland, without passports or luggage. An American foundation spirited them out of Europe, via Lisbon, and brought them to the United

States. Bernard joined the staff of the Boston Museum of Fine Arts until the army asserted its right of eminent domain over his person.

We soon discovered that ours was not the first meeting between members of our families. During World War I, Bernard's paternal grandmother, the wife of the grand chamberlain of the grand duke of Hesse-Darmstadt, and my maternal grandmother had managed the Red Cross station at the Frankfurt *Hauptbahnhof*. What brought us even closer, however, was the discovery that Bernard and my former Eerde teacher Billy Hilsley had been contemporaries at Schloss Salem on Lake Constance, a well-known boardingschool. He was, therefore, genuinely keen on seeing Eerde and meeting my mother and possibly Billy. (We did not know then that the latter was on tour with the Jooss ballet.)

Not wishing to waste a minute of the short leave, we set out early on a Sunday evening, using the night to travel. We reached Cologne just as dusk ended. No light or sound betrayed another human presence. Our jeep's battery appeared to be the only source of electricity for miles around. This feeble generator illuminated before our wondering eyes Germany's third-most-populous city, a silent moonscape of seemingly total destruction: chimneys without houses, bare walls without interiors, jagged outlines of shattered masonry pointing to the heavens. Only the familiar silhouette of the cathedral identified where we were, the only landmark that seemed to have escaped the terrible vengeance from the air.

We rattled on, across roads terminating without warning. Between Cologne and the Dutch border scarcely a bridge remained passable; no one had yet taken the time to put up barriers or warning signs. We moved slowly and cautiously, several times stopping just short of a sudden abyss. In the gray dawn we overtook some miners on their way to work, from whom we solicited fresh directions. We could not tell where these men had come from. There seemed to be no habitable dwelling in sight, but there they were, shabby, hollow eyed, and glum, on the way to or from their pits, most of them carrying briefcases, worn leather "brown bags" shapeless with age, holding a few crusts and some boiled potatoes to sustain them below. They appeared anxious to descend to an interior where the work of their hands dictated tempo and rhythm of change, a setting from which the war had been excluded.

At the Dutch border, a bizarre incident almost ended our trip. After crossing a small stream on a Bailey bridge built by British engineers, we wanted to make sure, once again, that we had not lost our way. Bernard called out to one of the British soldiers guarding the passage, "Tell me, is this the highway to the Netherlands?" Instead of replying, the soldier jerked his rifle from his shoulder, ran toward us, and stopped only when the tip of his bayonet grazed Bernard's throat. Had the man gone berserk?

Then we realized what had produced this dramatic reaction. Throughout the morning we had been talking to Germans, and as a result my companion had absentmindedly addressed the British soldier in the tongue of the enemy. The guard undoubtedly thought we were two Germans in stolen American uniforms, on an errand of flight or sabotage. Our nemesis was quickly joined by several other agitated and armed members of His Majesty's Royal Engineers, led by a sergeant. Only after we had produced our identification papers and our travel orders were we let go.

In Holland we made better time. Roads and bridges also showed the wounds of war, but highway markings had been restored, both by the Dutch and by the liberators, Canada's First Army. As we drove farther, my heart began to beat faster at the sight of familiar surroundings. The Overijssel countryside looked as level and green as ever, and there was a lively traffic of farm vehicles carrying loads of metal milk cans. Was it really seven years, almost one-third of my life, since I last saw this Arcadian plain? Peace had returned, a happy peace so it seemed, unlike the glum, apprehensive silence pervading life to the east.

We drove from Raalte to Ommen and finally saw in the distance the windmill looming over the last crossing before the turnoff to the castle. I asked Bernard to slow down; I examined closely every segment of the tree-shaded road—the only one in Holland marked on European road maps with symbols indicating a thoroughfare of unusual scenic beauty. We passed the forester's house and the two stone markers inscribed "Eerde," defining the land boundaries of the baron's fief along the public highway. Then we took another right and rolled down the unpaved avenue at the end of which stood the castle. The gate to the yard stood open—the war had not changed that—and the jeep springs creaked as we crossed the cobblestoned outer bridge. Then we rounded the front lawn and halted at the walled and flagstoned passage leading across the inner moat to the foot of the castle's staircase.

I stumbled from the jeep. I had by now received two letters from my mother and knew that she and my brother were alive, but until I had seen them I remained apprehensive. A small crowd of children gathered around our vehicle, and I inquired of one where I could find "Mevrouw Schmitt." The youngster told me she lived in the Pallandt House, the "California" villa situated about half a mile from the main building. We retraced our course through the castle yard and bore left on a gravel path meandering through more forest, then past an open field until the roadway ended at the entrance of the familiar low-slung house. Someone at the castle must have alerted my mother by phone, for she was standing in the door as we drove up. Out she rushed to embrace me. This time nobody cried. "You have gained weight," she said. She had not. She was gray and seemed smaller than I remembered her; but she bore no marks of extreme physical suffering, and a wave of relief washed over me. Presently I looked up and perceived a lank young man standing behind her, taller than I, with thick, curly black hair, wearing black-rimmed glasses: my brother, no longer a little boy, but the veteran of many silent battles.

Bernard, meanwhile, had tactfully turned his back on this private moment and begun unloading the jeep. These were the leanest of times, and we never went anywhere without sufficient rations to feed our hosts as well as ourselves. I introduced my friend to my mother, and then we all went into the house. We two soldiers had not slept since Sunday morning, and so my mother offered Bernard my brother's room, where he spread his sleeping bag and spent most of the day recuperating from the night ride. For me this was not the time to take a nap. We Schmitts are avid talkers at all times, and after seven years we hardly knew where to begin. I learned only now by what narrow margins my mother and brother had survived.

For more than a year after the German invasion, their life had continued fairly placidly. Then, in September, 1941, the Nuremberg laws breached the moat and invaded their refuge. Jewish faculty, staff, and children were separated from the other denizens of the school. Mr. Neuse, the headmaster, was forced to dismiss my mother with a letter in which every sentence revealed his sorrow and outrage at circumstances that had exacted from him this act of seeming disloyalty. He reviewed my mother's service as house-mother, her subsequent teaching of Latin, Greek, English, French,

227

and mathematics, and her preparation of classes for the Oxford School Certificate in the last two subjects. "Her intellectual gifts and interests are indeed so extensive," he went on to explain, "that she was able to provide fully competent instruction in these . . . many subjects." He concluded, "Because of prevailing conditions, Mrs. Schmitt was forced to leave the service of the school." Before signing the letter, Mr. Neuse apparently found this statement not sufficiently forthright and inserted the word *political* between *prevailing* and *conditions*. He added no verbal flourish of devotion to the conqueror.

This letter had, of course, little practical value. My mother's next mission was simply one of survival, both her own and that of her little band of outcasts. She set up housekeeping with these children in the quarters she still inhabited when I found her. The improvised household was left in peace until one day the following spring when she was awakened early by a persistent knock on the door. Upon opening it, she found on her doorstep the local *maréchaussée*—a kind of national highway policeman—in his neat blue uniform adorned with blue and white fourragères. His orders were to pick her up. "But," he added at once, "I know you need time to pack. I'll be back tomorrow." The question was, should she attempt to flee or stay? Without ado, she decided that she could not leave the children to an unknown fate in order to save herself, and remained. The Dutch gendarme returned the afternoon of the next day. "What, you are still here!" he exclaimed when he saw my mother, and added, before she could respond: "I know, I know, you need more time. I'll be back tomorrow." When he returned a third time and found that my mother had not budged, he arrested her with obvious reluctance.

Like many policemen in Holland, this well-intentioned enforcer of the rules of the road had also become an agent of Germany's machinery of extermination. Nothing in his past had prepared him for such a role. No government he had ever served had ordered him to arrest innocent people. His life had been devoted to serving the law, not breaking it. The collapse of a self-assured, orderly world, his since birth, left him mentally and physically defenseless. Protest could mean the firing squad; a decision "to dive" (*onderduiken* in Dutch, a slang term current during the occupation, meaning "to go into hiding") might save him but add his family to the ranks of the doomed. Was it worth taking such risks to protect the foreign refugees at Eerde? As my mother's experience showed, some of these functionaries nevertheless improvised a way out of their predicament by affording their quarry a reasonable chance for escape.[1]

My mother was sent to Westerbork, the Dutch camp from which Jews were dispatched to Auschwitz. I do not know exactly how long she stayed there. One day she was called to the office of an SS *Sturmbannführer* who had discovered that she was the widow of an Aryan man and the mother of his surviving minor son. The dignitary was much exercised because she had been detained, an error for which she was scarcely responsible. He explained that the führer did not wish the sons of pure-blooded Germans to be needlessly orphaned, even by the loss of a racially inferior mother. She would be reprieved to look after her child until he was of legal age. For the moment, the gas chamber could wait.

My mother's account of this detour through the underworld made me wonder whether she would have returned from Westerbork had my father still been alive. I also began to ask myself, for the first time, whether he had died a natural death. If he had known or suspected what fate awaited the Jews, despair and helplessness might well have prompted him to end his life. Franz Adorno, who lived until 1985, was the only survivor who knew at first hand something about the circumstances under which my father spent the last month of his life, and he has assured me that there was no evidence that my father died anything but a natural death. I shall never be sure.

At Westerbork my mother learned of several Pallandt House children who arrived after her. She knew, therefore, even before her return to Eerde, that few of her former charges would be left. She found that they were all gone, and most of them completed the final trip from which she had just been spared. I know of only one survivor who had returned when I visited the school in 1945. Some of the others, as I mentioned earlier, wrote regularly from their transit camp until their fatal departure to Poland.

My mother never spoke to me about the months following her release, when it became increasingly clear that she would not see her young wards again. By the time of my first postwar visit, she had become the object of some criticism. After the danger was past, some of her colleagues deplored her lack of foresight and initiative. The arrival of peace revealed that tens of thousands of the per-

---

1. A recent study of Jews in occupied Holland also covers this aspect on a broader scale, arriving at less charitable conclusions: Henry L. Mason, "Testing Human Bonds Within Nations: Jews in Occupied Holland," *Political Science Quarterly,* XCIX (1984), 315–43.

secuted had been concealed in countless Dutch households. In the more thinly populated rural provinces of eastern Holland, it had proved relatively easy to slip through the net of the occupation. There a considerable number of the twenty thousand Jewish "divers" had found asylum. In 1945 it seemed as if many, perhaps all, of Eerde's Jewish children might have been rescued by the same method. I can only speculate why my mother refused to scatter her brood. Most of her waifs were of grade-school age, already prematurely separated from their parents. Could they have endured being torn for a second time from the protection and company of familiar adults and roommates, this time under the additional strain of concealment? Hiding children, especially foreign ones, is more difficult than hiding adults. Frightened, vulnerable youngsters are more likely to give themselves away, and once discovered, they doom everyone who has played a part in their unsuccessful escape. The discovery of a Jewish underground railroad might also have prompted the Germans to take additional hostages, putting an even greater number of lives in jeopardy. There was no sure way of dealing with an enemy of unrestrained power and brutality.

There may have been other reasons for my mother's passivity, less rational and, I suspect, less conscious. By training and education she was a German jurist. Breaking the law, any law, was not part of her code; it took her time to adjust to the lawless ways slowly permeating the lives of the occupied. She was equally slow shedding the skin of her original nationality. At the time of her arrest, she may have retained some residual belief in a German humanity that would somehow permit the manifestly innocent to elude the traps set by official terrorism. In any case, she could not bring herself to put her charges out of sight and expose them and their rescuers, whoever they might be, to new, incalculable risks. When it became clear that her caution had availed nothing, it was too late to follow the counsel of second thought.

The hardier adult, who could map his own flight, was subject to fewer constraints. This explains why my brother escaped. In the autumn of 1944, he was seventeen and had been drafted by the enemy. A farmer nearby offered him shelter in his cattle barns, and there he spent the rest of the war, sleeping with cows and pigs, disguised as a Dutch farm laborer. One of the farmer's daughters even bicycled back and forth regularly, carrying letters from mother to son. Another successful "diver" was Mr. Neuse. A veteran of World

War I, he had been drafted—also late in 1944—to serve in a police battalion, and likewise refused to heed the call. His imperfect knowledge of Dutch, surprising in a linguist of his stature, and his scholarly eccentricities would have made it difficult to conceal him on a farm. He therefore chose a more perilous way out, hiding in a garret of Pallandt House. In a claustrophobically confined space under the roof, with barely room to sit up, he spent six months, preserving his sanity by translating Homeric epics into German hexameter. It never occurred to any search party to look for him in the house into which his family had moved after the Germans had taken over the castle. Who could imagine a deserter hiding in his own attic? One may ask why his wife and children were not held hostage. Perhaps it was the lateness of the hour; perhaps it was Mrs. Neuse's English birth. Who knows? Tyrannies are not only brutal; their actions are frequently unpredictable and inconsistent.

At war's end, Mr. Neuse's troubles were by no means over. Officially, he was now a German in a country whose population was filled with understandable bitterness against his nation. Before long, he expected to be deported to his native soil in the German east, now ruled by the Russians. Fortunately, his brother, for many years a professor at Middlebury College, eventually brought the entire family to safety in the United States.

Once again I discovered that peace brought greater relief to combatants, whom it removed from daily physical danger, than to civilians. The soldier could put away his weapons and his fears and wait for demobilization. Such peace of mind eluded many of the friends I had visited in Germany and those with whom I now celebrated a reunion in Holland.

When I visited the Neuse family and other Eerde inhabitants gathered in their living room, I discovered what new fears, real and imagined, troubled their minds. Before long, our talk turned to the cloudy future. Mrs. Neuse was particularly agitated. To her, Germany was still embodied in her husband, whom she worshipped. This country, which she had willingly exchanged for her own, had been betrayed by Hitler, and now the Allies were going him one better by putting an end to its existence. What outraged her most was to see the USSR sit in Germany's judgment. Once again a dialogue with friends forced me to say my piece about the Great Alliance of World War II. But my arguments carried even less weight here than in previous debates. To Mrs. Neuse the Russian presence ruled out a return to their home, a Germany delivered from Hitler. The family's eventual emigration to the United States meant exchanging one exile for another. She never became reconciled to this alternative.

Mr. Neuse also engaged me in a long, uncomfortable conversation about another emotional subject: the liquidation of Prussia, even then inevitable, although it would not be officially announced until 1947. He was a Prussian, more so perhaps than a German, and proud of his origins. He scoffed at the notion that his native culture represented only blind obedience on the drill field. He pointed to the philosopher Immanuel Kant, the incorruptible reformer Karl vom Stein, the progressive liberals of the nineteenth century and their immortal literary spokesman, Theodor Fontane, and even Käthe Kollwitz, with her dour, unbreakable spirit: spiritual ancestors of whom he had proved only too worthy. He argued for a Prussian renaissance and against the state's liquidation. As I rose to leave, my old taskmaster took from the shelf a book, which he put in my hands. It was Bismarck's correspondence with Leopold von Gerlach, the conservative leader who had launched the Iron Chancellor's political career. "Read it," he exhorted me, "and keep it as a souvenir of this reunion. Even these hidebound opponents of change had Prussian qualities on which we had better not turn our backs."

I was not prepared to find my country and cause cast in the role of a villain. Certainly most contemporary Americans were not at ease in Russian company, but from whatever viewpoint, it was too late for such squeamishness. The heroism of the Red Army had contributed as much to victory as we had. Every Russian casualty had reduced our own sacrifice, and I asked whether we would have been celebrating our reunion in the summer of 1945—or ever—without the USSR on our side. I also reminded my critics that Hitler had been the true engineer of our alliance with the Soviet Union when he invaded its "sacred borders" in 1941. By that time Germans, and/or Prussians, had long abandoned Mr. Neuse's house gods. That, too, had been their choice, not ours. In 1933 Prussian conservatives had been in the forefront of the führer's adulators; their subsequent, often silent repentance—no matter how heartfelt—had come too late to revive the civilization they had destroyed, long before the outcome of the war wrote its obituary.

A friend of my brother's, an alumnus of Eerde after my time, also unwittingly added to my vexation when he joined the critical chorus with a tirade against the disorderly behavior of Canadian troops in Amsterdam. He compared, unfavorably, their off-duty conduct with the discipline of the Nazi occupiers. Few people in the room were willing to go that far, and most agreed with me that intoxicated Canadians were better company than well-mannered German *Landser* on holiday. But this small concession failed to cool my rising anger. I did not know how many Canadians had died in the liberation of Holland, but I knew and told my listeners that although Canada, like all belligerents, drafted its sons, it did not force them to fight in Europe. Lt. Gen. Sir John Crerar's First Army consisted of volunteers. It was unfortunate that some of them now behaved in a way that reflected poorly on their country, and harassed a friendly population that had suffered enough, but these were trivial burdens for the Dutch to bear, compared with the deaths of countless Canadian citizens fighting for the freedom of Holland.

I was, of course, dealing with people who had not been able to speak their minds for five years and who took their own drunken pleasure in once again being able to criticize, needle, and nag. Before I left, all of us shook hands, and the next day met as if nothing had happened. After all, nothing really had.

But my forbearance, already at a low ebb, was to be tested once more. After I had recovered some of the sleep lost on my night ride through the Ruhr, I was invited to have tea with the baron. This could hardly be called a reunion. So far as I could remember, I had visited his home only once, for a formal farewell before my first departure for the United States. While I was a student, he had been the lord of the manor, where we lived by his sufferance (and I do not know how much rent). We children saw him from afar, a tall, lean, red-cheeked, and sharp-nosed gentleman, paying occasional calls on the headmistress to lodge complaints about some real or imagined maltreatment of his manor and its furnishings. He lived in a sphere different from that of us foreign earthlings, recognizable only by its outward trappings: a coat of arms whose components I have long forgotten, and the blue and yellow colors of his clan adorning the shutters of the ancestral palazzo.

My first reaction was to turn down the invitation. I had no penchant for the company of aristocracy, especially since this invitation did not include the remainder of my family, or "Graf" von Bothmer, whom the baron might have considered more respectable company. But my mother urged me to go. The future of the school remained as uncertain as it had been during the war. In view of Britain's poverty, it was unlikely that Friends' House could finance Eerde's reopening. Nor could one take for granted Holland's willingness to maintain a haven for the persecuted on its ravaged ground. This was no time to antagonize the landlord. If he should decide to look for another tenant (as he eventually did), many current inhabitants of the manor and Pallandt House would become homeless.

I polished my boots, put on my dress uniform, and made the only out-and-out courtesy call of my life, finding myself at the receiving end of another peppery lecture. The baron was incensed by American support for the independence movement in Indonesia, whose leaders my host considered nothing more than Japanese collaborators, no better than Nazis. These philippics, however, glanced off my hide without eliciting a reaction. To me and my generation the time for empire was past, and I was equally certain and satisfied that Europe's remaining aristocracy would play no part in shaping the postwar order. There was little I could contribute to the conversation anyway, since my current knowledge of events in the Far East depended entirely on the reports of the fighting carried by *Stars and Stripes.* Mindful of my goodwill mission, I let the baron speak without interrupting him. From time to time I emitted sympathetic grunts between genteel sips of tea. After a decent interval, I thanked the squire for his hospitality and went on my way. I was thoroughly weary of playing father confessor to the disgruntled.

My Dutch excursion contributed to the restoration of that "hard balance of spirit" of which I have earlier written. When one was with Germans, it was easy to forget that their present hardships fell short of the sufferings they had inflicted on their victims. Now that I had heard, firsthand, what my own family had borne, and seen what had been willfully visited on a nation so impeccably neutral as the Dutch, I became reconciled to some kind of retribution. As Bernard and I crossed the border back into enemy territory, I looked at Germans with different eyes. On our return it struck both of us that many people going about their business in the neat, prosperous rural communities of the Rhine Valley were still better dressed and visibly better fed than the countryfolk we had observed in Holland. They did not look as if they had gone hungry for five years. Two harsh, postwar winters would reduce these discrepancies in well-being, but in the late summer of 1945, many of our enemies still looked like victors, while their defeat had so far not put flesh on the ribs of their former ravin.

Christmas, 1945, provided another experience of life among the liberated. I obtained a week-long leave, just after the holidays, to visit my mother and brother a second time. I was now stationed in a prison enclosure on the outskirts of the drab little town of Stenay, halfway between Verdun and Sedan in northeastern France, on the edge of the great battlefield of World War I: a perfect place from which to study small-town life in the new but fragile Fourth Republic. The drive to Eerde took me, this time, through the more recent battlegrounds of Belgian Luxembourg—Marche, Bastogne, St. Hubert—where people huddled in primitive, temporary shacks, deprived of the most elementary comforts, until their towns could be rebuilt. The air was acid with the cold of an unusually severe winter, and the few people I saw resembled figures from the nightmare world of Hieronymus Bosch. Even a commodious villa like Pallandt House offered surprisingly little protection against the harshest season. After six months of peace, its modern appointments remained out of commission. (One went to the toilet armed with a bucket of water.) There was no coal and therefore no hot water. While the thermometer flirted with zero outside, I satisfied my inclination for personal cleanliness by taking a shower in my mother's bathroom. The water, like tiny ice pellets, stung my skin. An old-fashioned, wood-burning kitchen stove had been moved into the living room and did double duty as a cooking range and a fireplace. When evening fell and the thermometer sank out of sight, I often sat reading until late into the night, my combat-booted feet thrust into the glowing ashes, before leaping into my chilled sleeping bag. Even after three years of soldiering, I was ill prepared for such austerity. I wondered how the regular inhabitants had borne this comfortless life through five winters. They, of course, like millions of other Europeans, had long been weaned from regular bathing (an inviolate community rule at Eerde when I was a student), and even the cold seemed to affect them far less than it did me.

My second visit naturally caused far less excitement in the neighborhood than had my first. My family and I now had sufficient time to become reacquainted and to plan the future. Families of American servicemen were not subject to quota restrictions, and no waiting list could any longer impede their emigration. My mother and brother could therefore join my wife and me as soon as transport was available. But Hitler's legacy included one last obstacle for them. His laws had made my mother a person without a country and, more important, without identity papers. Before she could travel anywhere, she needed a so-called Nansen passport, named in memory of the Norwegian explorer who in the 1920s headed Norway's delegation to the League of Nations. At his instigation an international agreement had been signed at Geneva in 1922, establishing this identity document for stateless persons—at that time chiefly White Russians and Armenians.

To expedite the issuance of this indispensable document, I used another leave in the spring to visit the passport section of the Dutch foreign office in the Hague, as well as the recently reopened United States legation. In those days, any petition to the Dutch bureaucracy met the standard answer " 't word er aan gewerkt" ("We are working on it"), which local skeptics interpreted as meaning "Don't bother us, we have more important matters to consider." However, my mother received the proofs of her identity before I returned to the United States.

I also used this final leave to visit my uncle and his family in Amsterdam. Here I was spared the customary critique of Allied policy. Survival had been especially difficult for Amsterdamers. By April, 1945, local food supplies had shrunk to one pound of potatoes per person per week. Starvation and disease had become so rampant that the Germans had finally agreed to let Allied planes drop supplies, which they promised not to divert for their own use. No wonder that I encountered little predisposition to criticize the agents of the city's eleventh-hour liberation. In my uncle's house the hero of the hour was, however, not General Eisenhower, but Field Marshal Montgomery. He was credited with saving Allied fortunes at the Battle of the Bulge and hastening the end of the worst episode in Dutch history since the "Spanish Fury" of the duke of Alba in the late sixteenth century.

When I entered my relatives' apartment on Amsterdam's south side, I found myself in the presence of authentic war heroes. The occupation had reduced my uncle to wearing the Star of David and digging ditches for the Germans. My aunt took over the support of the family by opening a photo studio, putting to work a hobby in which she had acquired professional mastery. In a secret compartment under the staircase, she manufactured false identity cards and other documents for members of the resistance. What made this work doubly dangerous was the fact that the ground floor of their building housed the local offices of the Gestapo, whose staff was always on the lookout for lawbreakers among partners of mixed marriages. After the departure of the Germans, this contribution to the Allied cause was openly recognized, first, by my uncle's hero, Montgomery, in an official letter of thanks and, second, by the introduction of a bill into parliament that eventually bestowed Dutch citizenship on the entire family.

My relatives were also debating where to spend their future. After five years of enforced idleness—for my active and hitherto successful uncle, a fate leading to severe, if temporary, emotional problems—they rebounded and fell on their feet once more. They ultimately decided to stay in Holland. My uncle became special assistant to the minister for foreign economic relations and eventually joined the Dutch negotiating team whose members engineered Holland's accession to the European Coal and Steel Community. In the course of these events, he met and gained the confidence of Jean Monnet, the father of the European Community, who recruited him to become the first secretary-general of that agency and then head of its antitrust department. He, his wife, and children were to become our only remaining familial contact with the old world. Their bravery and good spirits increased my lifelong love and admiration for them, sentiments my wife has come to share. Florence has become especially devoted to my aunt, who proved herself so magnificently in silent service against the enemy, without betraying to this day any awareness of her extraordinary heroism. My uncle is gone now, but her home remains to all who know her a refuge from the imperfections of this world.

These imperfections were all too evident in Holland in 1946. Years spent in constant danger amidst miserable physical deprivations had invalidated existing moral standards. Fighting the occupier meant breaking the law. Illegality had become a way of life, a habit it was difficult to break, especially for young people who grew up in this anarchy. During my stay in their apartment, my relatives still received phone calls and visits from former resistance clients, requesting them to forge permits and ration cards. Children who had helped their families survive by stealing food could only with difficulty be broken of criminal habits rendered respectable by the ubiq- uitous presence of the common enemy. When I arrived, for instance, the first order of business was, not to celebrate, but to find a safe shelter for my jeep. "You can't leave it on the street," my uncle warned. "It will be stripped of engine and tires before morning." Garages were jammed with automobiles immobilized since the Ger- man invasion which cut off the supply of gasoline from the East Indies. Only after a prolonged search was an owner found who could give my vehicle sanctuary in the last vacant spot under his roof. Here again another infraction: My jeep blocked the exit, violat- ing fire regulations. However, this proved the last difficulty obstruct- ing our reunion, and we finally settled down, opened the bottle of champagne I had brought from France, and made our visit the grand occasion it deserved to be.

My own life did not become whole again until I returned home, in August, 1946. After sixteen months of separation, I embraced a near- stranger, my wife, and settled with her into the one-room apartment she had rented just before my departure. It was not the most roman- tic of homecomings, and there was no time for a second honey- moon. Although Florence was earning a good salary as a monotype operator, it was insufficient to pay for the passage across the Atlantic of my mother and brother, and for the larger apartment we would soon need.

The very next morning I put on my civilian clothes and, after my wife had hurried off to her job at the world's largest printer, R. R. Donnelly & Sons, set out to find a job of my own.

Finding work proved a lot easier than locating an apartment dur- ing this time of severe housing shortages. To leave open a possible return to graduate school, I took a position in the dispatch office of a large trucking firm on the 3 P.M. to midnight shift. This schedule left little time to reknit the threads of marital life. Florence and I scarcely saw each other. She returned from work as I was leaving. Often we only had time to touch hands as she emerged from the South Shore train on the same Illinois Central platform on which I was boarding a conveyance going in the opposite direction. I left just in time to grab a copy of the first morning edition of the Chicago *Tribune* and to map my apartment-hunting itinerary. At eight o'clock sharp the next morning I was on the phone calling every number listed in the sparse "Apartments for Rent" section. Often my call, even at this early hour, came too late. In other instances, I had to withdraw from the competition because the rent, coupled with a variety of under-the-table payments, placed a particular domicile beyond our financial reach.

About a week after my return, word arrived that my mother and brother would be sailing from Stockholm in December. There was no time to lose. After countless calls and inquiries, we learned of a three-bedroom apartment just around the corner from our cramped abode. The rent was surprisingly modest. It sounded too good to be true, and we discovered upon further investigation that we would have to provide more than our signatures on the lease. The furniture, fifteen hundred dollars' worth, went with the apartment. But the location was perfect and the size just what we needed, and we did have the money—thanks largely to the savings account my frugal wife acquired during my absence—though we had planned to spend it on furnishings of our own choice. A week later Florence and I moved our few belongings one block south and one block east and took possession of five rooms redolent with Grand Rapids renaissance. When we left Chicago two years later, we, in turn, sold the same household goods to the next tenant, paying the landlord his 20-percent share of the proceeds. We have often wondered how many times this blue-plush, walnut-veneered magnificence changed hands and how much the owner profited from these transfers of our apartment alone. On the other hand, our landlord was conscientious and maintained his property; the used-furniture business he conducted on the side was his hedge against rent control.

Acquisition of these expanded quarters also solved some subtler problems. Our dear and generous Chicago friends, the Morrisons, had appeared a trifle hurt when my wife, upon returning from her brief stint as camp follower, decided to set up housekeeping by herself. They had taken it for granted that she would remain under their roof until I returned. Now that my mother's and brother's arrival was imminent, Marian suggested, in the same vein, that my wife and I should have an opportunity to live by ourselves for a time and that the second wave of Schmitts should, like the first, start life in Chicago with them. I also discovered that my mother could not at once overcome her "helpless refugee" perspective. She was not prepared to let me take charge, and her letters were full of complicated stratagems: calls on "connections" in New York and visits to the American Friends' Service Committee before moving "out west" to Illinois. She, therefore, thought Marian Morrison's proposal an idea worth considering.

Looking back, I must agree that Marian's instincts were sound. To start a marriage in a household including two generations proved far more difficult than I could have anticipated. Living with a mother who had been widowed for several years, and who had always been accustomed to wield more authority than German mothers usually do, and a wife with whom I was only beginning to become attuned was not always idyllic. After her arrival it became evident that my mother, after a decade of communal life in a boardingschool, had difficulty understanding the need for newlyweds to be by themselves. She seemed intent on creating a new community of fellow refugees, whose members—often utter strangers to us—called on her as they came and went through Chicago. Our apartment soon became a busy way station for the uprooted, instead of a retreat for reunited lovers. Still, although I had not foreseen these complications, I was right in deciding to turn down Marian's offer. Even before my mother left Europe, I put a stop to her elaborate strategies by writing: "Mrs. Morrison's affection and helpfulness are indeed a marvel, and a gift only few humans receive. But I believe that she must be firmly, but gently, wrenched from the notion that we require constant help. You are my mother and Richard is my brother, and you will live with us, unless you prefer to live separately. Every good Samaritan has a streak of possessiveness, reflected in the way in which she [Marian] *assumed* that your staying with them was, more or less, a foregone conclusion." In the same vein I told my mother and brother to proceed directly from New York to Chicago, without pausing in Philadelphia. I had preceded them to this country, now my country, so that they would not enter it as helpless strangers, and I had kept that promise. No member of my family was to depend on charity, no matter how generous or well intentioned. My wife, who was born and raised in the United States, and whose immigrant parents had never touched a penny of philanthropy their whole lives, was even more determined on this issue. I should add that the Morrisons respected our independence, so in harmony with their own way of life. Our friendship continued uninterrupted to the end of their days.

It was a blustery Chicago day, on December 6, 1946, when I picked up the migrant remnants of my family at the Englewood Station on

63rd Street. In Holland, families were gathering for the feast of St. Nicholas; we were preparing for a Christmas often anticipated in letters but postponed year after year for almost a decade. My father had not lived to celebrate this reunion, and as we put up the tree in our living room we thought of him, the one person missing from our circle. The next year the gap would be closed at least as far as numbers went; our son Anthony, born June 10, 1947, would crawl among the presents, and my wife would wear the ring my grandmother had given my mother when I was born. My brother had begun his own distinguished scholarly career. He had won a three-year scholarship to the University of Chicago and begun to study philosophy. After many adventurous journeys and changes of direction, we had landed on our feet, lucky, happy to be alive, and once more in charge of our fortunes.

EPILOGUE

Almost forty years passed before I set down my recollections of the Hitler years. Writing them came easy. For a scholar it is a marvelous release to be able to write sentence after sentence, and page after page, without stopping for footnotes. Besides, I had at first nothing more ambitious in mind than to leave to my children and grandchildren a memoir of an ancestral world they would otherwise never know.

Since that unpretentious beginning, I have published some short pieces whose reception prompted me to turn these recollections into a more systematic chronicle. Having come to its conclusion, I find that a few loose ends remain: questions of meaning posed by the events themselves, questions from readers of those pieces, and gaps I have, in retrospect, decided need filling. Once set in motion, the process of recollection goes on, and a book drawing on memories almost insists on remaining ultimately unfinished.

Life, for many, is ordinary passage through high drama. The commonplace and the unique draw the boundaries of the historian's territory and, by their juxtaposition, feed his investigations. It is, of course, quite possible to be a historian without understanding what the parameters are and where they lie. The territory they enclose is sufficiently vast to permit endless varieties of narrow, as well as deluded, specialization. Some historians neglect the event deliberately; others deny the individual and pursue fictitious norms through dark statistical corridors. By still others' definitions, history remains the cataclysmic: winds fanned by the breath of power and of daring, fires bringing light as well as devastation.

Such reflections have forced me to relive my life as history, and now urge me to connect what I saw and sensed with what mankind has since added, withdrawn, and reinterpreted. I have recognized that my birth occurred in the middle of an important, if inconclusive, event: a great upheaval in Germany, remaining without issue because the state disappeared before the revolution ended. At its beginning that revolution seemed to change nothing (and the partisans of that viewpoint remain numerous), but its adversary successors also restored nothing, and eventually both revolutionaries and counterrevolutionaries found that they had lost control of their country and their destiny.

The world where my paternal grandmother knew her place and faced a cheerless destiny, where my maternal forebears clipped their coupons and performed good works, collapsed. No one had energy either to rebuild the old or to construct a new order animated by the liberal and egalitarian aspirations of the aborted revolution of 1848. German conservatives, like their French counterparts in the 1870s, recoiled from the complexities of restoration; liberals and Social Democrats dreaded the future, forecast by bolshevism, more than they mourned the past, whose elusive virtues they discovered too late. More important, the day-by-day quest for power had ended successfully for the purveyor of the most persuasive fantasies: Adolf Hitler.

All this happened in ritual rhythm, in a large country in central Europe, amidst a numerous people so clearly identified by language and achievement, and yet so ineffective, so diverse, so incapable of coming freely to a national consensus. In modern times the great German conflicts—the wars of religion, the disintegration of the Holy Roman Empire, the problems posed by the rapid modernization of the late nineteenth century—had eventually been settled by foreign intervention. Each time foreign powers decided what should be done and how: the French and Spaniards in 1648, the French in 1806, the alliance against Napoleon in 1815, the Paris Peace Conference in 1919. Only once, in 1871, did the defeat of France enable Germans to decide their own future. Throughout most of Germany's modern history, nationhood has been no more than a claim—never accepted by all German-speaking people—and now more than ever a goal beyond their reach as well as beyond their aspirations.

That was the historic nexus into which I was born a German. In turn, Hitler's victory—the last way station on the road to ultimate disintegration—coincided with my entry into adolescence. For me it was a fortunate coincidence, for my attendant state of rebellion found me readier to turn away from the problem-ridden universe of my birth than I would have been earlier, when my parents moved to Berlin, or later in life when I was totally uprooted.

This reflection provides another example of how remembrances force one to relive history, connecting what one saw with what others—both writers and makers of history—have since claimed. It adds that the coincidental convergence involves two variables: The encounter with history changes life, and the life crossing history's path changes history, or, at the very least, one's understanding of it.

My chronicle begins on a morning like any other and terminates after the threshold of yet another era has been crossed. On that first morning, I am a procrastinating boy with a sore throat; in the evening of the same day, I have been assigned, without yet knowing it, to join an epic migration across the Atlantic. Grand history calls to action, but ordinary people devise how to come to terms with it. During the first year of the Nazi onslaught, derisive laughter gives way to apprehension. The moment arrives when totalitarian politics ceases to be mere theater, when the pressure of tyranny becomes unbearable and "steps have to be taken."

From then on the protagonist can only look to the future, as his ties with Germany have been cut so summarily. A short train trip to Holland, merely a journey to another school, becomes the first installment of an itinerary without true returns. Occasional holiday visits to scenes of the past become forays into strange regions. At the heart of life is the need to belong, somewhere, anywhere, and during the search for this anchorage the migrant loses part of his identity.

As I was reliving my year in England, at sixes and sevens, and my arrival in the United States, I saw again my naturally changing self. I still possessed a German passport, but no longer a German home or allegiance—Holland and England only offered temporary hospitality to a stranger. America's welcome alone, I discovered next, was not enough to remove all barriers between the stranger and his new habitat. This country, too, was at first an alien ground, and only the open-endedness of my stay may explain why I finally came to see it as my home. In 1938 I was an exile; by 1945 I had, in my own eyes, become an American—before I was reunited with what was left of my European family.

Since the 1930s had not heard of culture shock, and the public at large was yet to discover the identity crisis, I passed through the

244

intervening metamorphosis fairly painlessly. I suppose that my transformation continues at this moment, to the extent that my origins will always remain part of my identity and force the process of assimilation to go on without ever becoming quite complete.

What subsequent years document, however, is not merely an individual change from one allegiance to another, but the way human bonds helped determine the ultimate course these allegiances took. What contributed most to my Americanization? My surrogate parents, the Morrisons, and my wife. Between 1940 and 1944, the human beings closest to me were all Americans. Without conscious effort I adopted their daily habits, their outlook, their values, and their aspirations. The moment I began to think about my nationality—probably when friends of my parents suggested that I return to Germany—I realized that I had become an American. America was home; everything else was a foreign country. Curiously, my reunion with my old schoolmate Fritz Ewald in Frankfurt revealed that our different paths through the war had, at this point at least, erected no barrier between us. Friends remained friends, although, in this case, distance and age has finally put an end to this childhood relationship, which no recent efforts of mine have succeeded in reviving.

There is, of course, another side to my individual experience: the life other members of my family led in occupied Holland during World War II. Germans all, they survived five years during which the government of the country of their birth hounded and ostracized them a second time, keeping them continuously suspended between a precarious safety and possible extermination. They had left Germany; they had accepted the verdict of their compatriots (how else could one see it at that time?) and agreed to give up their nationality, together with the civil and property rights issuing from their citizenship. Still, the Germans would not leave them alone. Holland's occupiers forced the Dutch to make these foreign Jews live through their nightmare a second time.

Not until I sat recently in the living room of my cousin Dorothea, my uncle's oldest child—like myself half Jew and half gentile—and heard her explain why she would never set foot on the soil of her native land, did the cruelty of this second persecution really penetrate my consciousness. One day in 1943 (she was sixteen then) she had gone downstairs to the Gestapo office—in the building where she lived with her parents—to renew her identity card. The transaction was routine and proceeded without difficulty. At the end of it, the German official looked at her reflectively and said, not unkindly: . "You are such a nice girl! What a pity that your father is a Jew!" The avuncular bureaucrat was telling her first, "What a pity that you are not like us," a questionable proposition in occupied Europe, and second, that the ancestry of her father—whom she dearly loved— constituted cause for personal degradation. Nothing ensued. She left the room and went back to her family's apartment; but the wound has festered ever since. In that moment she experienced, in her way, the full measure of cruelty the world around her could inflict. By outlawing a category of human being, it had become possible to place anyone, no matter how "nice," outside the pale of any society.

As a historian, I cannot help going beyond the personal response to such a shock and consider its collective implications. To persons like my cousin—refugees from Germany scattered over the surface of the European continent—their nation had become their most deadly enemy. It had declared war on them, civil war, and it was extending that conflict from the Arctic to the Mediterranean: between Nazis and other Germans, and between resistants and collaborators in every other nation drawn into the conflict. National loyalty had lost all meaning, either because their nation had driven them out or because the population of their homeland had divided into two irreconcilable factions at war with each other.

In the context of my relatives' fate, this particular turning point was papered over when the uprooted Germans in question acquired other passports. In my cousin's case, she, like the rest of her immediate family, became Dutch. How she views her Dutchness I do not know, except that it has been reinforced by a Dutch husband and children born and raised in the Netherlands.

Readers of some portions of this memoir previously published have been particularly curious about the eventual fate of my "droll uncle." He remained "droll" to the end. When my family and I visited him in Luxembourg, where he lived while directing the antitrust policies of the European Coal and Steel Community, he would recount to us his migrations to ever-smaller countries: from Germany to Austria in 1933, to Holland next, and finally, in 1952, to that picturesque grand duchy where a new Europe was to begin. "Watch out," he would conclude with a soft laugh, "Liechtenstein will be next." Retired in 1960, he returned to his earlier vocation of management consultant; a heart attack ended his life the following year.

My mother lived long enough to spend twenty-eight years—almost one-third of her four-score-and-three—in the United States, including more than two decades as an American citizen. When she arrived in Chicago in December, 1946, she had just turned fifty-five, but unlike most of her age group, she never succumbed to homesickness. She spent several extended holidays in Europe, yet no reunion with old friends tempted her to consider returning to Germany, anymore than it had me in 1945. On the contrary, I remember the indignant remonstrations she addressed to my teacher, her contemporary Hans Rothfels, when she learned in 1953 that he was planning to return to Germany and a professorship at the University of Tübingen. To me she said, "How can he crawl back, after they threw him out?"

Until her retirement in 1956, my mother's professional existence followed the peripatetic and haphazard course set in the last two years of World War I. An oddly assorted set of qualifications—a German *Doctor juris* together with experience in teaching the handicapped, editing a monthly magazine on management, running a dormitory, and instructing Eerde pupils in a bewildering array of subjects—impeded an easy entrance into the American academic world, even at a time when teachers were in demand at all levels. Yet when a Quaker college in Iowa offered her a post, she decided to stay in Chicago because my brother "needed her." Instead, she became secretary to the German department of the University of Chicago, eventually expanding that humble position into a hybrid job encompassing the teaching of courses on philological methods as well as a separate career as translator. When a stroke paralyzed her in 1967, eleven years after her retirement, she was halfway through a commissioned translation of a major work of Catholic theology. I well remember the consternation the news created among the faculty that had set her to work on this epic enterprise, and I have no idea whether they found anyone to finish the job.

No doubt future students of twentieth-century Western society, if they come upon my mother's voluminous papers, will find her a representative exponent (or victim?) of our age and its feminist pretensions. She had been fortunate that her parents possessed both the means and the broad views enabling her to enter a world of thought and enterprise hitherto closed to her gender. Yet she herself often wondered whether she had made the most of the resulting opportunities. Women like her—and her case is far from unique—

have often blamed their mediocre lives on social conditioning. They have claimed that admission to new intellectual and professional spheres did not change society's expectation that their generation retain, as its foremost obligation, the duty of motherhood, and that the resulting contradictions simply doomed them to lives of perpetual frustration. In rare, dark moments, I know that my mother saw my brother and me as major obstacles to a distinguished career. Late in life she sometimes viewed her motherhood as a sacrifice that we did not sufficiently appreciate. I understand why this should have been so, but am not entirely convinced that the proposition was that simple. In the Germany of 1918, women vastly outnumbered men, and the pressure to marry declined accordingly. Mrs. Petersen, Eerde's first headmistress, lost a fiancé in the war and never married. My mother hinted at a similar tragedy in her life, but why did this not determine her future in the same way, unless *she* decided otherwise? In a sense, the conflict between two ways of life was reenacted when she stayed in Chicago instead of taking the job offered her in Iowa. My brother was about twenty when the question arose, and a graduate student. He had long ceased to need the daily companionship of a mother, and only her dependence on his dependence may help explain her decision. Naturally, a dilemma remained in either case (for all I know, Mrs. Petersen may at times have regretted her single existence), but it puts credit or blame for its resolution squarely on the individual—where it should rest—and not on elusive and opaque social factors.

And what about other members of the cast? Bernard von Bothmer, my friend and partner in the army, eventually headed the Egyptological department at the Brooklyn Museum. Mr. Neuse reversed roles and ended his career teaching German to Americans at St. Lawrence University in Canton, New York. Since his new charges were under far less pressure to succeed than we Eerde students had been, the results of his work were, accordingly, less satisfying. He lived out his retirement in his wife's homeland, England, an exile to the end. Twenty years after the war I visited Hanover, where Mrs. Petersen had been living since the end of World War II. She had retired from a distinguished position in the educational hierarchy of the German state of Lower Saxony and sported an Order of the British Empire. Her home and hearth were in the care of Fräulein Emmy, the former deputy chief of Eerde's kitchen. Both insisted that I take my evening meals with them. The cuisine was several notches above Frau Kuck's of blessed memory; otherwise our meeting was just like old times.

My prototypal Aryan friend, Fritz Ewald, studied veterinary medicine and joined the Paul Ehrlich Institute in Frankfurt. I have lost all contact with my boon companion Rainer. After I discovered his father's sinister wartime activities, contact between our families ceased. In 1966, between trains on my way to Vienna, I took the old streetcar No. 23 (now part of the subway system) to Eschersheim and once more wandered past houses on my native street, now echoing with the shouts of a new generation of children for whom this old thoroughfare still seemed to be a safe playground. I also passed No. 15, where Rainer was born and raised and where I now descried him looking out a second-floor window. His round boyish countenance had not changed, but the shock of blond hair was gone, exposing a shining, bald expanse of ruddy skin. He did not appear to recognize me, and I could not muster the courage to call out to him. We had not seen each other for almost thirty years. What would we have to say? Rather than stumble awkwardly through an anticlimactic and pointless reunion, I walked briskly on. Fritz and Rainer, the only two persons, apart from parents and close relations, whom I have known as long as I can remember, apparently will live out the substance of their lives on the street on which all three of us were born. I have been tempted to speculate on who should envy whom, but that is foolish. None of us chose a particular life, either of rootedness or of transcontinental travel. We simply enjoy what chance tossed our way. Each one of us appears comfortable and fulfilled, and rather indifferent to the others. (From Fritz I gathered in 1956 that he rarely sees Rainer, who lives less than a block away.) Like so many human relationships, ours have turned into a story without a discernible ending.

Dieter Moeller's postwar peregrine life more closely paralleled mine. Once I returned home, we began exchanging letters, and my temporary association as correspondent with a German newspaper enabled me to subsidize his first painting trip to Italy, with earnings I could not transfer to America at that time. Then he emigrated to Canada, lost his first wife in a tragic accident, remarried, and returned with his second spouse to her native Switzerland. Here my family and I caught up with him in the late sixties in his studio at Altenrhein (St. Gallen) on the banks of Lake Constance. He told me then of a recent trip to the schoolhouse where his parents had instructed the children of Wittelsberg, his native village, in the three R's. There he found the old Nazi mayor back in office and decided never to set foot on German soil again. So far as I know, he has kept this resolve.

Paul and Marian Morrison spent the last years of their lives in Fulton, Missouri, where Paul, Sr., became the librarian of Westminster College. Paul, Jr., returned from the war before I did and decided to change careers. When I came back to our common stomping grounds in 1950 to get my doctorate, at a changed University of Chicago that was beginning to turn its back on Robert Hutchins' grand experiments, he was a graduate student in philosophy. A few years later our paths crossed once more, at Tulane University, where we both were young professors. After that, Paul, the southerner, moved north again, whereas I finally settled at the University of Virginia, only a short drive from the last capital of the Confederacy. He died of leukemia in 1978, seeking to the end to turn the secular revelations of his teacher, Rudolf Carnap, and their common idol, Ludwig Wittgenstein, into the perfect grammar of a language of impeccable logic.

Helene, the wife of Franz Calvelli-Adorno, reminded me in 1987 that it was then seventy-five years ago that she and my mother had met as students in Berlin on the eve of World War I. A few years after the second great conflict, the two children for whom the Adornos had found a refuge in England returned home. All three offspring have carved out significant careers and productive lives in public service, business, and the arts. Franz became, once more, a judge and lived long enough (until September 19, 1985) to enjoy almost two decades of retirement, playing his violin and giving music lessons to his grandchildren. His wife survived him three and one half years and died in February, 1988, at the age of ninety-three. Until Christmas, 1987, we corresponded regularly. In her old age she became a staunch rebel, although she had followed her husband into the Catholic church. She always felt uneasy among her countrymen, who had visited so many cruelties on her and her family merely because her husband had been half Jewish. When I wrote her—almost a year before her death—of a visit to Nuremberg, my father's birthplace, I received this reply: "When we were young, Franz and I were drawn to Italy and bypassed the old imperial city. Then everything about it was poisoned by Hitler and so, believe it or not, I have never visited Nuremberg, and most likely I never will."

Everything was poisoned by Hitler. Of how many lives has this sentence become the refrain?

Other loose ends concern episodes that keep surfacing in a mind suddenly focused on a personal rather than collective past. This secondary stream of reawakened consciousness threatens to become an ungovernable torrent. I promise to reduce its flow to a controlled trickle.

I finally revisited in 1986 the Berlin suburb of Frohnau, where my family had lived from 1928 to 1932, and showed my wife the two houses we inhabited, the roses in the park, and other childhood landmarks along the well-kept avenues. We also walked past the now no longer new 18. Primary School at the bottom of a hill, fronting on a side street named in my childhood after the World War I naval hero Maximilian von Spee. We found that the game of changing street names resumed after 1945. For a while this quiet thoroughfare became Edith Cavell Allee, in honor of the British nurse executed as a spy by German authorities administering Belgium during World War I. Then, for reasons unknown to me, the street sign changed once again, and the school's address is now Victor Gollancz Strasse, honoring the memory of a British publisher of Jewish descent and his philanthropic efforts on behalf of German children after 1945.

But this recollection bears not on the street's name but on the decision to place the school entrance off the main thoroughfare, now, as then, the Markgrafen Strasse, or Street of the Markgraves (of Brandenburg), so that children leaving and entering would not be endangered by traffic. As I stood there on the sidewalk, more than fifty years later, I suddenly remembered how that sensible measure had one day given rise to an angry exchange between me and my teacher, the redoubtable Herr Weber. One additional measure of traffic control prohibited students who bicycled to school from mounting their vehicles in front of the building; their conveyances had to be pushed first to either end of the block. One day, as I was leaving with my cronies, I saw our teacher, in flagrant violation of the rules, get on his bike, right in front of us, and then gingerly thread his way through the homebound multitudes on foot. "Look at that," I exclaimed to my buddies. "He can get on his bike anywhere he likes." Herr Weber abruptly stopped, dismounted, and motioned me to come over. "Don't let me hear you talk such nonsense again, Schmitt," he barked, and resumed his progress. For a moment I feared that my verbal assault on adult authority might incur a serious application of discipline. Only after Herr Weber had disappeared around the corner could I be sure that he had let me off with this brief reprimand. Years passed before I realized my teacher's disadvantage in this encounter, but at the time of the incident I suspected that God had granted adults immunity from rules applying to children. Not knowing where my parents stood on this issue, I was careful not to bring up the matter at home. I am still glad that I made this modest gesture of defiance; now I wish, of course, that I had possessed the courage to make more of an issue of it.

My recollections of the years in Eerde, unlike the Berlin years, could be continued almost indefinitely with the aid of surviving letters and photographs from a variety of sources. The two rather full chapters dedicated to my school years in Holland do not mention my friendships with several girls. In the long run these ephemeral passages have not affected my life as deeply as I was inclined to think at the time. Still, the fate of two of these young women provides insight into the history of the time.

The first girl with whom I thought I had fallen in love was an unusually quiet, retiring classmate with olive skin, straight black hair, and equally black eyes, perpetually downcast. I sat next to her in class whenever I could and, like Tom Sawyer in Becky Thatcher's presence, started clowning whenever she was within sight or hearing. Whether she recognized the impression she made on me I have no idea; I certainly never told her. In 1935 she and her family emigrated to Mexico, and I do not know what became of her. Her name was Marion Ballin, and she was the granddaughter of Albert Ballin, German shipping magnate, director of the Hamburg-Amerika Line, and adviser to Kaiser Wilhelm II, one of the few Jews welcomed at the imperial court. In 1918, after Germany lost World War I, Ballin committed suicide. Less than a generation later, the descendants of this passionate German patriot were cast out into the unknown.

The last and most durable of these friendships was with Marianne Josephs, who entered the school about the time Marion left. Marianne and I corresponded sporadically after I went to England and even after I had pitched my tent in Lexington, Virginia. She passed the examinations for the Oxford School Certificate a year or two after me and then emigrated with her family to Brazil. We made contact for the last time in 1956, while she was visiting Holland and my own family and I were spending a postdoctoral Fulbright year in Luxembourg. Illness kept her from paying us a promised visit, but we talked on the phone, and I remember being struck by her complaint that immigrants like her could not become Brazilians the way survivors in our family had become Americans. To become assimilated, she said, meant accepting a "cultural level" to which she was not prepared to descend. I was then put off by this *Kultur* snobbery, but in later years I have come to see this remark in a different light. The Josephs, like the Ballins—and my own Jewish forebears as well—had been Germans for generations and were completely unprepared for sudden ostracism. Twenty years after our adolescent friendship on the road into exile, their oldest daughter still had not come to terms with that personal and collective catastrophe. German civilization still provided the standards by which Marianne judged everything within her physical and spiritual purview. Her life, too, had been poisoned by Hitler. Even so, her Jewish heart continues to beat as German in Sao Paulo—where she has lived her adult life—as during her childhood in Germany.

The monstrous injustice done to hundreds of thousands of Germans with Jewish ancestors derived from the groundless assumption that they constituted another people. This notion has even survived Hitler: The desire to segregate Jews from the rest of society still has its supporters throughout the world. Such segregationists forget that a group certainly becomes different *after* its separation from the rest of society. Relegation to a ghetto, wholesale expropriation, or physical mistreatment forced German Jews to leave or die. The survivors became, indeed, a separate species, whatever their fate. They became people who left, people who returned, or people who emigrated to become strangers far from home. My maternal great-grandfather's and grandfather's expectation that Jewish emancipation under Napoleon would set in motion a process ending in complete assimilation was shattered, and nothing in our time can revive it.

The memories feeding this conclusion must not close one's mind to one of the pleasant surprises of subsequent history: the ease with which the outcast nations of World War II regained acceptance from former enemies, both east and west. In 1940, when I graduated from college, nazism was to many—both informed and ignorant—the sum of German history. Today I see it as an interlude, as was the Reign of Terror and the 1871 massacre of the Communards in the history of France. Germany has tried democracy a second time—

compelled, it is true, once again by foreign conquest rather than choice. Still, almost forty years after this second turning point, no domestic tyrant threatens liberty, and no upsurge of public discontent endangers constitutional government. Equally important, citizens of the German Democratic Republic continue "to vote with their feet" against oppression, at great personal risk, and the wistful glances the majority left behind the wall direct at passing Westerners tell us even more about their values than does the pluralism of the Federal Republic.

To be sure, this surprise provides no guarantees affecting a more distant future, nor does it enable us to forget what has gone wrong earlier. It cannot undo my separation from the country of my birth. It will not resurrect the dead or heal the wounds of oppression and torture. Still, it has opened the door to some amends. One of my mother's cousins and his wife, for instance, eventually came home from Israel to an idyllic retirement in Germany among their true people, the Germans. In the public sphere I cannot forget the Socialist Kurt Schumacher, crippled by years of Nazi torture, leading a new Social Democratic party, becoming the beacon, if not necessarily the leader, of a democratic Germany. A traditional love of liberty, long enjoyed and never disclaimed by millions of Germans in Alsace, Luxembourg, and Switzerland, and quite as much a part of the German past as the cult of authority, has reasserted itself east of the Rhine and in Austria. The German capable of great good and monstrous evil stands before us, not an outcast from, but a representative of, mankind.

With that conclusion we must continue to go about our business. Søren Kierkegaard recognized long ago that this is not easy considering that we know only the past while being forced to live in the future. Still, we lucky victims, privileged and all too few in number, always prepared for the worst though we may be, are not afraid to turn another corner on the road into the unknown.